DIVORCE

The Forgivable Sin?

DIVORCE

DIVORCE

The Forgivable Sin?

Ken Crispin

HODDER AND STOUGHTON
LONDON SYDNEY AUCKLAND TORONTO

British Library Cataloguing in Publication Data

Crispin, Ken
  Divorce
  1. Divorce. Personal adjustment. Christian viewpoints
  I. Title
261.8'3589

ISBN 0-340-50235-5

Copyright © Ken Crispin 1988. First published in Great Britain 1989. All rights reserved. No part of this publication may be reproduced or transmitted in any form or by any means, electronic or mechanical, including photocopying, recording, or any information storage and retrieval system, without either prior permission in writing from the publisher or a licence permitting restricted copying. In the United Kingdom such licences are issued by the Copyright Licensing Agency, 33–34 Alfred Place, London WC1E 7DP. Reproduced by arrangement with Hodder & Stoughton Australia. Published by Hodder and Stoughton Ltd, Mill Road, Dunton Green, Sevenoaks, Kent TN13 2YA. Editorial Office: 47 Bedford Square, London WC1B 3DP. Printed in Great Britain by Cox and Wyman Ltd, Reading, Berks.

"He hath sent me
to heal the broken-hearted"
(Luke 4:18)

To my wife Pamela who has loved, supported and borne patiently with me these past twenty years. With love.

Contents

Acknowledgements

It is not possible to acknowledge adequately my debt of gratitude to the hundreds of people who have contributed to my understanding as they struggled through the heartache of marital breakdown and divorce. They have included the stupid and intelligent, the ignorant and the informed, the cynical and the naive, the resentful and forgiving: in short, the whole gamut of human nature. It has been said that a lawyer sees people at their worst but what is frequently left unacknowledged is the fact that many people respond to the challenge of adversity with courage, tenacity and nobility of spirit. The example of such people has enriched my life immeasurably.

My understanding has also been helped by contact with many of those in the ''helping'' professions—court counsellors, marriage guidance counsellors, psychiatrists, psychologists, ministers, judges and fellow lawyers—who, in a hundred different ways have contributed insights borne of compassion and experience.

I am particularly grateful to a number of people who were kind enough to wade through the first disordered manuscript or otherwise contribute advice and encouragement. These include (in alphabetical order) Mr Justice R.W. Gee of the Family Court of Australia; Mrs Betty

Hocking, former member of the A.C.T. House of Assembly and President of the Freedom Council of Australia; Dr Don Lawrence, family psychiatrist, Canberra; Dr B. Ward Powers of United Theological College, Sydney; Mr Justice R.S. Watson, formerly of the Family Court of Australia and author of several books and articles on family law. That is not to say that each would endorse every word written and ultimately I must accept sole responsibilty for the opinions expressed.

I am also grateful to my wife Pamela for her patience and support and to Mrs Dona Turk and Mrs Jill Ross, each of whom invested an enormous amount of time in typing successive drafts.

Introduction

The break-up of a marriage is for many people the most agonising experience of their lives. The kind of anguish involved can be compared in intensity only to the grief caused by a sudden and tragic bereavement and, in many respects, even that analogy is inadequate. Such a bereavement is a devastating experience. It can produce almost unbearable grief, tinged frequently with regret for things left undone, and it can leave those left behind with a hollow aching void. There is no ready antidote for such feelings; they have to be worked through over a period of time. Even years later there will be times when memories trigger a sudden stab of grief thought long resolved. Yet despite all that, there is at least a note of finality about it. When the grieving is over those left behind can pick up the pieces and make a fresh start. It may be a tremulous start, without the financial or emotional security of former years; but it will at least be unfettered by a legacy of continuing legal, emotional and spiritual wrangles.

On the other hand, when a person is divorced the decree pronounced by the court is usually the culmination of a heart-rending process that has taken years, rather than months to come to finality. By then some people have reached that point of emotional exhaustion familiar to those who have nursed someone very dear to them through a long terminal illness. Yet for many people, particularly those with children, even that point offers no finality.

There may be disputes over access and custody, not only in the court but week by week. There may be almost ceaseless recriminations as a result of information "pumped" from the children during access periods. There may be constant haggling over the division of marital property or maintenance payments for the children or agonising on both sides about overtures of reconciliation. Countless issues constantly reopen the wounds even when both parties are reasonably mature and striving to sort out their differences as amicably as possible. Repeated confrontation with an estranged lover when picking up and delivering children can make it very difficult to put the pain of the divorce behind and start again. A friend of mine described meeting his ex-wife as confronting "a living ghost". He explained that no matter how much time he spent binding up his wounds during the week the very sight of her would "rip them open again".

One would have thought that these stresses would be well understood in these "enlightened days". Unhappily, this is often far from true.

Whilst people who are widowed usually receive a considerable amount of support and sympathy from friends, family and neighbours, those whose marriages break up are frequently treated with indifference and suspicion.

The church too, provides comfort for the bereaved. Even people who have had little interest in religion of any kind can find great solace in a new-found faith. But what of the divorced?

I think it is fair to say that most give the church a wide berth. After all, the only thing they ever hear from the church about divorce is that it is all terribly sinful. Regrettably, those who do seek Christian help and support frequently find that they are received with suspicion and ill-concealed condemnation. If they are lucky, they may be referred to a professional counselling service of some kind by a local congregation which assumes that such vicarious involvement is sufficient. If they are unlucky, they will encounter a morass of theological confusion and crippling guilt.

It is for those people that this book has been written. It is not intended to be a scholarly treatise on theology, law, psychology or anything else. It is intended rather to help those who have to walk that lonely and painful way through the morass. For there is a way and it leads not to despair but to new life.

It is also intended as a call to the church. Let us reconsider the burdens which we sometimes impose on people. Let us stop treating them as mere theological problems and let us instead seek to become caring communities in which they may receive comfort and healing.

Finally, let us remember that it was the lonely, the broken-hearted and those despised by the religious leaders of the day that Jesus sought out and befriended. Whatever your situation may be, he seeks you and he wants you to know that he cares!

Ken Crispin
April 1987

PART ONE

WHAT THE BIBLE SAYS — AND DOESN'T SAY

CHAPTER ONE

The Problem of Over-simplification

As a Christian, I have always accepted the authority of the Bible in matters of morality. Happily, I have found that throughout the Bible logic and compassion are consistently interwoven in the statements on the main moral issues. That is not to say that one accepts what the Bible says only because it is logical and compassionate but rather that, since those qualities epitomise God's very nature, they are inevitably reflected in his word.

On the other hand, as a lawyer dealing with people suffering the agonies of divorce, I have frequently found that advice given to them by Christian friends is devoid of both logic and compassion. The fact that such advice is given at all is regrettable but what is infinitely worse is that those responsible always seem able to claim uncompromising biblical authority for their views. It is one thing to have a friend say, "Well, this is what I think": it is altogether another to have to contend with someone who commences with the phrase, "Thus saith the Lord!" uttered in the tones one might imagine Elijah using to the priests of Baal.

Of course, there are many circumstances in which a dogmatic approach may be appropriate. I cannot imagine for example, how there could be any debate about the propriety of murder, rape, robbery or, for that matter, indifference to the suffering of others. Furthermore, despite

3

the seductive allure of tolerance, Christians are not philosophers free to vary their ethical position to accord with the social customs of the time. They are servants bound by the declared word of their master. Nonetheless, it is not a light matter to claim divine authority for any principle, especially one which is intended to be imposed on others. It seems reasonable to suggest that any phrase smacking of "Thus saith the Lord" should be used sparingly.

Since many of the things said by Christians about divorce are mutually inconsistent it is obvious that not all are stamped with the authority claimed. Dr Ward Powers has observed, for example, that within the Christian church there are eleven distinct theologies of divorce.[1] The main thing which these views have in common is that the proponents of each claim infallibility based on biblical authority.

Furthermore, much of the advice given is not merely wrong but callous and irresponsible. In many cases it condemns the recipient to distressing and quite unnecessary emotional trauma and in some cases it exposes the recipient or the children of the marriage to the risk of intolerable violence.

I vividly recall acting for one poor woman who had been savagely beaten at regular intervals by a psychotic husband. She had already survived two attempts on her life. One night he attempted to strangle her and left her unconscious on the floor, apparently believing that he had finally killed her. Whilst he was gone, she revived and staggered from the house to seek refuge in a women's hostel with her three children. Her husband returned home and, finding her gone, flew into a violent rage. He took an axe and chopped holes in all the internal walls of the house, smashed the windows, the light fittings, the crockery and even the refrigerator. Then, when there was nothing left to smash, he took a paintbrush and splashed obscenities on what was left of the walls.

The next day whilst still shaken and covered with bruises,

including welts around the throat, the distraught wife sought counselling from the minister of her church. The kindly, and doubtlessly sincere, minister expressed sympathy but then explained that marriage was, after all, until death did them part. Since neither of them was dead yet, she had a duty to return and live with her husband. He conceded that if she did so she might well be murdered but observed that that was, after all, better than losing her immortal soul!

This was an extreme but by no means isolated instance of someone being virtually blackmailed into exposing herself or her children to the risk of serious harm.

Another woman came to see me in a state of confusion about the attitude she should adopt towards her former husband. They had been divorced about ten years before and her husband had long since remarried. He and his new wife had three young children. The first wife had experienced no real difficulty in her attitude to her former husband over the years until a "helpful" pastor had taken her aside and offered his wise counsel. He explained that God did not recognise divorce and that her husband's second marriage really consisted of nothing more than living in flagrant adultery. Accordingly it was her Christian duty to do all she could to break up the relationship. She protested that if she succeeded in doing so it would mean a broken home for her former husband's three children but the pastor swept that consideration aside as being irrelevant. She did not want to ignore her pastor's advice but was dubious about the validity of any theological view which simply brushed aside the lives of three innocent young children as irrelevant. She was relieved to find that I shared her scepticism.

In other cases great anguish has been caused by well-meaning Christians leading emotionally vulnerable people into false expectations. Christians having trouble with wayward husbands or wives are frequently told, "Just pray in faith and God will heal your marriage".

A friend of mine had been an alcoholic before he became

a Christian and, after a great struggle, finally overcame his problem. He gradually rebuilt his life and, about four years after drying out, became a full-time Christian worker with an inner-city church. About that time his wife, who was quite antagonistic about his Christian faith, suddenly left him. He had been praying for her regularly and her sudden departure left him desolate. Yet despite his anguish he remained firm in his faith and didn't turn back to alcohol as his friends had feared. At that stage he was approached by another Christian who explained that he needed simply to trust God to bring his wife back and heal his marriage. He accepted that completely and for fifteen months prayed each day for his wife's return. At the end of that period she contacted him and offered a deal. She would come back if he would leave the church and ''give away this Christianity nonsense''. Within days he was back on skid row, a broken man. In time he recovered his faith but only after months of anguish.

I hasten to say that I do believe in the power of prayer. If it were not for prayer and God's healing, I would not be alive today. But marriage is a relationship between two people each of whom has been given the precious gift of free will which God does not overrule. Certainly the Holy Spirit brings conviction, changes attitudes, and rekindles cold hearts. I have seen beautiful reconciliations as the result of prayer. But ultimately, each person remains free to choose. A person who maintains a resolve to abandon a marriage, will not be dragged by God, kicking and screaming, back into the relationship.

Sometimes a person may feel that he has been given a real assurance from God that a reconciliation will occur. I have known a number of cases where one person has been sustained by such an assurance and, in time, seen it fulfilled. Unhappily, such precious and uniquely personal experiences do not account for most of the advice given. In most cases such advice is based upon nothing more substantial than an oversimplistic view of certain texts or mere presumptuousness. Many Christians seem almost unbelievably glib about claiming higher authority for some of their personal opinions. In reality, of course, one undertakes an awesome responsibility when one comforts a trusting friend with words which imply a promise on God's behalf to do something. People are encouraged to believe that the healing of the marriage is as sure a promise as salvation. I have known a number of people who have experienced the most crushing disillusionment and abandoned their faith completely at least for a substantial period of time. They had relied upon some such promise and when their hopes were ultimately dashed, concluded that if God had failed to honour one of his promises, then they could not put any faith in the others. Some turned to those who had raised these false expectations only to be told that they hadn't exercised enough faith. They, the victims, were made to bear the blame for their own grief.

It would be a mistake, however, to conclude that all problems of this nature are caused by the glib, the unfeeling or the irresponsible. There are many sincere and compassionate ministers and counsellors whose hearts go out to battered mothers and abused children. They are constrained to feel that God must make some provision for these people. Yet try as they might, they cannot find a theological basis for what they intuitively feel is the manner in which a compassionate God would respond to such a situation. Some seek to resolve this dilemma by simply assuming that the biblical statements reflect an ideal which is not always possible in an imperfect world. Others weep for the suffering of those involved but, ultimately, like the minister who sent the wife back to her psychotic husband, conclude that the biblical principle must be followed no matter what hardship ensues.

I fully accept that the correct view is to follow the biblical principles. However, that does not resolve the dilemma. It seems to me that the real difficulty lies not in determining whether the biblical principles should be followed but in determining what those principles are.

If one glances through the various English translations

of the relevant passages, one is immediately struck by apparent contradictions. For example, Mark 10:2-12 and Luke 16:18 seem to suggest that divorce will not be permitted on any ground; Matthew 5:21-31 seems to suggest it will be permitted for adultery but for no other cause; while 1 Corinthians 7:12-16 seems to suggest that divorce may be permitted on the grounds of desertion of a Christian by a non-Christian.

If Jesus, on one or more occasions, said that there was to be no divorce at all, then why did he say there could be divorce on the grounds of adultery? And, however that question is resolved, how could St Paul then permit divorce upon a further ground? Furthermore, one is left with an uneasy feeling that there must be more to it than is expressed in those passages as translated. Did Jesus really mean, for example, that a wife could divorce her husband for adultery but not for attempting to murder her? Did he really intend a marriage to continue at the expense of physical abuse of the children?

There are many books which seek to resolve some of these questions but whilst I have no wish to disparage the scholarship invested in them, most seem to reflect a purely linguistic approach with little attempt to come to grips with the practical implications of the principles espoused.

For example, if one accepts, as many such authors do, that God does not recognise a second marriage unless the first has been dissolved on some ground recognised by the Scriptures, then what advice can one validly give to a person involved in such a second marriage? The traditional answer and the only answer really consistent with such a view, is that if God does not recognise the marriage then it is an adulterous relationship. Logically that leads to a further step, namely that in order to receive forgiveness the person must repent and withdraw from the relationship immediately. That in itself causes a problem because one might be inclined to ask where the Bible suggests that it is any less sinful to break up a second marriage than a first?

But to illustrate the difficulty more starkly, let me pose

the example of the man who has three children as a result of his second marriage. In those circumstances is it really his Christian duty to break up the family? Is it really God's will that three young children be raised without the security of having their father live with them? This particular aspect is discussed more fully in Chapter 3. For the moment let me simply suggest that it is never God's will that families be split apart simply to comply with someone's pet theological theory.

Dilemmas of the kind which I have mentioned do not illustrate the fact that God's will can be hard, as some authors suggest, but rather that God's will can be misunderstood. Language, is at best, a clumsy tool for expressing concepts with precision and theologians, like lawyers, frequently disagree as to the construction of particular phrases. The passages dealing with divorce, are particularly susceptible to misunderstanding for two important reasons.

The first is that the concept of divorce has changed in one crucial respect since New Testament times. When Jesus spoke about divorce he was not concerned about a judicial decree but about the act of breaking up the relationship between a husband and wife. This aspect will be discussed in Chapter 2.

The second reason is that the English translations do not convey the subtleties of meaning in the original Greek text. Consequently the English translation suggests a far more rigid position than is justified by what Jesus actually said. This aspect will be discussed in Chapter 3.

The questions about the propriety of remarriage after divorce have also caused many Christians great anguish and these are discussed in Chapter 4.

However, if you have no problem about these things there may be no reason to wade through these chapters. I have set out a summary of conclusions in Chapter 5. You may find it helpful to go directly to those conclusions and come back to see how they are justified if you have some concern about them.

CHAPTER TWO

The Concept of Divorce

In most Western countries, we have become accustomed to a
legal system which involves inevitable delays in disen-
tangling the rights and obligations of the parties to a marriage when it has broken down.

In this context the termination of a marriage involves
two quite distinct stages. There is the stage of separation
where the actual marital relationship ceases and there is
a subsequent stage at which a judge makes a formal order
which has the effect of severing those legal rights and
obligations between the parties which were created by their
marriage. It is that later stage which is usually referred to
as the "divorce". In fact, the word is now so universally
used in that sense that it rarely occurs to anyone to wonder
whether it might have been used in the various New
Testament passages in a different sense. Accordingly, the
biblical restrictions against divorce are all assumed to relate
to that second stage.

This has led generations of theologians and Christian
leaders to teach that a married couple may separate where
the relationship between them has deteriorated to the point
where one or both feel they can no longer go on living
together but they must not "divorce" in the sense of
obtaining a judicial decree.

With the utmost deference to those who hold this view
I must say I have the greatest of difficulty in imagining

God regarding such a Christian "remedy" as anything but an unqualified tragedy. It does not require any profound theological scholarship to realise that God has a very great concern to keep families together. That aim is scarcely accomplished by a theology which treats the separation of a husband and wife as relatively unimportant. Yet, the "conventional" view involves the assumption that an order made by a judge severing certain legal rights and obligations is of infinitely more importance to God than the breaking up of a family and the resulting anguish caused not only to the husband and wife but to their children. These factors alone raise serious doubts as to the wisdom of assuming that comments made by Jesus concerning divorce were directed to the second rather than the first stage.

In fact this two-stage approach with which we are so familiar was quite simply unknown in biblical times. Divorce, which was available only to men, was accomplished by the simple expedient of ordering the wife out of the house. This kind of instant divorce by means of unilateral declaration still exists in Saudi Arabia and Afghanistan and other Islamic countries where, upon the utterance of a statement, "I divorce thee", repeated three times, the hapless wife will find that she is no longer married. The requirement of a bill of divorcement found in Deuteronomy 24:1 was not so much an essential requirement of the divorce itself but was necessary to facilitate the wife's remarriage at some later stage. This aspect will be discussed later. For the moment the point I wish to make is simply that when the parties stopped living together, they were regarded as divorced. It is apparent then, that at the time that Jesus spoke about divorce, he was referring not to two stages, but to a single event.

If that is so, then one must ask what justification there is for assuming that the remarks which Jesus made were directed exclusively or even primarily to the legal rights and obligations of the parties rather than to the maintenance of their marital relationship. Such a conclusion cannot follow from the mere meaning of the word which seems, in most languages, to be derived from words which mean to separate or to split apart. The English word "divorce", for example, is derived from the identical French word which in turn is derived from the Latin word *divortium* which means "separation". The corresponding verb is *diverto* which means "turn away".

If pressed for a definition most people would probably say that a divorce is simply the dissolution of a marriage. But to answer the question in that way is merely to introduce another question, namely, what is marriage?

If one were to ask one hundred people what was meant by the term marriage, one might well receive a hundred answers. To some it will be a passionate relationship of sexual and romantic love. To others it will evoke shared lives each complementing the other. To others it will mean the arrival of children and ultimately grandchildren to enrich their lives. To yet others it will mean settling down, a relationship of warm security. The answers will be as diverse as the people asked. Yet despite the diversity, all will have one thing in common, they will describe a relationship between a man and a woman. Not even the most unfeeling cold fish describes his marriage as a conjugation of legal rights and obligations.

It is important to realise that this concept of marriage as a relationship rather than a parcel of legal rights and obligations, or, for that matter, a kind of metaphysical or spiritual state, is the one which is reflected in the Bible.

In Genesis 2:24 is a statement later quoted by Jesus in Matthew 19:6 and by Paul in Ephesians 5:31: "Therefore a man leaves his father and mother and cleaves to his wife and they become one flesh" (RSV). This passage involves three propositions: Firstly the man leaves his parents and establishes a new home with his wife; secondly he "cleaves" to her, he sticks to her, it is a permanent relationship, not a transitory affair; thirdly, they become one flesh. The last expression has clear sexual connotations but it may also involve a more general intimacy and sharing of lives. These are the only characteristics which are given to distinguish a marriage from other sexual relationships. In New Testament times and through most of recorded history, they were the only requirements for a valid marriage.

Neither the Old nor the New Testament prescribes any kind of ceremony and the modern-day ceremonies required by law are a comparatively recent innovation. In England, for example, there was no requirement for a marriage ceremony until Lord Hardwick's ''Act for the Better Preventing of Clandestine Marriages'' was passed in 1753. When Isaac married Rebecca, he did so by the simple expedient of moving her into his tent and commencing married life.[2]

We know that by the time Jesus commenced his ministry there were weddings because he performed his first miracle at one.[3] However it seems unlikely that they were regarded as ceremonies necessary for the legal validity of the marriage. They were more likely to have been celebrations or, perhaps, services of a religious character at which the parties sought God's blessing upon their union.

In these days when the law does not recognise Aboriginal tribal marriages because they lack the modern trappings of Western weddings, and when churches query the validity of marriages because of ecclesiastical quibbles about the ceremonies, it may be instructive to remember that the Bible does not lay down any procedural requirements at all. It distinguishes between marriages and casual sexual encounters by virtue of the three characteristics referred to in Genesis, namely the creation of a separate household, the permanence of the relationship and the ''becoming one flesh''.

This concept is also enshrined in the marriage vows: one promises to ''love, honour and cherish'' or, to ''love, honour and obey''. In other words the very vow which one makes is to participate in a relationship in a particular manner.

Whilst the law imposes certain legal rights and obliga- tions in consequence of such a ceremony, it is apparent that the relationship is not primarily directed towards the creation of those rights and obligations. If it were, one would expect to see a series of vows along the following lines: "Do you, the party of the first part, covenant that you will faithfully observe the conditions set out in the 138 clauses appended to the marriage certificate?" A marriage is not a mere legal contract of concern only to the parties. It involves a covenant between the husband and wife in the presence of God.[4]

Nor, for that matter, do the marital vows create some purely metaphysical bond between the parties. If the relationship between them were purely a metaphysical one, then one would be entitled to ask why it should not continue beyond death? In fact, one does encounter Christians who seem to think it does. Such people will endeavour to remain faithful to their husbands or wives even after they have been widowed. The Bible contains, of course, no recognition of such a concept which is in fact expressly repudiated in Romans 7:2.

It is significant that when Jesus was asked about divorce he replied by referring to what the Bible said about marriage. His answer is recorded in Matthew 19:3-6, "Have you not read that he who made them from the beginning made them male and female, and said, 'For this reason a man shall leave his father and mother and be joined to his wife, and the two shall become one flesh?' ". He then continued, "What therefore God has joined together, let no man put asunder". The Greek word which is translated as "put asunder" is *chorizo* which means "divide" or "separate". Whilst there are other passages in the New Testament dealing with the question of divorce (and I will refer to them later), this is the only passage in which the reason for the restrictions imposed on divorce are explained. In terms as clear as one could ask for, Jesus answers the question about divorce by referring to the marital relationship, the effect of which is to join two people together as if they were one flesh, and then says, in essence, therefore let no one split them up! Despite the teaching espoused by some churches, you cannot glean from these words, by any feat of mental gymnastics, the proposition that it is right to separate providing one does not approach a judge to obtain a judicial decree. The words clearly mean the direct opposite. Reduced to its simplest terms, what Jesus was saying was that from the very beginning God created man to live with his wife in a particular kind of relationship and consequently, no one must break up that relationship.

Clearly it is that severance of the marriage relationship and not any judicial decree which Jesus has in mind when he speaks of divorce. That is not to strain the language as some might suggest. It simply reflects the plain meaning of divorce as "the dissolution of marriage: separation between things which should go together".[5] The contrary assumption is based upon little more than an accustomed distortion of the original meaning of the word to accommodate the two-stage process inherent in the modern legal system. I can find no passage in either the Old or the New Testament in which the word was ever used in that sense.

It was not until the Middle Ages that legal and ecclesiastical complications began to emerge. At that time an increasingly rigid attitude to divorce led to a kind of intermediate ground referred to as "divorce *a mensa et thoro*" which meant, literally, a separation from bed and board. That remedy permitted one party to the marriage to withdraw from the relationship whilst remaining bound in certain respects. It differed from a normal divorce in that both were unable to remarry.

This remedy was later incorporated in the civil law which until comparatively recently provided for decrees of judicial separation as an alternative to decrees of dissolution. There is, however, no scriptural support whatever for such remedies.

The understanding that the biblical statements about divorce relate not to a judicial decree but to the severance of the relationship should lead to a radical revision of the traditional attitudes to marital breakdown.

In the first place, I would suggest that the soul-searching that now occurs before starting legal proceedings should be done earlier—when one party is considering separating from the other. That is the crucial time. That is the time when the action which a person takes may sever the marital relationship and, to use the words of Jesus, "put asunder" those whom God has joined together. I have had one or two people respond to that proposition by saying, "But surely that means a breaking down of the standards". On the contrary, it involves an increase in the standards because it puts the emphasis back on the need to seek reconciliation. It seems to me that the statements concerning divorce taken as a whole reflect God's desire that we should make marriages work and not merely try to prevent the courts from recognising that they have broken down.

A second and equally important consequence of such a revision of attitudes is the recognition that, once one party to the marriage has walked out on a permanent basis and the relationship has been "sundered", then, in biblical terms, the parties have been divorced. True enough, the law may not recognise the validity of such a divorce but that is totally beside the point. What we are talking about is not the disentanglement of legal rights and obligations, but the morality of the position.

Let me reiterate: if a permanent separation has occurred, then the marital relationship has been sundered and in biblical terms that means that the parties are to be treated as divorced. Recognition of this fact should remove the need for a great deal of unnecessary anguish. Marriage is after all a voluntary relationship which exists only as long as the two people involved decide to continue in it. If one party decides to turn his back and resolutely and permanently renounces the relationship, then no matter how ardently the other longs for a reconciliation and regrets the separation, the relationship has come to an end.

Of course there are many cases in which people desert their husbands or wives for short periods but the parties are able to sort out their difficulties and come back together in an atmosphere of forgiveness and reconciliation. As Christians, we recognise that it is God's desire that we maintain that marital relationship and, if it is broken for some reason, then we should do what we can to restore it.

In many cases, however, even when it is abundantly clear that there is no chance of a reconciliation, Christians endure months or even years of agony over whether they may proceed to obtain a decree from the court, sort out their financial and legal affairs and start again. Such people are condemned to a kind of no man's land in which they are neither married, in any real sense, nor single in the sense of being free from an indefinable and incomprehensible bondage to their former husbands or wives. Some actually persuade themselves that they have been consigned to such a state as some kind of penance for real or imagined wrongs that they have committed either in marrying that particular person in the first place or subsequently during the marriage. The question of remarriage will be dealt with more fully in a later chapter. For the moment let me simply say, as emphatically as I can, that there is no basis disclosed in the Scriptures for such a "neither one thing nor the other" stage. In biblical terms one is married if one has a permanent relationship with a member of the opposite sex which involves living with him or her in the manner described in Genesis 2:24. One is divorced if that relationship terminates other than by death. There is simply no room for any kind of intermediate ground.

The circumstances in which a person may be justified in withdrawing from a viable marital relationship are considered in the next chapter. Before passing to that topic, however, it may be helpful to consider the implications of what has already been discussed. The following conclusions may be drawn:

(a) When the Bible speaks about marriage, it speaks about a marital relationship, that is, a relationship of the kind described in Genesis 2:24.

(b) When the Bible speaks about divorce, it means the "sundering" of that relationship.

(c) This means that it is the termination of the relationship which is of crucial importance and not the pronouncement of some judicial decree at some subsequent time.

(d) Consequently no Christian should withdraw from the marital relationship lightly nor permit it to be terminated without doing everything practicable to keep the relationship viable.

(e) If the relationship nonetheless terminates, then the parties should consider themselves already divorced in the biblical sense.

(f) Even then, any reasonable prospects of reconciliation should be pursued.

(g) If the prospects of reconciliation are exhausted and there is no reasonable likelihood of a resumption of the marital relationship, then the parties should feel free to sort out the legal rights and obligations which have come into being as the result of their marriage and proceed to obtain a legal decree recognising the termination of their marriage.

CHAPTER THREE

When is Divorce Permissible?

To understand that the Bible uses the word divorce to refer
to the severing of an existing marital relationship, rather
than to some judicial decree issued months or years after
that event, is extremely important. For some it may bring
a new awareness of the responsibility which we Christians
have towards maintaining the marital relationship. For
others who have experienced the pain of separation long
before, it may bring release from bondage to the peculiar
married-but-not-married state to which they have been
consigned by nothing more substantial than a misconception. Yet to understand the concept is only to cross the
threshold of the problem. We must still come to grips with
the question, "What does the Bible say about divorce?
When, if ever, is it permissible for a Christian to take the
step of breaking up a marital relationship?"

The New Testament passages which deal with this
question are all relatively short. Furthermore, each gives
the impression of being straightforward and unequivocal,
not the sort of thing which is likely to be misunderstood.
Unfortunately that impression is quite misleading. The
passages under examination raise serious doubts as to
whether the English translations may not paint a more
restrictive picture than is justified by the original Greek
text, particularly when considered in its historical context.
The relevant passages are as follows:

"It was also said, 'Whoever divorces his wife, let him give her a certificate of divorce.' But I say to you that every one who divorces his wife, except on the grounds of unchastity, makes her an adulteress; and whoever marries a divorced woman commits adultery."

(Matthew 5:31-32)

And Pharisees came up to him and tested him by asking, "Is it lawful to divorce one's wife for any cause?" He answered, "Have you not read that he who made them from the beginning made them male and female, and said, 'For this reason a man shall leave his father and mother and be joined to his wife, and the two shall become one flesh'? So they are no longer two but one flesh. What therefore God has joined together, let not man put asunder." They said to him, "Why then did Moses command one to give a certificate of divorce, and to put her away?" He said to them, "For your hardness of heart Moses allowed you to divorce your wives, but from the beginning it was not so. And I say to you: whoever divorces his wife, except for unchastity, and marries another, commits adultery".

(Matthew 19:3-9)

And Pharisees came up and in order to test him asked, "Is it lawful for a man to divorce his wife?" He answered them, "What did Moses command you?" They said "Moses allowed a man to write a certificate of divorce, and to put her away." But Jesus said to them, "For your hardness of heart he wrote you this commandment. But from the beginning of creation, 'God made them male and female'. 'For this reason a man shall leave his father and mother and be joined to his wife, and the two shall become one flesh.' So they are no longer two but one flesh. What therefore God has joined together, let not man put asunder."

(Mark 10:2-9)

"Every one who divorces his wife and marries another commits adultery, and he who marries a woman divorced from her husband commits adultery . . ."

(Luke 16:18)

To the married I give charge, not I but the Lord, that the wife should not separate from her husband (but if she does, let her remain single or else be reconciled to her husband)—and that the husband should not divorce his wife. To the rest I say, not the Lord, that if any brother has a wife who is an unbeliever, and she consents to live with him, he should not divorce her. If any woman has a husband who is an unbeliever, and he consents to live with her, she should not divorce him. For the unbelieving husband is consecrated through his wife, and the unbelieving wife is consecrated through her husband. Otherwise, your children would be unclean, but as it is they are holy. But if the unbelieving partner desires to separate, let it be so; in such a case the brother or sister is not bound. For God has called us to peace.

(1 Corinthians 7:10–15)

The first comment which might spring to mind on reading these texts is something along the lines of "That certainly puts the lid on that!" In fact there are numerous articles on this topic which do little more than list those texts and assert that they do, indeed, put the lid on the matter. Most then sanctimoniously intone that the word of God must be obeyed even if it is hard. As I hope I have already made clear, I agree completely with the last point. Christians are not free to depart from the declared will of their Lord merely because they disagree with it or because they find it distressingly onerous in some circumstances.

The question which I seek to address in this chapter is not, "Should the Lord's will be obeyed?" but, "What is the Lord's will?"

Despite, or perhaps because of, the emphatic and unequivocal nature of these scriptural passages there are very real difficulties in extracting from them a consistent series of principles faithful to all statements.

The first difficulty is that some of the passages appear to be mutually contradictory. As previously observed, the passages in Mark and Luke seem to exclude divorce for any cause, the passages in Matthew seem to suggest that there can be divorce but only on the grounds of unchastity whilst that in 1 Corinthians 7 seems to suggest that it may be permissible for a Christian to divorce a non-Christian husband or wife who desires to separate.

How does one resolve these contradictions?

Most of us who accept the authority of the Bible are prone to quote 2 Timothy 3:16 which reminds us "that all scripture is inspired by God and profitable for teaching, for reproof, for correction and for training in righteousness, that the man of God may be complete, equipped for every good work." If that is so, then it is not acceptable to endeavour to resolve this difficulty by simply asserting that one or more passages are correct and the others are not.

Some seek to resolve the difficulty by asserting that the prohibition of divorce contained in Mark and Luke is the true principle and that what is said in Matthew about unchastity is not an exception to the rule but simply a recognition that in those circumstances the wife will not be made an adulteress by divorce because she already is one. Some people would also seek to explain Paul's comments as recorded in 1 Corinthians 7 on the basis that he had prefaced his comments by making it clear that he was expressing his own view rather than God's declared will or, alternatively, on the basis that Paul was only permitting separation and not divorce. With the utmost deference to those who sincerely hold such views, the arguments that may be marshalled in support of them carry little weight.

The words that Jesus used in Matthew 19:9 assert in the clearest possible terms that a man will be guilty of adultery if he divorces his wife and marries another only if the divorce was not on the ground of unchastity. His

words could only be taken to mean that unchastity was a
valid ground for divorce. Certainly anyone familiar with
the Old Testament law would have construed it in that
manner. The attempt to brush aside the words of St Paul
by means of the arguments mentioned must also be
rejected. Whilst it is true that Paul was expressing his own
view, he was doing so in the course of a letter written in
an attempt to correct doctrinal errors creeping into the
Corinthian church. Paul was recognised as the great apostle
to the Gentiles and with his Pharisaic training, he was
scrupulous in ensuring correct doctrine was applied in the
churches to which he ministered. It is inconceivable that
he would not have been aware of Jesus' teaching on divorce
and that he would have suggested that the Corinthians
adopt a practice forbidden by it. Furthermore, how is such
an argument compatible with the proposition that all
Scripture is inspired by God? Can one really see God
inspiring Paul to write to the Corinthian church that its
members were free to act in a way that God had forbidden?

The suggestion that he was not permitting divorce but
merely separation is equally untenable. In the first place,
as we have already seen, separation and divorce mean
almost the same thing. Indeed in the same chapter, Paul
speaks of separated women remaining single, that is, not
remarrying. In other words, Paul saw people who were
separated as being single. The argument also overlooks
Paul's statement that in those circumstances the believer
is "not bound". In the context that word clearly means
"unfettered". The believer is no longer subject to the bonds
of marriage.

Another commonly espoused view is to accept that there
is an exception for adultery and another exception for
Christians married to non-Christians who wish to separate.
The statements in Mark and Luke are read as merely
expressing an ideal or a general principle subject to
exceptions, which for some reason, Jesus didn't mention
at the time. Whilst this explanation is superficially
attractive, it also encounters logical objections. If it is

legitimate to treat a straightforward and unequivocal command relating to divorce as a mere ideal or general principle subject to unspecified exceptions, then why is it not equally legitimate to treat other commands in the same way. Is it legitimate, for example, to suggest that the commandment not to commit adultery is a mere ideal to be disregarded if the attraction is sufficiently strong or, for that matter, to treat it as a general principle, subject to unstated exceptions which those of us with fertile minds should have little difficulty in devising for ourselves? If there were exceptions, then why didn't Jesus state them?

The question becomes even more inexplicable in relation to the passage recorded in Matthew 19 where Jesus did mention the exception for adultery.

How can one treat a statement that divorce is not permitted save in one situation as permitting St Paul to add another exception twenty or thirty years later?

The third commonly held view is to accept the exception for adultery and reject the exception given in 1 Corinthians. Whilst this view helps to overcome the distortion in the passage, it runs headlong into most of the obstacles encountered by both the first and the second views and is perhaps, the least tenable of the three.

These three views are those most commonly held among the mainstream denominations. All involve obvious difficulties.

How then are these passages to be reconciled? There is an answer and it is one which does not involve twisting the language to fit the concepts or other mental gymnastics. It is not, however, an explanation which can be stated in half a dozen words because it requires both an understanding of the historical context and an awareness that some of the words contained in the original Greek manuscript had particular shades of meaning which are not adequately conveyed by the English translation. For these reasons, I must ask you to bear with me whilst I try to fill in the background.

The first statement in the Bible concerning divorce is found in Deuteronomy 24:1-4 which reads as follows:

When a man takes a wife and marries her, if then she finds no favour in his eyes because he has found some indecency in her, and he writes her a bill of divorce and puts it in her hand and sends her out of his house, and she departs out of his house, and if she goes and becomes another man's wife, and the latter husband dislikes her and writes her a bill of divorce and puts it in her hand and sends her out of his house, or if the latter husband dies, who took her to be his wife, then her former husband, who sent her away, may not take her again to be his wife, after she has been defiled; for that is an abomination before the Lord; you shall not bring guilt upon the land which the Lord your God gives you for an inheritance.

A number of significant things may be gleaned from this passage.

Firstly, it seems certain that this law did not introduce the practice of divorce but merely sought to regulate, and to a degree, restrict a practice that was already in existence.

However, the formal requirement of a bill of divorce was an innovation. The purpose seems to have been to provide some protection for the woman concerned and, quite possibly, for any man she may wish to marry. The importance of this kind of protection may be readily appreciated when one considers that the law applied to a nation which had no provision for marriage ceremonies or records, and the death penalty for adultery. In those circumstances it was understandable that a man might have been wary of marrying a woman by simply taking her into his tent and commencing married life unless there was very strong evidence to establish that the earlier marriage had been terminated by divorce and that she was free to marry him. If he had made a mistake he might have found that what he thought was a marriage was regarded as an adulterous relationship and that those who did not share his view, stoned him to death outside the city gates. A bill of divorce, therefore, would facilitate the woman's remarriage.

Although it is now an historic anachronism some Jews still insist upon a bill of divorcement as a pre-condition to a woman's remarrying, even though the earlier divorce is regarded as valid without such a bill.

Secondly, the woman's remarriage to some other man was not prohibited; all that was prohibited was her subsequent return to the original husband. The law was thus diametrically opposed to the view held by many modern Christians who would say that because God does not recognise divorce, only the first marriage is valid, the second constitutes nothing more than an adulterous relationship and the woman's clear duty is to return to the original husband. It is thought that the purpose of this law was to raise the standards of marital and sexual behaviour among the people by preventing husbands and wives from leaving the original marriage relationships for other marriages of short duration and then returning to the original relationship. The restriction may, therefore, have been directed at a process akin to wife-swapping.

The third significant thing about this passage is that it states the ground for divorce, namely, that he has found "some indecency" in her. The Hebrew words so translated were *ervath dabhar*. That phrase has been translated as "the nakedness of a thing", "some uncleanness" (according to the Authorised Version) or "some indecency" (according to the RSV). This passage was the subject of controversy, and divergent views are described in the Talmud.[6]

Stated shortly, those who followed the teaching of Shammai held that a man should not divorce his wife unless she had been unfaithful. The followers of Hillel taught that a man should divorce his wife only if she had been guilty of some misconduct but the misconduct might be quite minor. Rabbi Akiba had the wonderfully straightforward view that a man may divorce his wife for no other reason than he found another woman more beautiful. Presumably he could trade them in annually if he were so inclined. That view was justified by stressing the words in Deuteronomy 24:1, ". . . if then she finds no favour in his eyes. . ."

The controversy still existed at the time of Jesus' ministry. Indeed it was almost certainly the reason for the Pharisees asking Jesus about divorce.

The first comments which Jesus made about the subject were made during the course of his Sermon on the Mount. Jesus said, "It was also said, 'Whoever divorces his wife, let him give her a certificate of divorce.' But I say to you, that anyone who divorces his wife except on the ground of unchastity, makes her an adulteress; and whoever marries a divorced woman commits adultery."[7]

The opening phrases of this passage are usually taken to mean that Jesus was quoting the Old Testament position and changing it by introducing a new and more strict commandment. Some translations, which have the happy propensity to record what the translator thinks Jesus should have said, rather than what he did, confirm that impression.

The *Living Bible*, for example, translates the opening phrase as the "The Law of Moses says, 'If anyone wants to be rid of his wife, he can divorce her merely by giving her a letter of dismissal'."

Mercifully, the RSV is rather more accurate. It is significant that Jesus did not commence his comments on this subject with the words, "The Law of Moses says" or even "It has been written", but rather, "It was also said". What then follows does not accurately reflect the passage in Deuteronomy 24:1 because it contains no reference to the ground for divorce; that is, the requirement of *ervath dabhar*. Accordingly, if Jesus was purporting to quote the Law of Moses, then he was doing so in a completely inaccurate manner which picked up the superficial and formal requirement and omitted the matter of substance. That Jesus, who described himself as the "word of God" should have done so during the course of the Sermon on the Mount in which he stated so many truths with profound precision seems simply incredible. In the context of the controversy concerning the meaning of Deuteronomy 24:1, it seems far more likely that when Jesus used the phrase, "it was also said", he was referring to what had been said by Rabbi

Akiba, namely that a man might divorce his wife, even though there had been no fault on her part so long as he gave her a bill of divorce. It was not the Law of Moses that he was correcting, but that particularly lax view of it which omitted the need for *ervath dabhar*.

Ervath dabhar is a term which refers to a range of misconduct.[8] It has definite sexual connotations and would include not only adultery, but other kinds of lewd or immoral or indecent behaviour. There is no English word with a comparable meaning but there is a Greek word which expresses a similar concept. That word is *porneia* from which, I understand, we derive the modern word pornography. That word referred to sexual immorality and, like the Hebrew concept of *ervath dabhar* would have included adultery but have extended to other forms of misconduct. The precise meaning of this term has also been the subject of considerable debate.

It is interesting to note that in that part of the passage quoted from Matthew 5 in which Jesus is normally assumed to be correcting the Old Testament, the word which is translated as "adultery" or "unchastity" is actually *poerneia*. In other words, Jesus did not impose a new and more restrictive commandment but corrected the lax view of Akiba and restated and confirmed the original commandment. In fact, he had just finished saying, "Think not that I have come to abolish the law and the prophets; I have come not to abolish them but to fulfil them".[9]

The concept has become confused because of the lack of any English equivalent and translators have opted to use "adultery" or "unchastity" probably because those words have been thought to be the closest in meaning. *Porneia*, nonetheless, had a wider meaning than adultery and the normal English translations are expressed too narrowly. There was a Greek word which meant simply adultery and that word *moichea* was used only three sentences earlier when Jesus said, "But I say to you that everyone who looks at a woman lustfully has already committed adultery with her in his heart". If Jesus intended to permit divorce only in cases of adultery, why did he change to the more general word only three sentences later? The only possible answer to that question is that he did so because he wanted to express a wider concept, namely the concept of shameful or indecent conduct already contained in the law that had been given to Moses.

What then are the limits of this ground of shameful or indecent conduct? Neither the Old nor the New Testament contains any further explanation other than that implicit in the meaning of the Hebrew and Greek words.

The most difficult question is whether it has to be misconduct of a specifically sexual nature. Both the Hebrew and Greek words have strong sexual connotations and that seems to have prompted the various translators to pick words such as "unchastity" or "adultery" as the closest English synonyms available. It seems to me, however, that the concept should not be looked at in the abstract but in the context of a marriage which is, of course, an essentially sexual relationship. In that context it seems to me that the word may be taken to include any kind of misconduct or immorality which is so serious that it pollutes or perverts the marital relationship. If that construction is correct, it would mean that a Christian should not contemplate divorce unless there was misconduct so serious that it virtually undermined the whole marriage. On the other hand, it would mean that a wife need not feel locked into a marital relationship with a man who was repeatedly guilty of gross violence towards her and/or their children merely because he had not committed adultery. That is more the kind of principle we would expect a wise and loving father to impose upon his children. I must confess I have always had the greatest difficulty in persuading myself that God intended that women would be free to withdraw from a marital relationship if their husbands committed adultery but not if their husbands tried to kill them.

This construction is confirmed by an Old Testament incident, the significance of which is normally overlooked because of the common, but incorrect assumption that Jesus

had overruled the Law of Moses in this respect and that
the Old Testament was therefore irrelevant. The incident
is recorded in Ezra, 9 and 10. The people of Israel,
including priests and Levites, had married foreign wives,
despite the Lord's commandment that they were not to do
so. The races concerned practised "abominations" and
when Ezra heard of the marriages, he was absolutely
appalled at the faithlessness of his people. The matter was
only resolved after a great assembly of the men of Judah
and Benjamin who confessed their sin, resolved to be
obedient to the Lord's will and to separate themselves from
their foreign wives. There is no suggestion whatever that
these women had committed adultery, yet each man was
commanded to divorce his foreign wife and send her back
to her people. Was this an act committed in defiance of
the law of God? Ezra and the people concerned were so
convicted of their guilt that they "wept bitterly". They
divorced their wives as an act of repentance, out of an overwhelming need to restore a right relationship with God.
One could scarcely imagine that they would attempt to do
so by deliberately flouting his law. Clearly then, there was
immediate and unanimous agreement that to divorce their
wives in these circumstances, was an act permitted by God's
law. Indeed they were not only permitted, but constrained,
to divorce them.

How could that be so if the uncleanness referred to in
Deuteronomy 24:1 was of an exclusively sexual nature?
It is apparent from the Old Testament context that the
uncleanness of which these women were guilty was not
sexual misconduct, but their practice of idolatry and of
leading the people of Israel into idolatrous practices. Some
may protest that these idolatrous practices involved sexual
immorality. Yet there is no suggestion of any inquiry to
determine which women, if any, were guilty of sexual
immorality. Ezra's concern was idolatry, not the form of
its practices. He clearly regarded that as falling within the
ambit of the grounds specified in Deuteronomy 24.

Of course there can be dangers in trying to establish

principles by reference to a single incident but even a single incident may be sufficient to show that a principle must have wider application than has been suggested. As a wise man once observed, if you find one black swan, you can no longer assert that all swans are white. The incident recorded in the Book of Ezra clearly refutes any dogmatic assertion that divorce was only allowed for sexual misconduct. Furthermore, there is another factor which makes it difficult to imagine that Jesus could have intended to limit divorce to cases of adultery or other sexual immorality.

All the main kinds of sexual immorality, whether adultery, homosexuality, or bestiality, were punishable by death. The story of the woman taken in adultery whose life was spared only because of Jesus' penetrating command, "Let him who is without sin among you be the first to throw a stone at her!"[10] confirms not only that the law was still in existence at the time Jesus spoke, but that it was applied. The consequence of that practice was that the husband of a woman taken in adultery was promptly widowed.

If Jesus had really intended to limit the grounds for divorce in the manner suggested, then his words might be paraphrased, "You can divorce your wife only when you don't need to, because you are about to be widowed". Furthermore, since gross violence would not fall within such grounds, the paraphrase might well continue, ". . . but not if she is about to widow herself by killing you". Clearly, Jesus did not say and did not mean anything so devoid of compassion, understanding and commonsense.

If then, the Old Testament concept of *ervath dabhar*, confirmed as it was by the use of the New Testament equivalent of *porneia*, was not limited to sexual misconduct, then what did it mean?

The only answer to that question which may be given with any real confidence is that the misconduct concerned must be very serious. The denunciation of the lax approach adopted by Rabbi Akiba and the strong statements to the effect that to divorce your wife unjustly was tantamount to adultery, clearly establish that. Even if those words had not been used, it should have been evident from the very nature of marriage and, in particular, from the concept of a man cleaving to his wife. That means sticking with her in good times and in bad. In these circumstances it seems clear that only something which struck at the very heart of the marital relationship could be a sufficient justification for divorce.

In fact, some theologians have sought to justify their contention that adultery is the only valid ground for divorce by reference to this very argument. They have suggested that the only thing sufficiently serious to strike at the very heart of a marital relationship is adultery. The only response that needs to be given to such an assertion is gratitude to God that he has permitted theologians to enjoy sheltered lives. Anyone who has spent much time counselling divorced people or dragging their unhappy sagas through the courts can recount incident after incident of the most savage brutality and unspeakable cruelty. I do not for one moment suggest that adultery is not a very serious matter, but there are many things worse. A child battered to death by a psychotic husband is one of the many instances which I wish did not spring to mind quite so readily.

The frailty of human nature is such that a person who is normally a good husband who cherishes his wife and does his best to maintain the marital relationship may, in a moment of particular weakness or temptation, commit adultery. Shakespeare recognised that when he asked the famous question, ''Who so firm that he cannot be seduced?'' If followed by a proper Christian response of reconciliation and forgiveness, an act of adultery, though undoubtedly the cause of great distress, may pose nowhere the same threat to the long-term future of a marriage as a pattern of persistent brutality or more subtle forms of cruelty, or even callous indifference.

John Stott has sought to support an argument that only sexual infidelity can be a ground for divorce by reference to the Old Testament. In Ezekiel 16:8ff, we read of God's covenant with Jerusalem: "...I plighted my troth to you and entered into a covenant with you...and you became mine... But you trusted in your beauty, and played the harlot..." Therefore God said he would judge Jerusalem as women who break [the bonds of] wedlock and shed blood are judged..." Yet although her behaviour was worse than her "sister Sodom" and although she had despised the covenant, God said, "...yet I will remember my covenant with you in the days of your youth, and I will establish with you an everlasting covenant..." and "...forgive you all that you have done..." This is said to be consistent with the proposition that only sexual infidelity breaks the marriage covenant but, with due deference to a very learned author, I would have thought that it indicated precisely the opposite. Ezekiel 16 was concerned with the sins of Jerusalem and, in particular, with unfaithfulness to God by means of idolatry. Sexual infidelity is used simply as a metaphor for spiritual infidelity. One could no more extract from this passage the view that divorce was only permissible on the ground of adultery than one could legitimately infer that the ceilings of all churches should be covered with feathers because Jesus said that he longed to gather the people of Jerusalem together "as a hen gathers her brood under her wings".

There is, however, some significance which can be gleaned from the fact that sexual sin is used as a metaphor for unfaithfulness to God. Clearly God was saying through the words recorded in Ezekiel 16 that other sins involved the same breach of faith as adultery. This is precisely what one would expect because sin is simply rebellion against God. It is the fact of that rebellion or lack of faithfulness which is of critical importance rather than the particular form it takes. Equally it is the fact of a serious and persistent violation of faithfulness to the other party which is important. That lack of faithfulness will undermine and ultimately destroy the marriage. It matters not one whit whether that unfaithfulness is reflected in adultery, desertion or violent and cruel behaviour.

Marriage is a relationship of shared lives which extends over many years. Within such a relationship, there is ample opportunity for conduct of all kinds; from the most noble to which human nature aspires, to the depths of depravity. I suspect that God chose the words *ervath dabhar* and *porneia* for their very generality because he wished to avoid the kind of legalism so practised by the Pharisees. He simply made it plain that he was speaking of serious conduct that struck at the heart of the marital relationship. In fact, it may well be that in speaking of *porneia*, Jesus was not really creating an exception permitting the termination of a marital relationship, but merely recognising that such conduct may itself destroy the relationship. Within the parameters of the general concept may fall many different kinds of misconduct.

I believe that each person must evaluate the situation and decide prayerfully and conscientiously whether the conduct of the other spouse has been so serious that the marriage is at an end, or whether, with patience, understanding and forgiveness, it may yet be revived.

In this context, it is easy to understand the comments of Paul in 1 Corinthians 7. Paul was not intending to contradict what Jesus had said. He was well aware that Christians, like Jews, were not permitted to divorce their husbands or wives unless they had been guilty of such misconduct. I would suggest that he was also very conscious of the fact that it was a matter for individual judgement whether particular kinds of misconduct came within that area or not. It is obvious that a number of Christian converts were troubled about where their duty lay when their husbands or wives wished to separate from them following Christian conversion. That was a question not specifically dealt with by Jesus and one referred to Paul because of his apostolic role. Accordingly, the answer he gave should be understood not as the imposition of some new rule, but as a guideline intended to assist his fellow Christians to understand how the existing rule applied to those particular circumstances. No doubt it was for that reason that Paul made it plain that he was not expressing a new revelation of God's law but his own judgement.

In other words, Paul was saying, "If your husband or wife insists on leaving you because of your conversion to Christianity then, in my opinion, that is conduct which constitutes *porneia* and you are justified in treating the marriage as being at an end."

At this point I would ask you to pause and consider the two conclusions so far expressed.

Those conclusions are, firstly, that when the Bible speaks about divorce, it speaks about breaking up a marital relationship; and secondly, that divorce is only permitted upon the ground of serious misconduct which strikes at the very heart of the marital relationship. When those conclusions are considered together they give rise to one further question. Suppose a Christian woman with a number of small children is married to a drunken thug who regularly beats her and the children. As time goes by she repeatedly seeks help from marriage guidance counsellors and others expert in advising on alcoholism and violent behaviour. She is also faithful in prayer about the situation and has Christian friends also supporting her in prayer. Yet despite all these efforts, her husband becomes increasingly antagonistic, is openly derisive of her involvement in church and Christian affairs and his violent outbursts become so uncontrollable that the children are in a constant state of terror at home. Ultimately, she has two alternatives. The first is to remain in the marital relationship, knowing that her husband has no intention of permitting a real marriage and that sooner or later either she or one of the children is likely to be seriously injured, if not killed. The other alternative is to leave him and take the children to a new home where they will be safe. Eventually, after much soul-searching and anguish, she decides to leave him.

At that stage when they are occupying separate households and there is no likelihood of reconciliation, they are already divorced, using that word in the sense that was used in the Bible. Yet who has divorced whom? It is true that she left him in the sense that she withdrew from the roof under which they were both living. Yet if one looks at the word divorce in the wider sense of the destruction of a viable marital relationship, might one not fairly conclude that it was the husband who had divorced the wife? The extremity of his misconduct over many years had struck at the heart of the marital relationship and virtually destroyed it months or even years before she actually left the home.

There are many cases like this where husbands and wives agonise over whether they are entitled to divorce their spouses but, in reality, arguments as to the meaning of *porneia* are irrelevant because the marital relationships really ended years earlier and, for all practical purposes, the parties are already "divorced". Similar considerations may arise when a person is confronted by the harsh reality that a viable marital relationship is no longer possible, not as a result of some particular misconduct but because of some other factor such as insanity.

With that in mind, let us return to the problem of reconciling the various New Testament statements.

Chronologically the first statement made is recorded in Matthew 5:31 where Jesus affirmed the Old Testament law by the use of a word recorded in all of the early Greek texts as *porneia*, the equivalent concept to the Old Testament's *ervath dabhar*. That statement was a public pronouncement made in the early stages of Jesus' ministry. It was uttered during a portion of the Sermon on the Mount in which he was calling for greater holiness by adherence not only to the letter of the law, but to the heart of it. Any suggestions that he included the exception by error, that he stated it more widely than he intended to or that he later changed his mind are nonsense.

The subsequent statements in Mark and Luke must therefore be understood as having been made at a time when Jesus' position on divorce was already public knowledge. Consequently they may be regarded as occasions upon which Jesus emphasised or re-emphasised a particular part of a teaching that he had already fully expounded. The part that he was re-emphasising was that for a man to divorce his wife unjustly was tantamount to adultery; it was a serious wrong. There was no need to pursue a digression about some exception which had already been part of God's law for centuries and which Jesus, himself, had specifically affirmed. Furthermore, in one sense, the reference to *porneia* is scarcely an exception at all. It may be that a person who withdraws from a relationship because of such serious misconduct by the other party does not thereby commit the act of divorce because that kind of relationship has already been destroyed. Whichever way the matter is looked at, there is no basis for treating these later statements as being inconsistent with the earlier affirmation of the Old Testament principle during the course of the Sermon on the Mount.

The words of St Paul in 1 Corinthians 1:7 were also consistent with the views that I have expressed because, for the reasons discussed, they reflect not the imposition of a new and contradictory rule, but simply a guideline as to whether or not particular conduct falls within the parameters of the old rule.

CHAPTER FOUR

The Right to Remarry

The question of whether divorced Christians may remarry and, if so, in what circumstances, has been a source not only of great controversy but also of very great anguish and heartache. In this area, too, there are a number of commonly espoused views, to use an unfortunate term. As with divorce the only factor common to the various views seems to be that the proponents claim infallible scriptural authority.

Unhappily, this area is also somewhat confusing and it is necessary to examine the matter in depth by reference to the historical context and to the precise meaning of the particular language employed in the various scriptural passages.

To gain some appreciation of the proper historical setting, one must again return to Deuteronomy 24:1. That passage clearly sets out the Old Testament position, namely, that a divorced person was free to remarry. Perhaps the most striking thing about the passage is that it clearly contemplates a woman having the right to remarry even though her husband had divorced her after he had genuinely found some "uncleanness in her". In other words, the passage makes it plain that even the guilty party was free to remarry. Indeed, the husband who was properly exercising his right to divorce was commanded to give the

guilty wife a bill of divorce and, as discussed earlier, it seems
clear that the purpose of giving her that document was to
facilitate her remarriage (to someone else). There can be
no suggestion that the Law of Moses prevented remarriage
or restricted it to innocent parties. It simply prohibited a
husband from remarrying his former wife if her subsequent
marriage was terminated.

That, in a nutshell, was the Old Testament law concerning remarriage after divorce. It was clearly understood
in the sense which I have mentioned and was applied in
that fashion. There was no Jewish tradition of formal
separation akin to the Middle Ages development of divorce
a mensa et thoro or any other middle-of-the-road obligation
without the right to remarry.

The crucial New Testament passage, Matthew 5:31–32,
consequently presents an enigma. For the reasons discussed
in the previous chapter, it seems abundantly clear that in
making this statement, Jesus was refuting the lax teaching
propounded by Rabbi Akiba and emphatically affirming
the Old Testament law. He was also re-emphasising the
principle that divorce was only permitted on the grounds
of serious misconduct. That being the case, one would
naturally expect an affirmation of the whole of the Old
Testament principles set out in Deuteronomy 24:1. Jesus,
after all, had just announced that he had not come to abolish
the law and the prophets, but to fulfil them. After those
words of general affirmation and after a specific affirmation of the Old Testament law concerning divorce, it would
be surprising indeed to find Jesus abolishing part of the
law concerning divorce and instituting something diametrically opposite in its place.

Yet, at first blush, that is precisely what he seems to
have done when he said, ''But I say to you that every one
who divorces his wife, except on the grounds of unchastity, makes her an adulteress; and whoever marries a
divorced woman commits adultery''.[12]

The conventional explanation of this passage runs along
these lines:

(a) Jesus is explaining that God does not recognise the validity of divorce based upon any ground other than adultery (or, at least, *porneia*);

(b) a divorced woman will necessarily be forced into a further marriage;

(c) because God does not recognise divorce he will not recognise the validity of her further marriage and will regard her relationship with her second husband as adultery;

(d) consequently the wife will become an adulteress because of the divorce;

(e) the exception for unchastity is explained by the proposition that in those circumstances the wife was not made an adulteress, because she already was one.

That explanation is superficially attractive. Closer examination, however, reveals serious objections.

In the first place the argument is totally dependent upon the assumption that divorced women would inevitably be forced into a subsequent marriage. Attempts are usually made to bolster this assumption by reference to the Jewish lifestyle existing in Palestine at the time. There were, after all, no twentieth-century innovations such as deserted wives' pensions, supporting mothers' benefits or other kinds of social welfare assistance which might have sustained unmarried women. Yet, as superficially plausible as that explanation may be, it simply does not hold water.

Divorced women usually received back their dowries and there is no reason to suppose that, as a class, they would have been any more underprivileged economically than the widows of the day. There was always the possibility of the widow of a wealthy man inheriting a substantial estate but it was obvious that in a pre-industrial civilisation where most people supported themselves by manual labour, the overwhelming majority of the population would have been relatively poor and large estates rare. Under those circumstances life may have been difficult for widows as well as divorcees.

Why could not a divorced woman have pursued the courses which were obviously open to widows? Why could she not return to her parents' home, for example? Why could she not live in the household of a married brother? Certainly Ruth and Naomi managed to survive notwithstanding their widowhood and, what is more, they managed to do so after returning to an area in which they were not well known. The New Testament also contains reference to a number of widowed or single women. Anna the prophetess, for example, had been widowed for many years. Philip the Evangelist had four unmarried daughters who were prophetesses. There is no suggestion that any of these women were forced into marriages, remarriages or prostitution by economic or other circumstances. Of course there may have been some women whether widowed, divorced or single who felt constrained to marry someone able to support them adequately. But it cannot be said that remarriage was an inevitable consequence of divorce.

In the second place, the argument assumes that God regards the first marriage as continuing notwithstanding the divorce. There are no biblical statements in either the Old or the New Testament which support this view other than the words of the passage itself. Consequently, in this respect at least, the argument has to hold itself up by its own bootstraps. The argument may be paraphrased in these terms. Remarriage is adultery. How do we know that? Well it stands to reason—after all God regards the first marriage as continuing notwithstanding the divorce. How do we know that? Well, it stands to reason; after all, remarriage is adultery.

Upon such wonderful flights of circular logic people attempt to justify assumptions about God's will which condemn men and women, frequently still in their twenties, into remaining single for the rest of their lives. It is clear that the Old Testament law did not treat remarriage as adultery. Accordingly, those who seek to support this view have to assert that the assumption based upon this circular logic is sufficient to outweigh clear biblical statements.

In the third place Jesus did not say the woman would be made an adulteress by the act of remarriage. What he said was that her husband, by divorcing her, made her an adulteress.

The conventional argument therefore depends upon a distortion of the words used or, at least, the assumption that Jesus did not express himself very clearly and that he said one thing but really meant another. This difficulty is implicitly recognised in the *Living Bible*, in which a phrase has simply been added to the first sentence of verse 32 so that it reads, "But I say that a man who divorces his wife, except for fornication, causes her to commit adultery, if she marries again". Those last four words do not appear in the original Greek text nor, for that matter, in most English translations and are a classic example of a translator recording what he thought Jesus should have said, rather than what he did say. They no doubt reflect the author's understanding of what he thought Jesus was trying to say but the very fact that he felt obliged to add to what Jesus said in order to "make it clear" is eloquent of the difficulty of this construction.

As previously discussed, I believe that the key to the interpretation of this passage lies in understanding that Jesus was speaking in denunciation of the hypocritical and immoral practices of those Pharisees who followed the teaching of Akiba and who divorced their wives frequently, for no other reason than they had found other women who, for the time being, they found more attractive. Having referred to this practice in verse 31, he then proceeded to restate the Old Testament law and then said that those who unjustly divorce their wives thereby make them adulteresses. How could that be so? Well, the law provided only one lawful ground for divorce, namely some "uncleanness". That would usually, though not exclusively, have been adultery. The husbands were

Pharisees, men who were religious leaders and who were
seen by the community as pillars of moral rectitude. If such
a man divorced his wife surely there could be only one
explanation: his wife had been guilty of adultery. In the
eyes of the community, therefore, the very fact of a divorce
was sufficient to brand the woman as an adulteress. Dr
Ward Powers, in his paper "Divorce and the Bible",
explains it in these terms,

> ". . . what the divorce causes is that the wife is stig-
> matised as an adulteress, given the status of an adulteress
> (because under the law *ervath dabhar* is the only acceptable
> ground for divorce). Jesus is making the accusation that
> the Jews are changing the import of the laws of Moses,
> and when a wife is divorced in accordance with their
> lax view, she is placed in a position as being regarded
> as an adulteress in terms of the actual wording of the
> law. Moreover, the man who married her in such
> circumstances would be regarded as the lover who
> provoked the divorce and thus stigmatised as an
> adulterer. In what Jesus says, the blame in this situation
> is not being placed upon the divorced wife, nor upon
> the man she next marries (if she does), but upon the
> first husband who thus lightly cast her aside, and beyond
> that, upon the Pharisees for their laxity about the law
> which has accepted this situation."[13]

Viewed in this light the passage offers a confirmation
of the Old Testament law coupled with a stinging rebuke
of the practices of the Pharisees. It commences with a
statement of the emasculated version of the law by which
the Pharisees sought to justify their actions. It continues
with an emphatic statement of the true position and
concludes by pointing out the evil that is caused by their
unjust practices and distortion of the law. That evil is that
an innocent woman is stigmatised as an adulteress and any
subsequent marriage sullied by the suspicion that her new
husband was an adulterer who had broken up the first
marriage.

The passages in Matthew 19, Mark 10 and Luke 16 must

be treated as relating to situations where a man has sent his wife away not because she has been guilty of gross misconduct but because of some trivial fault or for some reason unjustified by the law. The reasons for this conclusion have been canvassed in the previous chapter. Understood in this light, passages such as that recorded in Mark 10:11, "Whoever divorces his wife and marries another commits adultery against her," can be readily understood. The man is breaking the marriage bond without justification so that he may enter into a sexual relationship with another woman. It is hardly surprising that Jesus regards that as being tantamount to adultery.

It must be candidly conceded that there is no evidence which conclusively proves the correctness of this view. However for the reasons already expressed, there are several quite serious objections to the alternative view and strong grounds for concluding that Dr Powers is almost certainly correct. Those reasons include the following:

(a) It provides a logical explanation for a statement which can otherwise be explained only by a combination of unwarranted assumptions and distortion of language.

(b) It rings true in the sense that it reflects the justice and compassion that one would have expected from Jesus.

(c) It represents a logical culmination of Jesus' comments which are then seen to consist of a statement of the error followed by a correction, followed by explanation of the harm caused by the error.

(e) It is consistent with the Old Testament law concerning divorce which Jesus had just affirmed.

Another significant New Testament passage concerning marriage appears in 1 Corinthians 7. In that chapter, verse 10 is one which, if not kept in its context, can also be seen to be prohibiting marriage after divorce, "To the married I give charge, not I but the Lord, that the wife should not separate from her husband (but if she does let her remain single or else be reconciled to her husband) and that the husband should not divorce his wife".

For a proper understanding of that verse, however, it is crucial to remember that it immediately follows verses 8 and 9 which state, "To the unmarried and the widows I say that it is well for them to remain single as I do. But if they cannot exercise self-control, they should marry. For it is better to marry than to be aflame with passion".

There are two Greek words, both of which are translated in the Revised Standard Version by the word "unmarried". Those words are *parthenos* and *agamos*. The word *parthenos* means a person who has never had sexual intercourse, a virgin. The other word, *agamos*, refers to a person who is no longer married but who may have been married in the past. Later in 1 Corinthians 7—in verse 25—Paul commences a lengthy narrative of advice to the single person. That narrative commences with the phrase "the unmarried" and the word there translated as "unmarried" is *parthenos*. The advice which Paul gives in verses 25 to 40 is accordingly confined to those who have never married, the virgins.

On the other hand, in 1 Corinthians 7:8 the word *agamos* has been used. Now it is important to note that Paul has referred to the widows quite separately and, consequently, did not have to use the word *agamos* in order to include them. If he had used the word *parthenos* he would have made it plain that he was referring to those who were widowed and to those who had never married and could have excluded the divorced from consideration. Yet he did not do so. The word used is *agamos*. Not only was Paul a Pharisee but he was an outstanding student; one who had the rare distinction of being permitted to sit at the feet of Gamaliel. It is scarcely likely that his use of the word *agamos* in preference to *parthenos* can have been explained by mere clumsiness of expression, especially since he used the word *parthenos* only a sentence later. It must be assumed that he chose the word deliberately and that he did so conscious of its wider meaning. Accordingly, verses 8 and 9 might be expressed more clearly in the following terms, "To those who have never married, those who are divorced and to the widows I say to them that it is as well for them to remain single as I do. But if they cannot exercise self-control, they should marry".

Paul has already made it plain that he really wished that all people would remain single as he was, but he recognises that whilst some are called to celibacy, others are not. His summation in verses 8 and 9 indicates with the greatest possible clarity that those who cannot exercise self-control, that is those whom the Lord has not called to celibacy, should marry whether they are single, divorced or widowed.

Following that clear indication that so far as remarriage is concerned the divorced are to adopt the same principle as single people and widows, Paul turns to deal with the married.

In verse 10, Paul clearly uses the term "the married" in contradistinction to those referred to in the previous verses. He has dealt with the unmarried, including the divorced, and now he is passing on to deal with married people. It is to those people that he conveys Jesus' charge that the wife should not separate from her husband and that the husband should not remove or abandon his wife. Here again, the traditional English translation is confusing. The word used in verse 11 is not *apoluo* which means divorce but *aphiemi* which means remove or abandon. There is no reason to suppose that this passage was written in an attempt to lay down an inflexible rule concerning divorce. Such a construction would be quite inconsistent with what he says in verse 25.

In laying down an instruction for married Christians, Paul was clearly concerned to remind them that Jesus had charged them to try to sort out their differences and remain in a proper marital relationship. In that context Paul said that if the wife did leave she should remain single or be reconciled to her husband. Clearly what Paul has in mind was a short-term situation immediately following separation. There may have been some estrangement and one party may have stormed out but the marriage has not been irretrievably destroyed. Whilst there is still hope it is the wife's duty to seek a reconciliation with her husband. Equally, it is the husband's duty to seek a reconciliation and not to abandon his wife.

No doubt that is the advice which any modern Christian counsellor would offer a woman, or a man for that matter, in similar circumstances. But it is important to remember that the commandment was given as advice to the married. Clearly then Paul was contemplating a period immediately following separation when the prospect of a reconciliation existed and it had not become clear that the marital relationship had terminated. If, despite the wife's efforts, the relationship was finally extinguished then without any further step being taken both the husband and the wife would be regarded as *agamos*, that is, unmarried. They would then be subject, not to the commandments in verses 10 and 11, but to those in verses 8 and 9. In other words, once it was clear that the marital relationship had been terminated then each would be free to marry.

As in Deuteronomy 24, there is no suggestion in any portion of 1 Corinthians 7 that the right to remarry is limited to the person who was the innocent party in the original divorce. It is clear from Matthew 5:31 that a person who divorces a husband or wife without justification of the kind recognised in the concept of *porneia* commits a serious sin. His conduct is tantamount to adultery. If a Christian has been guilty of such a sin in terminating his marriage then he should confess it and obtain forgiveness.

Having done so he must treat it in the same manner as he would treat any other sin that he has had to confess; that is, he should accept God's forgiveness and put his sin behind him, secure in the knowledge of Christ's atonement. He must not, under any circumstances, permit it to cripple or restrict his future life. If he later contemplates remarriage there may be many factors which he needs to consider (some of which will be discussed later) but he need not ever feel that he may be held back from remarriage by some real or imagined sin either in his former marriage or in the act of divorce.

If, after fully weighing the historical context and the precise meaning of the words used, you are still in any real doubt as to the views which I have expressed, then I would invite you to pause for a moment and consider the consequences of the more simplistic views held by many churches.

What are the consequences of applying a theology which holds that the first marriage is either indissoluble on any ground or dissoluble only on the ground of adultery? To be blunt, they are appalling. The righteous remain held in bondage and sin becomes the only way to freedom.

Let us suppose that a proponent of such a view is seeking to counsel Anne, a young mother married to a brutal and domineering man who has made life virtually unbearable for her and her children over a period of many years. If he were completely candid he would confide that it is a very great pity that she married the man instead of "living in sin". If she had merely lived with him in a de-facto relationship that conduct would have been sinful but she could have immediately received forgiveness for that. Her withdrawal from the relationship would not only have been untainted by any suspicion of sin but could actually have been acclaimed as a virtuous act of repentance. Once out of the situation she would, of course, have been free to marry someone else. After all, in those circumstances it would have been her first marriage and there would have been no suggestion that such a union would not have been pleasing in God's sight. Indeed, the very bells of heaven would have rung for joy at the thought of this woman with the sinful past now entering into a proper and virtuous marriage. Having made that clear, he would then proceed to shake his head sadly and say that—because she had insisted on following her conscience and marrying the man in the manner she believed God had ordained—she was now irretrievably imprisoned in that relationship.

She might, with some justification, retort, ''That can't

be right. Why, for heaven's sake, should I be forever locked into an intolerable situation because I kept his law instead of breaking it? Doesn't the Bible suggest that God rewards the righteous and punishes the wicked? If you are right then that should be reversed''. One could not really expect the poor man to offer direct answers to such questions. However, he might choose his words with great care and, in tones at once patient and pious, explain that God's will can be very hard but that we are not meant to question it. Of course, if the woman had sufficient spirit and sufficient confidence in the character of God, she might retort with some feeling, ''Look, that may be so, but he is neither unjust nor illogical and the nonsense that you have just attributed to him, paints him as both''.

Faced with a young woman looking at the situation with such distressing clarity and logic, the dear gentleman might decide that it is prudent to change tack and mollify her. He might point out that the marriage need not be indissoluble for ever. After all, at some stage in the future her husband may stop beating her up and being cruel to the children and, just for variety, go out and commit adultery. In that event she would experience the glorious liberty to leave him.

Unfortunately, logical young women are not so easily mollified and the poor man might hear her exclaim, in tones dripping with incredulity, ''You expect me to believe that the only right and proper Christian solution to the bondage that I am enduring is to wait until I am set free by my husband's sin? Is that the answer God has for me? If so, is it right and proper for me to pray that God will hasten the solution by sending along an appropriately seductive woman at an early date?''

I trust that you will forgive the emotively laden way in which I have sought to make these points. I have done so only because these views seem to have become so well entrenched in the church that they are rarely questioned and to challenge entrenched views sometimes requires a cutlass rather than a rapier. I make no apology for pointing out, as bluntly as I can, that advice of the kind given to Anne is totally inconsistent with everything the Bible says about justice and mercy.

Advice of that kind may also place a person in a position in which he feels that his divorce has become an unforgivable sin.

Let us take another example of a man whom we shall call Len. He had a brief but unsatisfactory first marriage which terminated in divorce. He has subsequently re-married and has a good relationship with his second wife and the three young children of that marriage. At that stage he becomes a Christian and seeks advice from a counsellor who holds traditionally restrictive views on divorce. If the counsellor holds those views with sincerity and if he is a man of integrity then the only advice that he can give Len is that God does not recognise divorce from his first wife and regards him as still married to her. Consequently his marriage to his second wife is not recognised in God's sight and, indeed, is nothing more than an adulterous affair. True, he may be forgiven for what he has done but the price of that forgiveness must be repentance. In this case repentance means that he must forever withdraw from any sexual relationship with his wife. Furthermore, since to live with her under the one roof would impose an intolerable temptation, his clear Christian duty is to move out of the house. At this stage poor Len may look somewhat aghast and protest. "But surely it can't be my Christian duty to leave my wife and kids?" The counsellor, whom I have described as a sincere fellow, may sympathise but he will have to be firm. "I'm afraid it is. After all, you don't obtain the right to commit adultery just because you have done it long enough."

In a desperate search for safer ground, Len might bring up the subject of the children and suggest if God intended him to move out of the house they would be deprived of the support and security derived from living with their father. However, that might cause little concern to the counsellor who would be free to explain that none of the

THE RIGHT TO REMARRY

biblical passages dealing with divorce mentions children.
Consequently, like the pastor I mentioned in Chapter 1,
he would be entitled to disregard them.

This situation is by no means fanciful. People with
children of a second marriage are converted every day of
the week and whether or not they are counselled to separate,
most of them go through months and years of agony
concerning their position with God as a consequence of their
second marriage.

It is a very real and a very serious problem. I know of
actual cases in which advice of the kind attributed to those
counselling Anne and Len has been given to sincere and
anguished people with disastrous consequences. Whilst one
may be critical of such advice one should nonetheless have
some sympathy for the counsellors. The advice may not
spring from a lack of compassion or sensitivity but simply
from the acceptance of views which make an absurdity
inevitable whenever one encounters a particular set of
circumstances. How do you solve these problems whilst
remaining faithful to such views? As suggested in the
dialogue above, it is scarcely legitimate to claim that whilst
God does not recognise the subsequent marriage initially,
there will come a point at which he suddenly does, even
though the first wife is still living. What basis in scripture
or in logic could there be for such an assertion?

Personally, I have no doubt whatsoever that such advice
is completely misconceived and reflects a travesty of God's
word. Quite apart from the theological principles which
I have canvassed in earlier chapters, it flies in the face of
everything which the Bible tells us about God's character.
We are told that God is just, merciful and the father of
the fatherless. If we are presented with a view of his word
which involves him imposing upon a man a duty to break
his marriage vows, betray his wife's trust and cause serious
emotional harm to innocent children, then we must ask
whether his word has not been misrepresented.

The argument also assumes that nothing the Bible says
about divorce applies to second marriages. Nowhere in

either the Old Testament or the New Testament is there anything to support such a proposition. When, in Malachi 2:16, God said, ''For I hate divorce. . .'', he did so in the context of the Old Testament law which clearly permitted remarriage. He did not, for one moment, suggest that what he hated was only divorce which terminated a first marriage. Clearly, what he meant was that he hated an act which terminated a precious relationship between a man and a woman of the kind which he himself had ordained. The effect of much of the advice given by ministers and other Christian counsellors is actually to encourage divorce where it relates to second marriages. To be blunt about it, that is not only wrong, but sinful. Jesus said that what God had put together, man should not put asunder. If someone disagrees with me, well and good. God, during the course of eternity, will no doubt reveal which of us is right. But if he seeks to encourage someone to leave his second wife because of some theological quibble about the validity of an earlier divorce, then let him beware that he does not find himself cast in the role of one who has presumed to put asunder that which God has joined together.

I am absolutely convinced that this peculiar concept that the first marriage exists beyond the divorce, a view not stated in either the Old or the New Testament, is clearly wrong. Worse, it is the source of the utmost heartache and anguish to thousands of families where husbands or wives have been previously married. These people should long since have accepted God's forgiveness and put the past behind them. Indeed, like Paul, they should be ''straining forward to what lies ahead''.

This kind of advice has imposed a great strain on second marriages and, even if the couple are not actually counselled to separate, the strain can be a contributing cause to the failure of such marriages. One does not atone for the failure of one marriage by destroying another any more than a murderer may atone for killing one person by killing another.

Let us not encourage immorality or a watered-down commitment to marriage but, on the other hand, let us not emulate the Pharisees by putting great burdens on the shoulders of those least able to bear them.

CHAPTER FIVE

Some Conclusions

The strength and diversity of views on this unhappy topic and the need to dispel unnecessary guilt have caused me to deal with these arguments in detail and to take far more time than I would have wished. In conclusion, it seems to me that the position may be summarised in the following terms:

(a) Where the Bible speaks of marriage it speaks not of the legal rights and obligations which flow from such a relationship but of the marital relationship itself. The three elements which characterise such a relationship are the establishment of a separate household, the permanence of the relationship and the intimate nature of the relationship, including the sexual union of the parties.

(b) When the Bible speaks of divorce it speaks of the termination of that marital relationship. It does not speak of some subsequent time at which the legal rights and obligations of the parties are disentangled. For that reason the advice so frequently given to Christians, namely that it is all right to separate as long as they don't proceed to divorce in the sense of having a judicial decree of dissolution pronounced, is completely wrong and un-scriptural. The true position is that Christians are obliged to do all that they can to nurture and preserve their marital relationship. God is concerned with keeping the families together, not with a legal shell.

(c) If a marriage becomes intolerable to one party in the sense that the conduct of the other party is such that a proper marital relationship is no longer viable, then a Christian husband or wife may proceed to divorce, that is, proceed to sever the marital relationship. Even after actually leaving, however, any reasonable areas of reconciliation should be explored and it is only when it has become clear that no reconciliation can be achieved that the marriage should be regarded as at an end.

(d) Once that point has been reached, then, in biblical terms, the couple is already divorced and may feel free to regularise the situation by proceeding to obtain a legal decree and to resolve any issues concerning the children of the marriage and any matrimonial property.

(e) If a person is at fault in the breakdown of his (or her) first marriage, and everyone is to some extent, then he will need to seek forgiveness for his part. No matter how responsible he may have been for the termination of that marriage, however, God will forgive him and he will be free to remarry and to start a new life.

PART TWO

THE CLIMATE FOR DECISION

CHAPTER SIX

Seeing Through the Fog

Stripping aside some of the misconceptions concerning the biblical statements on divorce may, of itself, bring liberation to some people.

To know that God loves you and offers forgiveness and acceptance no matter what your background is heady wine. Yet it is completely true. If your marriage has broken down, you may be assured that God is neither glaring down at you like a stern headmaster nor gloating that he has caught you out. You don't need tearfully to implore forgiveness. He has seen and heard everything and has shared your anguish. Whether you realise it or not, you are entitled to approach him as a favourite child approaches a benevolent father.

Of course there are rules which he has laid down and he expects them to be obeyed. Yet if we look at these carefully we will see that his commandments also reflect his love. They are for our benefit individually and collectively. If we follow them we find that we have followed the path that will lead in the long run to peace and contentment. If, from time to time, we fail, then he readily forgives us.

Unhappily these simple truths have frequently been obscured by a pharisaical adherence to a number of rules which are said to follow from what Jesus said about divorce. These rules and the climate of emotional blackmail surrounding them locks people into a prison of guilt and despair. Yet, as I have sought to demonstrate, many of them are completely misconceived.

As you emerge from this fog of pharisaism, new options open up. Yet options give rise to the need to make decisions and the decisions you may be called upon to make may have far-reaching consequences, not only for you, but for other members of your family. At this point you may find that you have emerged from one fog only to become lost in another. This is a fog of confusion in which any accurate assessment is shrouded in the swirling mists of strong emotions, dubious advice and general insecurity. Hope and resignation may jostle for supremacy. The desire for the freedom of a new life may fight daily battles with factors such as loyalty, regret and a reluctance to forsake the familiar and to some degree, perhaps, the secure.

You may find yourself so confused you don't even know what course you would like to pursue. Alternatively, you may know what you want but have no idea how to achieve it or whether such a course would be morally defensible. Whatever stage you have reached, you are likely to find yourself crying out, "How can I get out of the mess?"

There is, of course, no magic formula which will provide the right answer in every situation. If there were some straightforward solution you would probably have adopted it long ago. That is part of the agony. People frequently feel that every alternative involves hurting someone and every opportunity is plagued by risk and uncertainty. In this climate it is not surprising that so many decisions are made, not as a result of any sober evaluation, but simply as a response to emotional pressure. Typically, a person under this kind of pressure will procrastinate, and, not knowing the right decision, make none at all. Yet, in a sense, that is a decision because it involves electing to accept the status quo. Things usually go from bad to worse and finally after a particularly angry scene, the person storms out.

Unhappily, neither simple indecisiveness nor an angry

demonstration of defiance is likely to guarantee a course that is right for you and pleasing to God.

The first step towards any rational decision must be to make some attempt to control the emotional turmoil and take a cold, hard look at the facts. Despite the difficulty, this is essential to the resolution of every problem. Your future and the future of your children demands the most rational and careful consideration.

At this point, the advice of friends usually proves to be of little value. They may offer encouragement, support and sympathy, but they are unlikely to understand your situation with clarity. In fact, friends are more likely to be misled by their own reaction to your distress which they rightly or wrongly attribute to the conduct of your spouse. There will be a sense in which you are acutely alone. You have never been through a situation like this before and no one else really understands.

Despite this, you need not succumb to despair. Whilst there is no magic formula, it is possible to evaluate your situation and make the right decision. To do so requires, not a flash of intuition, but a step-by-step approach.

The first step is to endeavour to put your marital situation in context. That may give you greater insight into your present situation. It may show you how this situation developed and it may throw some light on what is likely to happen in the future. If it does nothing else it should bring home to you the fact that you are not alone. Thousands of people are embroiled in the same kind of anguish.

Intriguingly enough it was Don Juan who came out with the immortal lines, "Marriage is like a besieged city. Those inside want to get out and those outside want to get in". Generations of readers have smiled at this splendidly cynical observation but the concept of being under siege will strike a responsive chord in the minds of many married people. Marital relationships are based upon intimacy and trust. Consequently, they are vulnerable. Certainly, some are more robust than others. Some husbands and wives are more mature, better adjusted and more compatible. Some have built up a strong relationship over many years and some are strong because of their common faith and Christian commitment. Yet sooner or later, they will encounter pressures sufficient to buffet the strongest city walls.

It may be helpful to identify some of these pressures and to consider what can be done to alleviate them. In many books pressures of this kind are discussed under headings such as ''causes of divorce'', but I believe that such a classification tends to imply that divorce is an inevitable result. This is both unfortunate and misleading. One meets couples who have not only remained together but overcome the hurts caused by alcoholism, adultery and even violence to forge a strong and enduring marriage. Conduct of that kind can have a devastating effect on a relationship, but in the long run, it is the state of the relationship itself which is crucial and not specific acts. Of course one may be a pointer to the other, but it is important not to slide into the assumption that divorce is inevitable merely because some ''ground'' has been established.

When one seeks to analyse the factors involved in marital breakdown, one encounters a broad spectrum of human experience and almost the whole gamut of human emotions. Marriage is the most intimate and revealing of relationships. Each person brings to it his personality and his needs and problems. Accordingly, marriages are as diverse as the natures of the people who form them. The same is true of marital breakdown. Lawyers, court counsellors and other people involved in handling divorced people on a day-to-day basis may reach a stage where they think they have heard everything, yet there is always something new, something that does not fit into any recognised pigeonhole. Any categorisation involves the risk of sweeping generalisations. This can lead one to confuse cause and effect and to overlook other problems which may be equally serious. Furthermore, every marriage goes through a stage of disillusionment and it is easy to read too much into conduct which is relatively normal for that stage.

However, one has to start somewhere and it seems appropriate to begin with a discussion of some factors which seriously undermine marriages.

CHAPTER SEVEN

Common Marital Problems

1 Conflict of loyalty

Problems with in-laws tend to be one of the most notorious features of married life. So well known is this problem that whole books of mother-in-law jokes are published. Many of them are in appallingly bad taste and they unjustly malign the majority of mothers-in-law (and fathers-in-law for that matter) who are genuinely delighted to have a new member of the family and do everything they can to support the marriage. The fact that such wonderfully pejorative phrases as "mean as a mother-in-law" abound is, however, eloquent testimony to the incidence of marital problems caused by the parents of the husband or wife or, in some cases, both sets of parents.

Difficulties usually commence with an attitude adopted by the parents for the best of motives. Sometimes there is a concern that the newly-weds lack the maturity and experience to make some of the important decisions which confront them. The parents may smile indulgently, say, "Well, you can't put an old head on young shoulders," and give the younger folk the benefit of their advice. As time goes by advice is given more fully and more frequently. The parents are pleased to have the opportunity of "helping" the newly-weds in this fashion. They may be quite shocked to discover that the advice is not appreciated by one or both of the recipients. They may become aware of that fact only when someone's patience reaches breaking point and he bluntly tells them to stop interfering and let them manage their own lives. Whether it is the husband or the wife who erupts, the resulting blast will usually be directed at that person's mother-in-law or father-in-law rather than at his or her own parents. That is also to be expected. Even if she feels that her own parents are interfering in the marriage to an unacceptable degree, a young wife is more likely to be understanding of them simply because she knows them better and can more readily attribute charitable motives to them. That difference in perceptions of each other's parents can cause bitter disagreements between the husband and wife at a relatively early stage of a marriage. The husband may see his independence at risk. He may have visions of spending the next twenty years trying to justify every decision he makes or feeling like an errant schoolboy whose homework is constantly being found deficient. For him it is necessary to take a stand or a declaration of independence. If "the interfering old busy-bodies" aren't put in their place now he is never going to have any peace. His wife, on the other hand, may be acutely conscious of her parents' good intentions. She may see her husband's "declaration of independence" as a petulant outburst which has caused unnecessary hurt to two kindly middle-aged people who only wanted to help.

How serious such a rift becomes will depend largely on how it is handled. If the husband and wife can themselves discuss the problem and come to some agreement as to how they should handle it then the problem will usually be short-lived. A joint approach to the parents can usually enable ruffled feelings to be healed but also gain the necessary degree of independence.

The real problem arises when the wife (or the husband as the case may be) decides that her primary loyalty lies with her parents. She may not think of it in those terms but as time goes by, successive incidents will confirm the battle lines drawn between "him" and "them". Sometimes the problem does not commence with the parents but with the husband or wife. What frequently occurs is that the wife goes home to mother after an argument and regales her parents with stories of her husband's unreasonable behaviour. When things go wrong, they get the full story. When the couple subsequently make up and she does not need any support, mother and father may not be informed. If they are, it is likely to be a throwaway line such as, "Oh, by the way, Bob and I made up" or some other generalised comment which does little to balance the bitter and detailed denunciations to which her parents have been treated. From the parents' point of view, therefore, there may be a constant litany of complaints demonstrating the unworthiness of their new son-in-law and the fact that their daughter's marriage to him was an appalling mistake. This process will very naturally lead to their being supportive of their daughter and antagonistic towards their son-in-law.

However the alienation occurs, if it becomes clear that one party to the marriage has a primary loyalty to his or her parents rather than to the other spouse then there is a serious risk to the marriage. The extent of that risk may not be immediately apparent. It may take months or even years for the position to deteriorate to the point where that becomes obvious. In some cases it never becomes obvious to one party until the other leaves him and goes back to her parents. In other cases there will be a series of bitter arguments between a man and his in-laws and it will become steadily apparent that his wife has chosen her side.

As mentioned earlier, Jesus reminded his disciples of what the Bible said, as early as the second chapter of Genesis, namely that a man shall leave his mother and father and cleave unto his wife and the two shall become one flesh. The concept of leaving one's mother and father and cleaving unto one's spouse clearly involves a transference of primary loyalty. That transfer of loyalty is absolutely vital to any marriage. Many marriages encounter

serious trouble because the husband or wife has been very
dependent upon his or her parents and is unwilling to sever
the umbilical cord and transfer that dependency to the
spouse. In a very real sense it is true to say that the problem
with many marriages is simply that one party has never
"left". "She wants to be married but she still wants to be
Mummy's and Daddy's little girl," is the way one
frustrated husband put it.

Situations may well arise in which you feel that your
spouse has over-reacted and your parents have been
unnecessarily hurt. If that is so then, by all means, talk
to your spouse about it and try to make him see your point
of view. The fact that you have transferred your primary
commitment to your spouse does not mean that you have
to ignore the feelings of others or that you have to pretend
to agree with a completely unreasonable attitude. To
"cleave unto" someone does not mean undertaking to agree
with him about everything. What it does mean is giving
that person your loyalty. It means regarding yourself as
being in "his camp" rather than in "their camp". A
diplomat may sometimes feel that he has to walk a tightrope in endeavouring to balance the tensions between two
countries but he never loses sight of the country to which
he owes his loyalty.

Unhappily, many people seek to justify this confusion
of loyalties and will sweep aside any criticism from their
spouses as being exaggerated or unreasonable. In reality,
however, the criticism is valid. If your husband or wife
does not have your primary loyalty, then you have failed
to live up to your marriage vows as surely as if you had
committed adultery and the effect on your marriage is likely
to be just as serious.

2 Disillusionment

As mentioned earlier, it is a normal part of married life
to encounter and work through a period of disillusionment
before progressing to a deeper and more mature

relationship. Unhappily, in some cases the couple never make that progression. For one or both of them this dis-illusionment quickly leads to erosion and, ultimately, to the decision to get out of the marriage and start again with someone who will live up to expectations. This is by no means a new phenomenon.

In the Old Testament it was commonplace for a man who had married a woman and subsequently found out that she was not a virgin summarily to divorce her. The fact that she was not a virgin was regarded as grounds for divorce, within the concept of *evarth dabhar*. What more frequently happens these days is that a man marries a wife in the full confidence of her innocence in a wider sense and, as the weeks and months unfold, discovers that she is prone to be selfish and unreasonable or to display other unpleasant characteristics from time to time. In short, he discovers that she has feet of clay like the rest of us. If he is an immature individual he may react to that discovery with resentment and bitterness. There may be a feeling of having been deceived or cheated. Some people seem incapable of making the mental adjustment from their quite unrealistic image of their spouses to the flesh and blood people they married. For them it is not a case of coming to terms with reality and lowering their expectations. That would be to embrace the cheats who defrauded them. It is usually a case of one spouse demanding that the other shape up or ship out. Human nature being what it is the other spouse will, more commonly than not, find that he or she is unable to shape up to the extent demanded and in due course will either ship out or be shipped out.

Because this problem is due primarily to immaturity it is frequently characteristic of young marriages. Nonethe-less, there are people who seem incapable of progressing beyond this immature attitude. Such people may have two or three short marriages and then subside into a sullen and cynical single life style punctuated by the odd affair. The stage of disillusionment is discussed more fully in Part III.

3 The other person

Many Christians seem to find great difficulty in discussing anything of a sexual nature even in purely abstract terms. In Old Testament times devout Jews would not refer to God directly, and he was denoted by a series of consonants which has loosely been translated as Yahweh. These days the church rarely displays such reverence for God but it does have a somewhat similar approach to sex. The subject is simply so taboo that a prickle of uneasiness is likely to run through a group when the topic is mentioned even though all those present are adults and the topic is mentioned for quite compelling reasons. One may joke in Christian company about heaven and hell and, if it is done with sufficient tact, even about God himself but under no circumstances can one joke about sex. To do so would be to act like a "vulgar fellow".

In the permissive society in which we presently live it is understandable that the church should wish to distance itself from the crude and immature attitude to sex presented by those who seem to acknowledge no God but unbridled hedonism. Furthermore, St Paul, in particular, refers to the need for purity not only of conduct but of speech. Yet I believe that in many areas of the church the desire for purity of speech has produced an atmosphere in which it is almost impossible for anyone to mention the subject of sex, much less to admit that he has a problem and requires help.

It is, perhaps for this reason that married Christians who find themselves attracted to someone else find it almost impossible to talk the matter over with Christian friends who might be able to support them and pray for them. You don't raise the subject even with a close friend if you fear that she may treat you as a brazen harlot seeking to justify succumbing to the lusts of the flesh!. You don't approach your minister if you fear that he will mentally transliterate your request for help as a request that he endorse your heartfelt desire to ignore your marriage bonds, betray your wife and children and go off on an orgy of debauching innocent maidens. Consequently, Christians who find themselves torn between loyalty to their family and to God on the one hand and a passionate longing for some other person on the other usually feel they are condemned to wrestle with this appalling dilemma alone.

The agony of decision is further compounded by an enormous overlay of guilt. There is the feeling that decent Christian men and women don't feel like this. There is a feeling that "the very fact I am going through this struggle must indicate some terrible moral weakness on my part" or, to put it another way, "I can't be much of a Christian if I still have these desires". Although the person concerned may not be consciously aware of it, there will frequently be an underlying agony of spirit which stems from the belief that to leave one's husband or wife would be a sin so grave that it could never be forgiven. It is not quite clear what the origins of this belief are. They may lie in the fact that Christian marriages are supposed to be for life and in the belief that divorce gives rise to a continuous state of sinfulness which subsists throughout the joint lives of the parties. Alternatively it may be based upon the assumption that God is the third party in a marriage and that to leave one's husband or wife also means that one has, in a sense, deserted God as well. Whatever the origins of the problem may be, the fact remains that many Christians who forsake their spouses and slip into an adulterous relationship find that they leave their Christian faith behind in the process.

When a situation is so emotionally charged it is sometimes difficult to see the wood for the trees. Nevertheless a number of comments can be made with confidence:

(a) Sexuality is a normal part of human nature. Its expression is governed by several biblical directives just as other forms of conduct are regulated, but there is no basis for suggesting that the whole topic is either too sacred or abhorrent to be discussed by decent people. The conversational taboo evident in so many of our churches is certainly not displayed in the Bible which is strikingly earthy by comparison. St Paul, for example, in his letter to the Galatians 5:12 says that he wishes those who insist on circumcision would go the whole way and castrate themselves. Can you imagine the furore that would erupt in your synod or presbytery if your minister tabled a paper in which he suggested that those who disagreed with him should castrate themselves?

Please don't misunderstand me. I am not advocating salacious language. What I am advocating is that we stop pretending that a perfectly normal and God-given part of our lives does not exist. It is time we cultivated an attitude of honesty in which people who have encountered some particular problem in the area of sexuality can discuss it frankly without being made to feel that they are the only ones who do not have divine dispensation from "that sort of thing"!

(b) Christians are attracted by members of the opposite sex as much as other people with red blood in their veins. That is also a normal part of human life. Keith Miller in his book *A Second Touch* relates his initial horror at reading what Jesus has said in Matthew 5:28, about a man who looks at a woman lustfully having already committed adultery with her in his heart. He said to himself, "Man, if giving up noticing good-looking women is a pre-requisite for getting into heaven, I know three things:

(i)   I'll never make it
(ii)   there is no need for me to witness to my friends because they would never make it either
(iii) what kind of men will there be in heaven with whom I would want to spend an eternity?"

He went on to point out that what Jesus was speaking about was not the recognition of beauty or the attractiveness of the opposite sex but fantasising about an act of adultery with the person concerned.

Recognition or appreciation of beauty is not, in my
view, sinful in any way. If I enter an art gallery and
admire a beautiful painting, I have done nothing more
than appreciate a beautiful thing. Yes, I know that
women are not mere paintings and, yes, I know that
when I look at them I frequently experience an attraction that cannot be dismissed as mere aesthetic
appreciation. Yet God, in his wisdom, chose to make
women sexually attractive to men and vice versa.
Despite some Christian teaching to the contrary, the
fact that God's chosen system works and men and
women are attracted to each other is not an unqualified disaster. In creating that system of mutual attraction, God really did know what he was doing. And
people who are attracted to others do not, for that
reason alone, become guilty of sin.

Furthermore, to return to the analogy of the art
gallery, if I am tempted to steal the painting but resist
the temptation I have still committed no sin. Temptation is not sinful. It is an experience common to all
mankind. Even Jesus experienced it. If, however, I
succumb to the temptation and begin to fantasise as
to how I might steal the painting and how wonderful
life would be if it were all mine then, and only then,
have I moved into the area of sin.

(c) Every now and again a person comes into contact with
someone to whom he or she is immensely attracted.
It is not merely a matter of recognising the other person
as someone who is sexually attractive nor even as
someone who is intelligent and personable. There is
a feeling which seems to transcend such considerations.
Something deep within seems to cry out for the other
person. There may be a feeling of destiny; that you
have always been waiting for this meeting. If you try
to describe your feeling for the person, words seem
hopelessly inadequate and you are forced to fall back
on clichés like ''head over heels''. You may try to

reason with yourself but you will quickly find that reason offers little answer to the strength of your feelings. Friends may suggest that is a mere infatuation but you know that it is not a "mere" anything. The only word adequate to describe such a feeling is love; pure, romantic, story-book-kind love, or so it seems at the time.

Such an experience may shatter a lot of pre-conceptions. You may have thought that you were immune from feelings of that kind because you were a Christian, you were married and you loved your spouse. Yet it has happened. Duty, loyalty, logic and everything that you believe tells you that it is wrong but there is a need deep within you which cries out to be filled.

Your guilt may try to persuade you to the contrary but the fact of the matter is that this experience is also common to mankind. It is not a day-by-day occurrence as simple sexual attraction may be, but at some stage during the lives of most Christians this kind of situation will be encountered. Furthermore, as in the case of the more simple attraction, there is nothing sinful in being attracted or for that matter about the temptation that attraction may bring.

(d) No matter how strong your need for this person may be you will not be justified in breaking up an existing marriage for that reason alone. Jesus himself made it quite clear that to divorce a spouse for no other reason than that you wish to marry someone else is tantamount to adultery. If that seems somewhat harsh then I would urge you to think about the situation. Your spouse may be far from perfect but if he has kept his marriage vows and tried to maintain the marriage then how can you justify betraying his trust and hurting him so very deeply? If you have children are you prepared to try to take them away from your innocent spouse or, for that matter, are you prepared to leave them behind when you go? In either event they will be deprived of the opportunity of living with their mother and their father together.

(e) Yet to decide that one cannot, in conscience, leave one's spouse does not solve the problem. In fact, the problem has no ready solution. No doctor can prescribe a couple of pills and assure you that in the morning the other person will seem revolting. However, in this area too, it may help to gain some understanding of the problem. I do not for one moment suggest that I am able to offer any definitive explanation of the reasons for which people become passionately attracted to each other. If I were to claim that kind of expertise, I fear my wife might rupture something in her paroxysms of laughter. Whatever the causes may be, two important things may be noted.

In the first place the new person is usually somebody who meets a deep need. You may never have appreciated that you had such a need until you met that person, but now, when you think of him, you are aware of an aching void in various areas of your life. Frequently someone who is married to a good steady reliable spouse, the sort of person who expresses love by providing material things, may have a great unfulfilled need for a romantic kind of love. A woman may be confident that her husband loves her in his own way but may nonetheless feel the need to be wooed. She may feel that it has all become a bit boring. Her heart may go out to a more dashing and less predictable type of man. A man may feel an immense attraction to a woman who seems to understand and who has an empathy for his deeper concerns. The range of needs may be immense but very frequently the person to whom this immense attraction is felt will be someone who offers hope of their fulfilment.

In the second place any comparison between the new person and the existing spouse is certain to be an unfair one. Any romantic relationship is characterised by a series of stages commencing with the intoxication of a fairytale romance. Your attitude to this new person will almost certainly fit into that category. There is an inevitable degree of unreality about this stage—faults are not really seen. The idealised image shines so brightly that it obscures the real person. On the other hand, your relationship with your spouse is probably in the disillusionment stage, or to put it more accurately, in a stage which includes some element of disillusionment. You may very well be comparing the pinnacle of your feelings for this new person with the lowest ebb of your feelings for your spouse. Furthermore, it will be natural that you will compare the two in the areas in which the new person is most attractive to you and that is likely to be the areas in which your spouse is most deficient. While it is natural that your attention should be focused on those areas it is obvious that such a comparison is unfair. Your present husband or wife may have many good qualities which this new person cannot emulate.

In trading in your spouse you may well find that one set of needs is being met but only at the expense of another set, which, in the long run, may prove of even greater importance to you.

(f) Whilst desire may flare almost instantaneously, a relationship does not. A relationship of any kind usually commences with fairly subtle overtures by one party. Sometimes a deliberate ambiguity is used as a device to enable one party to "test the waters" before making an unequivocal declaration of interest which might prove embarrassing should it not be reciprocated. This may produce an equally ambiguous response but if the by-play between the parties develops it will become evident that there is a degree of mutual attraction. The person may participate in it to boost his ego by establishing that he is still attractive to members of the opposite sex. Others may participate in it in order to relieve the boredom, as a conditioned reflex acquired during their single years, or simply because it is an enjoyable game. The initial flirtation may, however, lead to a pattern of flirtation with a particular person and that may create an atmosphere for some declaration of interest in establishing some kind of romantic relationship. Such a declaration may be effected by an invitation for a quiet dinner, a bunch of flowers, or in a hundred and one more subtle ways. From there the relationship may develop either quickly or slowly depending upon the nature and degree of contact between the parties and any inhibiting factors such as competing loyalties to other people.

(g) Whilst no one in his right mind would endeavour to reduce the magic of courtship to a cold-blooded formula, a moment's reflection will be sufficient to reveal one characteristic of almost all romances. Whilst you may smile at the analogy, the experience is not unlike riding a slippery dip. You commence very tentatively and move forward only to the extent to which you push. Then you pick up speed and experience an exhilarating rush while being carried along by your own momentum. If you change your mind at the start you have no momentum to overcome. If you have only just pushed off you may still be able to grab the side rails and pull yourself back, but once you are in full flight down the slippery dip it is very difficult to pull out. If you have become emotionally attached to someone other than your husband or wife then make the decision to pull out now. The longer you leave that decision the harder it will be. If you have not told the other person or made your feeling evident to him, then don't. If you have reached the stage of a regular flirtation but there has been no actual declaration of interest then don't make one and don't respond to one. In fact stop flirting. If there is an acknowledged relationship between you then terminate it. If possible tell the person face-to-face that whatever your feelings for each other the relationship cannot continue because you are married and your faith simply demands that you be loyal to your spouse. If you don't feel that you can handle such a face-to-face confrontation then write. However you break the news do so firmly and unequivocally.

(h) If you have had a sexual relationship with the other person then don't embark upon a great debate with yourself about whether or not your conduct is excusable. It isn't. On the other hand don't wallow in shame and guilt. Jesus was criticised by the Pharisees of his day because he sought out the prostitutes and swindlers like Zaccheus. I suspect that he still finds it easier to deal with an honest sinner than a sanctimonious hypocrite. All that he requires is that you acknowledge the wrongness of your conduct, ask for his forgiveness and receive it by faith.

God's promise of forgiveness is succinctly stated in 1 John 1:8-9, ''If we say we have no sin, we deceive ourselves and the truth is not in us. If we confess our sins, he is faithful and just, and will forgive our sins and cleanse us from all sin and unrighteousness''. If guilt is a problem for you then memorise that passage and use it as an emphatic answer to every twinge of guilt that arises during the day.

The Bible is full of stories of God's forgiveness of people who had committed adultery. Perhaps the most striking example is Psalm 51 which David wrote when he was seeking forgiveness not only for his adultery but for arranging for the death of Bathsheba's husband, Uriah the Hittite. You will find that, although the psalm is essentially a prayer for forgiveness, it has a note of confidence about it. ''The sacrifice acceptable to God is a broken spirit; a broken and contrite heart, O God, thou wilt not despise''. David is confident that, as he is coming with a contrite heart, he will not be turned away. Neither will you!

(i) The Bible contains no clear guidelines as to when it is appropriate to tell someone else about your extra-marital involvement. Don't feel justified in doing so simply because of the New Testament emphasis upon confession. In some cases people who have a serious problem with feelings of guilt may feel something akin to a compulsion to get it off their chest. On the other hand, there is an old adage that "no man is an island". If the desire to get it off your chest means that half the church finds out that you have had an adulterous relationship with another person, then not only that person but both families and a whole series of people who care for one or both of you are likely to be deeply hurt. If you do feel the need to confide in someone either because of the need for confession or because you need someone to support you in your resolve to terminate the relationship then pick a close friend who can be trusted to keep the matter in the strictest confidence. Even then, divulge the name of the other person only if it is strictly necessary.

More difficult considerations arise in relation to the question of whether you should tell your spouse what has occurred. There are some Christians who feel that marriage must be founded upon truth and that no matter what the cost may be you must tell your spouse and seek his forgiveness. I have great respect for people who hold that view and one would find it very difficult to cavil at the underlying principle. Nonetheless I do not believe that it is possible to lay down an inflexible rule of universal application.

My own view is that one must balance the distress that is inevitably caused by such a revelation against the advantages which may be seen in a particular situation. It is not something that can be approached superficially. If people in this situation examine their motives carefully they will sometimes find that a disclosure has not been made in the interests of simple candour but for more subtle reasons. Sometimes it is done because the disclosure brings a sense of release from tension; the feeling that "at last it is all out in the open". In certain cases there can be a transference of the emotional burden and sense of guilt to the innocent spouse who may respond to the news with questions such as, "Where did I go wrong?" In other cases the disclosure is made with the subconscious hope that the news will trigger bitter recriminations and that the marital relationship will deteriorate to the point where the person making the disclosure will feel justified in withdrawing from it. Even if your motives are completely pure, I believe that you should pause and ask yourself, "What is to be gained that will compensate for the tremendous distress likely to be caused?"

Of course it may be that your spouse needs to know. You might have had an affair or be contemplating one with one of your spouse's close friends who is likely to be constantly invited around to your home or otherwise expose you to added temptation. It can be an agonising decision to make and there is no short-cut to the right solution. You simply have to weigh the pros and cons, perhaps take advice from a trusted friend and, ultimately, trust that God will guide you.

j) If you are not certain you can handle your feelings then sever all association with the other person. There may be any number of valid and indeed compelling reasons why you should continue to see the other person, but unless the reasons are completely overwhelming, you should dismiss them out of hand. It is simply a question of priorities. Even if you cannot avoid the other person altogether, you should be able to eliminate any private meetings and restrict your contact to those you simply cannot avoid.

(k) Pray fervently that God will heal the pain caused by your infatuation for this other person and, in its place rekindle your love for your spouse. God will answer your prayer but he may require persistence on your part. Don't give up if you don't feel a warm glow for your wife or husband in the first five minutes. These things take time.

(l) Analyse your feelings for the other person. Ask yourself what is it about this person that you find attractive. By doing so you may reveal areas of need you had not previously identified. Whilst it may sound like a sweeping and unfair generalisation it is true that, in most cases a person's affections wander because some emotional need is not being adequately met in the present relationship.

I hasten to add that this does not mean that the other partner is uncaring or insensitive. We human beings are complex emotional creatures. It is easy to overlook a deep longing in a partner whose character and temperament may be quite different from your own. In fact, if you have not been able to identify it yourself, then how can you blame your spouse for a similar failure? Many men, in particular, pride themselves on being down-to-earth practical types. They may be kind, considerate and well mannered. They may display their love for their wives by meeting their material needs, and by endeavouring to provide a secure lifestyle. However, no storybook has described Prince Charming in those terms.

A woman may genuinely appreciate those qualities in her husband and may have great affection for him, yet at the same time, be conscious of the lack of romance in her life. She may be a complete sucker for some dashing young swain who sends her flowers and suggests romantic dinners by candlelight. Another woman may have great affection for her husband, but the strictness of her upbringing may have engrained within her the concept that sex is a shameful thing to such an extent that she subconsciously keeps her husband at arm's length. This kind of problem tends to be more prevalent among people who marry for the first time when they are already well into their thirties but may occur in quite young marriages. The husband may totally fail to understand the causes of this inhibition and may perceive his wife's attitudes as a personal rejection. He might go off to work day after day sexually frustrated and feeling hurt and perhaps a trifle resentful. He may be immensely attracted to a new woman who simply oozes immense availability. Some people may have a great unfulfilled need or greater sensitivity or understanding. Others may have a spouse who is never really home and when he is, is too busy to listen.

Whatever the need may be, if you can identify it, you have gone some distance towards solving the problem, or at least coming to terms with it. Once the need has been identified, you should prayerfully consider ways of filling the void. In this situation, a frank discussion with your spouse may be helpful. It may be difficult because an over-sensitive spouse may read into your comments far more than you intend but it is worth the effort. Frequently the problem goes unresolved for no other reason than that a spouse does not understand the need. As a result of such a discussion, you may also find that your partner has needs of which you have not been aware. Openness frequently permits a new depth of intimacy. You may find that you don't need a new marriage, you simply need to recycle the old one. Do be sensitive about such a discussion. You are not a trade unionist serving a log of claims upon an employer and your spouse may experience great difficulty in understanding precisely what you are trying to convey. Remember that you both have limitations. We don't marry saints, perfect in every respect, but mere men and women with all the frailties of mankind. If your husband is short, bald and chubby, he is unlikely to fulfil your dreams of a latter-day Valentino no matter how well motivated he may be.

Some of your needs may also be met in other ways. Many sensitive people find a great emotional release in music, others gain a great sense of fulfilment in being able to help others. People frequently become involved in romantic liaisons because of the emptiness in their lives. Every one has a burning need for fulfilment, a need to be needed. A Christian community should provide the opportunity for you to move into new areas of involvement with people, to learn more about yourself and to enable you to feel that your life has a worthwhile purpose. If it doesn't, you can at least take comfort in the promise that "every one who has left houses or brothers or sisters or father or mother or children or lands, for my name's sake, will receive a hundredfold, and inherit eternal life".[14] Whilst some may protest that this list does not include mistresses, I believe that the principle which Jesus was expressing is simply that any sacrifice which a person makes because of his Christian commitment will be rewarded. If you do the right thing it may hurt, but in the long run God will make it up to you.

4 The mid-life or emotional crisis

In recent years considerable attention has been focused on the phenomenon of the so-called mid-life crisis. Phrases such as the "male menopause" have captured the imagination. The malady itself is hardly new. Most people, as they go through their teenage years, begin to collect a series of aspirations for the future. As time goes by, there will be a degree of weeding out. Some aspirations will have been realised, others will have given way to new ones and yet others will have taken subtle changes in direction. Yet underlying all this process will be one essential assumption which might be loosely termed the "when I" principle. In a very real sense younger people live for the future. Their sense of self-esteem is inextricably bound up with the things which they aspire to achieve at some stage in the future. There is a great deal of emotional investment in this kind of thinking. Even the person concerned may not appreciate how much because it is contributed over a period of many years. Thoughts about future happiness are so often expressed in sentences which commence with the magic word, "when". "When I finish my degree". "When I achieve the next promotion". "When I start my own business".

The emotional investment in all of these aspirations inevitably generates an accompanying set of anxieties. "What if I fail?" "What if I don't make it?" "What if I'm not accepted?" It is perhaps largely for this reason that the suicide rate among the young is so high. My wife and I exchanged smiles not so long ago when we couldn't help but overhear the conversation at the next table in a restaurant. The young lady turned to her companion and with a note of near panic in her voice exclaimed, "I'm nearly twenty-two years old and still haven't had my first novel published!"

This kind of anxiety is hard to live with because it is not merely anxiety that a particular goal will not be realised but, at a subliminal level at least, anxiety that a lack of personal worth will be revealed. As time goes by these fears may accumulate. There may be a sense of desperation, of having missed the boat. The years have rolled by and the opportunities have been lost. This may bring a devastating feeling that you were not the man (or woman) that you thought you were. Naturally enough this stage is accompanied by wide mood swings, between depression and despair on the one hand and a kind of desperate optimism on the other. Intermingled with this may be a different, but related, feeling. The investment of time and energy lavished upon the pursuit of life goals may have carried with it the "promise" of future happiness. One may feel that he has postponed the good times enjoyed by his less ambitious mates rather than sacrificed them. There may be a feeling of having "promised" oneself. The grudging admission that some goals will never be realised may augment an awareness that youth is fast running out. The time for dreams to come true is limited.

At this stage of life people frequently exhibit unpredictable behaviour. A man may suddenly leave a job he has held for more than twenty years and buy a market garden even if his agricultural knowledge scarcely permits him to distinguish grass from green cement. He may also decide to abandon his marriage in favour of a younger spouse or simply to rid himself of marital constraints so that he may pursue a new life style.

Such a step is not necessarily indicative of any perceived fault on the part of the deserted spouse. In fact he may still have considerable affection and concern for her.

Before I commenced practice as a barrister, I was employed by a superannuation board and, at one time, acted as an advisor to people with superannuation problems of various kinds. During that period I was approached by a man in his late fifties who was living with a twenty-six year old woman. He had deserted his wife some six years before and he and his new partner now had three children, the oldest of which was four. The problem which concerned him arose from his early retirement, due to a bad back. The scheme under which he was entitled to superannuation benefits provided that in the event of his death, his widow would receive a pension for the balance of her life, provided that he had been married to her prior to his retirement. He explained that he would like to divorce his first wife and marry his new partner but was concerned that if he took such a step it might deprive his first wife of that pension. I explained that the divorce would, indeed, have such an effect and, perhaps untactfully, expressed surprise at his concern for a wife whom he had abandoned years before. He smiled gently and explained that his first wife was a very nice person for whom he still had the greatest respect and affection. He had left not because of anything she had done but simply because he had reached a stage where he felt a need to find someone "younger and racier". His premature retirement had made him realise that time was running out. There were not going to be many years before the opportunity for a last fling was irretrievably lost. He had been faithful to his wife for twenty-five years but thought that he had to pursue this last chance for happiness. His decision to leave his wife had obviously been tinged with considerable regret and it was almost as though one part of his personality had debated the matter with another and persuaded it, somewhat reluctantly, that he owed it to himself.

Regrettably most people who experience a mid-life crisis are incapable of the same perception and intellectual honesty as the man with the superannuation query. The overwhelming majority simply know that they are in the grip of some very powerful emotions which they can neither understand nor articulate. Yet, I believe, many people leave their spouses at the time of a mid-life crisis because of the longings which he expressed so vividly.

It is very difficult to know how to deal with a threatened or actual departure due to a mid-life crisis. If the marriage is threatened by a series of bitter arguments or acrimony over particular issues it may be possible to discuss the deteriorating situation and, possibly, achieve a resolution by mutual understanding and by hammering out a compromise solution in which each party makes concessions. Central to that kind of resolution, however, is the fact that you do, at least, have something to give. You can endeavour to see things your partner's way and to change in order to meet at least some of the grievances. But when the root cause of the problem is a mid-life crisis there may be a series of grievances but they are likely to be merely superficial complaints stemming from the need for self-justification. In reality there is no substantial grievance to be redressed.

One may endeavour to win back the errant spouse in a variety of ways. One may try to inveigle him into participating in some counselling sessions or, at least, discussing the matter with a mutual friend. It is certainly wise to be supportive and, in particular, to make him aware that he is valued as a person. Sarcastic jibes at this time are likely to prove fatal to the marriage. Ultimately, one can only wait and pray.

If you are the person experiencing this type of crisis then take heart! It may be difficult but you will live through it. There is no instant cure. These things take time. My wife claims that I've been going through a mid-life crisis for the past ten years. It may also be necessary for you to take a good honest look at your life. Perhaps this experience can be a useful catalyst. You may find yourself in a rut so deep you can scarcely peep over the edge. It may be time for you to make a decisive change of some kind.

May I suggest that you engage in a spring-clean of your life. Pray firstly about your attitudes. It may help to analyse your feelings and come to terms with them in the context of your Christian beliefs. The emotional drives that cause such a crisis are really incompatible with a proper Christian view of life. If you believe, as Christians do, that you are an immortal being who will still have a meaningful existence in a billion years time, it is difficult to become consumed with fear that time is running out. If you have a proper realisation of your inexpressible status as a child of God and a "fellow heir with Christ"[15] as St Paul puts it, then it is difficult to be crushed by your failure to attain the next rung on the corporate ladder. If you know that Christ is coming again, you need not give way to the desperate urge to wring the last dregs of pleasure from the cup of life.

Pray that God will help you make a sober evaluation of your life. What are the aspirations that seem so important? How do they measure up to a proper understanding of your relationship with God? If they are unworthy of a Christian then they should be discarded. Ask yourself whether you are prepared to give up each aspiration should that be God's will for you. As John the Baptist said, "A man can only have what the Lord gives him".[15] Are you prepared to entrust your future to him?

I am not, of course, suggesting that you should abandon any sense of responsibility and wait for God to drop success into your lap. My concern is the emotional investment in these aspirations. Ultimately each person has to answer the question, ''Whose life is it?'' The only answer a Christian may give is that his life belongs to God. If that is so, then you need not try to win his favour. You already have it! Equally, you need not try to prove yourself. One of the tragedies of modern life is that we tend to judge ourselves not so much by what we are but by what we can do. The Bible makes it plain that God is more sensible. He judges according to our hearts.

A re-evaluation will not, of itself, provide an anodyne for your distress. That will require time. In the interim you must do the best you can to remember that God loves you and will sustain you through this difficult time. You should also remember that you have undertaken certain obligations, including obligations towards your spouse and your children.

To succumb to the temptation to leave your spouse for no better reason than to pursue some elusive dream of re-capturing lost youth or having a last fling while time still remains is not only wrong but tragic. So many people who cast aside wife, family or career in the pursuit of this elusive kind of goal find that their dreams crumble, leaving them with nothing but remorse and bitter regret.

5 The problem divorce

This, perhaps, is a misnomer because every divorce is caused by problems. However, it is a convenient way to refer to a marital breakdown as a result of a particular problem afflicting one of the parties. It may be alcoholism, the proclivity to chase anything in skirts or trousers, as the case may be, gambling, financial irresponsibility, violent outbursts or any of the whole range of emotional or psychological disturbances. It can be difficult to get behind the symptoms and uncover the underlying cause.

Furthermore, the problem is not always that of a particular person. Sometimes the problems arise from a clash of temperaments or from the family dynamics, sometimes a problem is imposed upon a person by force of circumstances. In a discussion of this nature it is not possible to analyse exhaustively the various kinds of problems likely to arise within a marriage or offer suggestions on how to deal with each of them. The topic is far too wide for that. The approach which you should adopt in these circumstances will be discussed later.

6 The walk-out divorce

Sometimes this can be the most shattering. A person may come home to find a curt note on the kitchen table announcing that the marriage is over. In many cases, he will have had no warning that this was likely to occur and, if asked, would have described his marriage as secure.

Surveys in Britain, the United States and Australia have all found that three women leave their husbands for every man who leaves his wife.[17] Even in China, traditionally a male dominated society, it has been estimated that seventy per cent of divorces are initiated by women and in the city of Taiyuan a survey of 5401 divorces between 1981 and 1986 put the figure as high as 81.4%.[18] This almost certainly reflects the profound changes in the perceptions and expectations of women over the past two decades and in the traditional husband and wife roles.

Our grandparents accepted a type of partnership in which the husband was the bread-winner, protector, disciplinarian, and in the main, the decision-maker. The wife was the homemaker, cook, nurse, and the main source of encouragement and emotional support. Whilst the husband was the sole breadwinner, it was understandable that most of the housework would be done by the wife. Women themselves saw motherhood as the prime source of fulfilment and took pride in cookery, needlework and other domestic skills. The protector/provider, male half of the partnership left such things to her, secure in the knowledge that they were women's work.

All this has changed dramatically. With the rising tide of feminism, women have come to review their perceptions of life and their expectations of their role in marriage. Women have increasingly sought satisfaction from careers and other interests outside the traditional role of wife and mother. Helen Glezer of the Institute of Family Studies in Melbourne has found that whilst in 1971 sixty-eight per cent of women felt that they could find fulfilment through motherhood, only thirty per cent of those interviewed in 1982 held that view. Equally, support for the view that "wives who don't have to work should not do so" fell from seventy-two per cent to forty-six per cent in the same period. At the same time the economic decline has conscripted into the workforce many women who would have preferred to be full-time mothers and homemakers. In fact the movement of women into the workforce, whether for fulfil- ment or economic necessity, has, to some extent, masked the full impact of the economic decline. Families may be as affluent as they were twenty or thirty years ago, in some cases more so, but it requires two incomes instead of one. Changes in the taxation system, including the abolition of allowable deductions for dependent wives and children have also contributed to this economic conscription.

The liberation of women to pursue fulfilment in the manner they choose and to live at the level of their expectations and aspirations has been rightly acclaimed. The old diehards who assert that a woman's place is in the kitchen may not yet be extinct but the World Heritage Commission could justifiably list them as an endangered species.

Unhappily, whilst there has been a great deal of publicity concerning the positive value of the breakthroughs in this area, little attention has been given to the need for social adjustments to accommodate the wide-ranging changes involved. This is particularly true in marriage.

Men have tended to respond to all this with tolerance

rather than real support. A husband may greet the news of his wife's new job with the comment, ''That's nice, dear,'' but he is not likely to come up with a comprehensive arrangement whereby he takes over half of the family chores formerly shouldered by his wife. An American survey has found that whilst the average working wife spends twenty-six hours per week on housework, her husband spends thirty-six minutes.[18] The London *Sunday Times* found that only two per cent of men took any part in housework. This is obviously an immense source of dissatisfaction to women.

At the same time changes in levels of education and career prospects, a growing awareness of rights and an increase in expectations generally have lead to changes in the balance of power in marriage.[20] As Helen Glezer found, the percentage of women who believed that important decisions should be made by the husband dropped from forty-four in 1971 to sixteen by 1982. As the willingness of women to accept male leadership has diminished, their financial emancipation has released them from economic domination. One frequently encounters a relationship which has gone sour because of changes in the wife's perception of her husband's attitude toward her. That attitude may not have changed but what may once have seemed acceptable, perhaps even a source of security, now seems dictatorial and unreasonable.

A further change has occurred as a result of women becoming less willing to bear the prime responsibility for the emotional wellbeing of the relationship. Men have traditionally been the strong, silent types or at least that has been the image they have had of themselves. Women have tended to be far better at communicating feelings and, perhaps because of the experience of motherhood, were more inclined to be sensitive to the emotional needs of others. With increasing levels of self-esteem and an increasing awareness of the quality of relationships, women are demanding more sensitivity to their emotional needs. In this area too, men have missed the boat. Many find it extremely difficult to express strong emotions. There is a feeling that it is not manly. Buried deep within the forty-five-year-old executive may be the fumbling youth who would hide the flowers behind his back until he could thrust them into his girlfriend's hands and blurt out something romantic like, "Here!" or "I bought these for you". Thirty years later he may not express his feelings by buying her flowers but by the provision of a house, car and other items. She is supposed to understand how he feels. As one man put it, "She keeps saying I don't seem to care because I don't talk about things but I beat my brains out trying to get her everything she wants. What more can I do?" The answer was that she wanted him to relate to her. In fact, many wives perceive that long hours may be more indicative of workaholism than devotion and that they may indicate at least a subconscious desire to avoid them.

Men are notoriously prone to missing signals from their wives of difficulties in the relationship. One constantly hears husbands protest, "But why didn't you tell me?" In most cases the wife has tried to tell him in a hundred subtle ways that went over his head. Consequently, men are frequently unaware that there is a problem, let alone a major threat to the marriage until it is over.

From a Christian perspective, it is an unqualified tragedy when two people who genuinely love each other are driven apart through different perceptions and a failure to communicate.

From a man's viewpoint, let me say that men do not understand many of the things which their wives assume they do. They are preoccupied, operate substantially on the basis of an understanding of their role gleaned from their fathers and other traditional male figures and are frequently inarticulate, at least when it comes to expressing deep feelings. Films and television entrench rather than ameliorate the traditional male role. Furthermore, whilst the enormous changes in the roles of women have caused virtually every woman to reconsider her own role in life, the role of women has not been a central issue in the minds of most men. It is frequently not selfishness, chauvinism or lack of love which is the problem, but lack of under-standing. If you want to save your marriage, then you must try to communicate with your husband in a way which he will understand. The subtle or not-so-subtle signals which might be as clear as day to another woman may be lost on him. Sit down with him and tell him bluntly that there is a problem and that it is so serious that it is undermining your whole relationship with him. If he brushes that aside, persist. If things have become so bad that you are considering leaving him, tell him so. Make him listen, if it is at all possible.

Men, for their part, need to take a good hard look at their role in their marriages. If you both work, how much of the overall workload involved in running a house do you accept? Do you see your efforts as helping your wife with *her* housework or do you really see it as a joint responsibility? How sensitive are you to her needs? Do you consult her? Do you ask how she feels about particular issues and really care about the answers? Do you confide in her with your innermost feelings, your fears, aspirations, disappoint-ments? Do you tell her how you feel about her? Do you share your thoughts with her as candidly as you would with your best friend? If not, you had better spend some time asking God to show you what it means to be "one flesh" with someone.

CHAPTER EIGHT

Some Aberrations

In addition to the pressures which have already been discussed, there are a number of attitudes which bedevil Christian marriages in particular. Most are not unique to Christian marriages but are particularly prevalent amongst them. They are also likely to prove more intractable among Christians because they involve strong moral convictions. Many people become very defensive when such sacred cows are challenged. Others simply dismiss the challenge out of hand but do so in a kindly, regretful manner and you abandon the conversation knowing that they are sure to pray that God will show you the error of your ways.

Once again I would ask you to read this section with an open mind. If you remain of a different view on some issue then so be it, but I believe that none of us are so mature as Christians that God is unable to reveal to us fresh insights into his love and concern for us.

1 The problem of the domineering "head of the house"

One of the most destructive attitudes is frequently passed off as a virtue. These days nearly every church seems to contain a smattering of men who justify arrogance by reference to texts such as Ephesians 5:22 which exhorts wives to submit themselves to their husbands ''as to the Lord''. In recent years there has been a great deal of emphasis upon the concept of submission, both within the church and the family. Unfortunately that emphasis seems to have produced enormous numbers of Christian husbands who see their roles as being something akin to that of a domestic sergeant major, charged with the duty of barking orders at a female recruit until she comes neatly into line with an appropriate click of the heels. This kind of nonsense is tearing families apart and causing great distress and tension in marriages even when there is no actual separation.

If the men in question were to continue reading the chapter they would strike verse 25 which reads, "Husbands, love your wives just as Christ loved the church and gave his life for it". If you want to lead your family then you have to acknowledge that your leadership is not to be an excuse for arrogance or self-aggrandisement. It is rather the kind of leadership practised by Jesus who had absolute authority but never exploited it for his own interests. On the contrary, he treated his followers with kindness, humility and self-sacrificing service. He was prepared to get down on his hands and knees and wash their feet as if he were a mere domestic servant. Ultimately, he was prepared to die for them. When a dispute broke out about leadership among his disciples, Jesus dismissed the matter with the simple but profound statement that "he who would be first must be the servant of all". That is the kind of God-given leadership referred to in Ephesians. If you think that it offers any excuse for you to adopt a dictatorial condescending attitude towards your wife, then you have missed the point entirely.

2 The problem of sex

The proper Christian attitude to this topic has already been discussed. Nonetheless, one regularly encounters the most bizarre attitudes to sex in marriage. The view is expressed that marriage is for the purpose of nurturing children, not for satisfying the lusts of the flesh. One encounters extremists who argue that sexual intercourse should take place only when it is desired to conceive a child and not at any other time. Some mutter darkly that even on those occasions the participants should try not to enjoy it too much. Other people caution young wives to beware of lust in marriage. This kind of attitude can produce guilt feelings leading, ultimately, to serious repression of the proper sexual function within marriage.

All these concepts are completely foreign to the Bible. St Paul deals with the topic in 1 Corinthians 7:3-5 where he says: "A man should fulfil his duty as a husband and a woman should fulfil her duty as a wife, and each should satisfy the other's needs. The wife is not the master of her own body, but her husband is; in the same way the husband is not the master of his own body, but the wife is. Do not deny yourselves to each other, unless you first agree to do so for a while, in order to spend your time in prayer; but then resume normal marital relations, to keep you from giving in to Satan's temptation because of your lack of self-control". It may be seen from this passage that the Bible fails to offer any support for these ridiculous calls for sexual abstinence but lays upon married people the positive duty to meet each other's sexual needs.

The reason given by St Paul is the avoidance of temptation. Temptation may come in a variety of circumstances. The only thing which can be said with any confidence about it is that it is inevitable that both you and your spouse will encounter it from time to time. The Bible makes it perfectly clear that Christ himself encountered temptation. The expectation among some Christians that one will reach a stage where one is free from such things has no biblical support whatever.

The important question is how will we handle temptation? Some of us seem to have great faith in our own willpower or, as my father used to say, in our "won't power". Some of us may admire those made of sterner stuff but acknowledge our own frailty and take what steps we can to minimise our exposure to temptation.

In the sexual area however, temptation arises in the most mundane circumstances. Men, in particular, are very susceptible to visual stimulation. One female jogger can do more for the cardiovascular systems of her male colleagues than the heart specialist in the medical clinic around the corner can accomplish in a month. The point which St Paul makes is simply that whichever form the temptation may take the person is far more likely to succumb to it if he is already sexually frustrated. For a wife to cut off sexual contact with her husband can be similar to refusing to give him breakfast and sending him off to work in a pie factory where his salivary glands are constantly stimulated by the enticing sights and aromas. Even in the average office there are a few dainty morsels floating about. I hasten to add that I am not suggesting that husbands and wives have some sort of duty to meet every demand made by their spouses. Proper sexual balance in marriage is achieved through sensitivity and mutual consideration, not through submission to demands.

A further area of sexual difficulty is frequently caused by male impatience or lack of consideration. Women are usually aroused more slowly than men. If sexual intercourse is truly to be a precious experience of shared intimacy, then it, like other aspects of marriage, should involve each spouse seeking to fulfil the needs of the other. In many marriages this doesn't happen. What occurs is that the husband gratifies his own needs and assumes that his wife's needs have been met in the process. When this occurs in a Christian marriage the wife is unlikely to protest either because "she doesn't know what she is missing" or because she is terrified that her husband will think she is over-sexed, a veritable Jezebel. This means that the problem is likely to go unresolved and in fact unrecognised.

Sexual inhibitions can be both a symptom of other problems and a cause of further problems. But whether a cause or symptom, they can impose a great strain upon a marriage. Problems of this kind may be solved in much the same way as any other marital problems. It is quite

proper to pray about them: God is not likely to be shocked.
It is also proper to talk about them. Sex should never be
a taboo subject between husband and wife. In fact, if there
is a problem in this area, it is absolutely imperative that
the matter be discussed frankly. To do so requires both
sensitivity and a certain degree of courage but it will pay
off in the long run.

3 The problem of time and priorities

In 1975, my wife and I moved into an inner-city area of
Sydney with our two young children. We were attending
a church only a few hundred metres from Kings Cross
which had an exciting ministry to people who were society's
outcasts—drug addicts, alcoholics, prostitutes, criminals
and people with all kinds of emotional and psychiatric
problems. I was already working long hours as a barrister
but my wife and I were both convinced that God wanted
us to become involved in this work and we threw ourselves
into it wholeheartedly. It was an exhilarating time.

In that kind of environment the veneer of respectability
that one constantly encounters in suburbia has been
stripped away by the extremity of the need. Dishonesty
is endemic to anyone addicted to alcohol or drugs, but at
least the problems were obvious. A person would look you
straight in the eye and say something like, "Look man,
don't give me that new-life stuff. I'm mainlining heroin.
I'll be dead in six months!" That kind of a challenge is
hard to resist.

Apart from the activities of the church itself, we had
groups of people meeting at our home. For a time we lived
as an extended family. We had people dropping in at all
hours of the day or night to discuss problems which were
simply too urgent to be left. Some nights we would come
home from a meeting at midnight to find someone sitting
on the doorstep waiting for us. On other occasions I would
get up in the morning and sleepily open the front door to
retrieve the milk bottles only to find someone had been

patiently waiting for me to wake up and ask me to pray
with him before I went to work.

Because of my legal background and contact with people
in trouble, I was invited to join a number of Christian
bodies concerned with social responsibility and from time
to time was invited to address groups of concerned
Christians on a variety of topics ranging from drug
addiction to a Christian attitude to criminology.

All of this took an immense amount of time and as the
months rolled by, my children saw less and less of me. I
was concerned that they were growing older without the
fathering which I had always promised myself I would give
to them. Yet, surely God had to come first? Besides, people
in desperate need are hard to refuse. We couldn't ignore
the problem but gradually persuaded ourselves that if we
were putting God first then he would ensure that our
children did not suffer as a result of having insufficient time
with their father.

That was a wonderful theory. It sounded so spiritual,
so full of faith. The only thing wrong was that it didn't
seem to work. Christians seemed to be having enormous
problems with their children simply because they were
never home with them. The "minister's kids" syndrome
has long been a problem within churches. Ironically enough,
some congregations can be very critical when, in fact, it has
frequently been the minister's concern for the congregation
which has taken him away from his family and contributed to
his children's attitudes.

The problem is, of course, by no means confined to the
children of ministers. In the early seventies I was teaching
Sunday School at a church which was in the throes of
building a new church complex. One fifteen-year-old boy
in my group was particularly sullen and unresponsive and
I could see that he was deeply troubled. When I took him
aside privately to ask him what was troubling him, he
reacted angrily. "We were a happy family until my dad
got tied up with this church. Now we're all torn apart.
Mum and Dad are getting divorced and it's all because

of this rotten place!'' In those days before the introduction of the Family Law Act a person petitioning the court for a divorce had to file a document setting out the grounds relied upon. It seems that this lad's mother had filed a petition seeking a divorce from his father upon the legal ground of cruelty and in support of that ground had asserted that the husband had simply ignored his family for months on end whilst he spent the whole of each weekend and each evening Monday to Friday, working upon the new church building.

At the time we moved into the city that incident was fresh in my mind and I was determined that I was not going to make the same mistake. Despite this caution, I was quickly able to persuade myself that the situations were really completely different. My young friend's father had become totally consumed with what was a mere building whilst I was concerned with people in genuine need. Besides, he had spent virtually no time at home at all. I would make sure that I didn't slip into that trap.

Yet, within about twelve months of making that resolution, I had six regular evening commitments per week and was virtually inundated by these regular demands. I think I knew, deep down, that any system of priorities which left me virtually no time for the children, let alone my wife, was not compatible with the teaching of Jesus. He had actually rebuked his disciples for imagining that he was too busy to speak to children and had said, ''Suffer the little children to come unto me for such is the Kingdom of Heaven''.

I don't think I quite realised how bad the situation had become until one night when I was putting my daughter to bed. She was then nearing her ninth birthday. As I tucked the sheets and blankets around her, she took my hand, looked at me seriously and said, ''Dad, do you remember when we used to go out for picnics or go to the beach? Do you remember how we used to spend whole days together?'' The list of things that we ''used to do'' went on and on, then, with tears in her eyes she concluded, ''I know you are always too busy now, Daddy, and we'll never be able to do those things again. But I really miss them''. It was as if an eight-year-old prophet had said, like Nathan, ''Thou art the man''.[21] I went out and bled all over my living-room floor.

Christians, in common with many other members of the community, frequently find themselves joining in the despairing refrain, ''If only I had more time''.

On a day-by-day basis at least, time is one area in which all men are created equal. Everyone gets twenty-four hours a day. You get exactly the same amount of time as, say, the Prime Minister of Australia, the President of the USA, or the Secretary-General of the United Nations. You simply have to allocate priorities and make the best of it in the same manner as they do. Unhappily, the principle is easy to express but very difficult to implement.

Lawyers, the professional group with which I am most familiar, are almost invariably workaholics. I have fond memories of a colleague in Sydney whom I encountered on every single occasion I went into my chambers on weekends. I began to chide him about never going home and on one occasion said, ''I'll bet you even came in here on Christmas day''. The poor man looked a trifle embarrassed and then said, ''Well, only for a couple of hours''.

It's a trap that's particularly easy to slip into because there are always good reasons for working long hours. When I first became concerned about this problem, I remember making a resolution that I would leave my chambers punctually at 6.00 pm each evening, unless some emergency occurred. A fortnight later I realised that I had had an emergency on each night in the fortnight.

The sources of this time pressure, whether related to one's profession or to one's ministry, are many and varied. They include a sense of duty, security, a pride in doing the job as well as it can be done, hunger for acceptance, recognition or prestige, and simply lack of discipline. Whatever the causes may be, the result is the same. Unless we are particularly careful, we find that our lives are not proceeding according to some pattern which we have determined but simply rolling on as a series of push-button responses to an incessant stream of demands. This frequently means that the demands which are the most immediate are the ones that are met.

It is possible to reach the end of the year and realise that the things that we really regard as important have received almost no attention at all simply because less important things are more pressing in the sense that they require immediate response. Unhappily, our families frequently fall into the category of important things that get little time.

This causes enormous strain on marriages. Perhaps this is why lawyers are so frequently divorced. A lot of the problems stem from the fact that no matter how valid the reasons for spending so much time away from home seem to us, they may not be understood by our spouses who may feel that we simply don't want to come home. Furthermore, there is a sense in which our priorities, or lack of them, implicitly say to our spouse, "Look, these clients (or these people in need of ministry) are more important than you are!" We may not say or even think such a thing, but our conduct silently asserts that it is so.

This is particularly difficult when it comes to ministry because, as I have already observed, there is a temptation to resolve the matter by telling oneself that "God comes first". Whilst I do not deny the truth of that statement, it is possible for people to use devotion to God as an excuse for neglecting their families. Jesus asked Peter three times if he loved him; each time Peter answered, that he did. And each time Jesus' response was a command. "Feed my lambs"; "Tend my sheep"; "Feed my sheep". (John 21:15–17)[22] He made it perfectly plain not only in that incident but in many other statements that true love for God is reflected in a concern and care for his people. Consequently, if this is a problem in your life, it is not a question of God versus your family but simply your God-given duty toward your family compared with your God-given duty towards other people for whom you have some responsibility.

Within the catalogue of human relationships your marriage must be given the highest priority, higher even than your relationship with your children. Few Christians would argue about that in theory though many might splutter a little when it came to putting it into practice. What it really requires is both planning and determination.

You need to set aside blocks of time which are sacrosanct save in dire emergencies. In my home, for example, it became almost impossible to have a quiet dinner with my family because the telephone would ring constantly. Now I have an answering machine fitted which records the incoming calls so that they may be returned later. I'm also far more selective about the time at which I invite or permit people to come around for counselling. I even make an effort to master my own sense of insecurity and begin turning away work when the load becomes so great that it is intruding into my family life to an unacceptable degree.

You may have to make some hard decisions. You may find it necessary to pull out of particular activities altogether. In other areas you may find that you don't need to do anywhere near as much as you have been doing. There may be all manner of people who are willing to help. Perhaps you could be even more effective in your ministry by training others to share it.

Think about it, pray about it, but don't simpy permit your marriage to be swamped in a deluge of activity.

4 The problem of the non-Christian spouse

The only New Testament passage dealing specifically with the attitude which a Christian should have toward a non-Christian spouse is 1 Corinthians 7:12–16.

"To the rest I say, not the Lord, that if any brother has a wife who is an unbeliever, and she consents to live with him, he should not divorce her. If any woman who has a husband who is an unbeliever, and he consents to live with her, she should not divorce him. For the unbelieving husband is consecrated through his wife, and the unbelieving wife is consecrated through her husband. Otherwise, your children would be unclean, but as it is they are holy. But if the unbelieving partner desires to separate, let it be so; in such a case the brother or sister is not bound. For God has called us to peace. Wife, how do you know whether you will save your husband? Husband, how do you know whether you will save your wife?''

This passage is widely recognised as authority for the proposition that a Christian has a duty to try to maintain his marriage to a non-Christian spouse, provided that the spouse is also willing to continue with the marriage. It is also a passage which some people treat as involving a promise that if a Christian remains married to a non-Christian spouse, God will haul that spouse into the Kingdom of Heaven, even if it means leaving drag marks all the way. Others have disagreed and suggested that what is involved in the passage is not a promise but an exhortation that the Christian partner should convert the non-Christian one. Both views are over-simplistic. The assertion of a promise is totally incompatible with the words, ''how do you know...''? That phrase, involving as it does the possibility that the spouse will not be saved, also seems inconsistent with a firm commandment to go out and achieve the spouse's salvation.

Surely what St Paul is saying is simply that through marriage to a Christian the non-Christian spouse will constantly be exposed to the Gospel and may, in due course, turn to God. Experience suggests that this frequently happens. However, it is a natural thing which does not need to be forced. It happens simply because the person has the opportunity to see the reality of God in a Christian life. The process can be assisted by a genuine love and a certain degree of sensitivity but never by a hard sell. Ultimately, of course, individuals must make up their own minds.

Unfortunately many Christians seem to feel that they need to cajole, threaten or bludgeon their spouses into the Kingdom of Heaven. In time the marital relationship itself may come to be used as a means of exerting a subtle pressure. In a hundred different ways a wife may be made to feel that her Christian spouse no longer accepts her in an unreserved manner. A husband may come to feel that he is being subjected to a degree of emotional blackmail; that his spouse's love is to some degree, conditional upon his fulfilling her demands for a Christian commitment.

If you love someone and you are convinced that you have found the real meaning of life, a source of forgiveness, peace and eternal salvation, then it is only natural that you would want to share it. In some cases the fear that a spouse will miss out on that salvation may lead to a sense of desperation. Yet the attitude which it engenders is not only unhelpful, it is quite unfair.

As the years roll by the barrier created by your demand that your spouse should adhere to your views about Christianity may be extended into increasing numbers of areas. The manner in which your children are raised is likely to become a particular area of conflict. It is easy to slip into the habit of assuming that any disagreement between you stems from your spouse's failure to understand "the proper Christian position". In some cases that may be true but if you are not careful you can slip into the habit of simply assuming that you are always right and that your spouse is always wrong. The corollary of that temptation is, of course, to assume that because your spouse does not have that proper Christian "perspective", then his opinion is not worth considering. For his part, he may regard these attitudes as little more than presumptuous arrogance and, to be blunt, he may be right.

It is not possible to lay down a set of precisely formulated principles which will cover every situation. As a general guide, however, you might consider the following suggestions:

(a) Explain to your spouse candidly just what your faith means.

(b) Say that you'd be happy to discuss your beliefs with him at any time but that you don't wish to pressure him and if he ever feels that you are, then he should feel free to rap you over the knuckles.

(c) Make it very plain that your love is not conditional on what he may or may not believe.

(d) Remind yourself repeatedly that he is an equal partner with you in that family and that his views are entitled to as much respect as yours.

(e) If you got off to a bad start, then frankly admit that you haven't been really fair to him.

(f) Specifically ask for his understanding.

(g) When disputes arise, try to put yourself in his shoes and imagine how he would feel about the situation.

(h) Make it plain that you love and respect him as he is.

(i) Pray for him regularly, not merely for his salvation, but for him personally, that God will bless him and enrich your lives together.

(j) Pray also that God will help you to be sensitive. It is not merely a matter of what you say but of what you make your spouse feel.

CHAPTER NINE

The Stage of Disillusionment

In Western societies at least, it is true to say that most people marry in a state of mind that scarcely permits a searching and realistic appraisal of the qualities and character of the person they are marrying or, for that matter, any realistic appreciation of what they can expect from the marital relationship. That is scarcely surprising. Marriage is a culmination of a thrilling romantic adventure. It is heady wine. Prince Charming has wooed his beauty. All of the anxiety of losing the lover, the fear of being rejected, have been overcome.

The lover has said "Yes". Now it is time for the "happy ever after". In the euphoric intoxication of that wonderful anticipation there is boundless optimism and a fierce loyalty to an idealised image of the lover.

Of course there are those, older and more cynical, who "commit matrimony" in a far more detached and businesslike way. Many such people have been hurt before and their optimism is tempered by an awareness of the pain that can be inflicted by a broken relationship. Others have ulterior motives: money, prestige, or the fact that a new wife or husband might help with custody of children of an earlier relationship. Some older couples, though deeply in love, may approach their relationships with a more mature understanding of each other and a less idealised set of expectations about their marriages. Such people may even realise that Sir Lancelot has to get off his white charger to put the garbage out on a Tuesday night. Yet those who are able to maintain a realistic image of their betrothed throughout the period leading up to their wedding and who realise that marriage is not an idyllic and perpetual state of bliss are rare individuals indeed.

For this reason, a stage of disillusionment develops in every marriage. This stage commences as the true nature of the other person begins to emerge from the mist of romantic idealism in which he has been shrouded. Sir Lancelot may still cut a pretty romantic figure but he snores, sometimes smells like a horse, and isn't much fun when he forgets to take his spurs off before coming to bed. Guinevere may still be a pretty stunning woman in her flowing gown and medieval headdress but she has a tongue like a battle axe, never seems to get around to polishing his chain mail underpants and keeps leaving those wonderful veils sodden with water and strewn all over the ancestral bathroom.

When this stage commences one, and usually both, parties will feel hurt, angry, bewildered and, frequently, resentful. He had always been so wonderful. He promised to love, honour and cherish you. Then what happened? He turned out to be an insensitive, domineering, oversexed brute who could not even remember your birthday. And after you trusted him! How could you have been so blind?

In the early part of this stage, people frequently spend some effort trying to bolster the romantic image they have of their partners by trying to explain away particular instances or by blocking them out of their mind. As time goes by, however, the image becomes increasingly frayed as successive incidents confirm that the knight in shining armour or the vision of loveliness, as the case may be, does indeed have feet of clay. As this awareness grows there may be frequent and drastic swings in attitude to the other party. One moment she may still be the girl of his dreams whose few minor foibles only serve to add to her charm. The next moment she will seem selfish and unreasonable, a mere caricature of the delightful girl he thought he had married. As time goes by one or both of the hurt and bewildered spouses may find themselves concentrating on the negative side of the relationship.

Some people will bottle up these feelings and do their utmost to conceal them from their spouses. More commonly, however, the hurt will produce resentful reactions of one kind or another. There will be recriminations about real or imagined misconduct. This may be expressed in any manner from quiet nagging to a full-blown screaming match. At this stage the wife may go home to her mother or the husband might decide to put in some time at the pub with his mates, "who you can at least talk to!"

It is important to remember that this stage is not only an almost universal experience but an understanding of it is absolutely essential to the establishment of any mature relationship. There is always a difference between the romantic, idealised image and the true nature of the persons we have married.

That difference is not their fault. They may have contributed, to some degree, to the falsity of the image but not with any real attempt to deceive. It is only natural for a young man to be particuarly attentive and considerate during the courtship period and equally natural that he will be unable to sustain that attitude twenty-four hours a day, seven days a week for ever after. In any event, much of the falsity of the image had been due to your own hopes and dreams, the mental casting of him in the role of the lover you had always hoped to meet. How many girls in love have shared the news of their engagement with phrases such as, "He is the sort of man I always dreamed about"? Of course it is perfectly natural for them to think that way. Although men are far more reticent in expressing their innermost feelings, most of them feel the same way about their intended brides. Nonetheless, the result of that kind of thinking is to create quite unrealistic expectations. Many newly married people have expectations of their husbands or wives that no mortal person could ever fulfil.

The same comments could be made concerning the marriage itself. So many people seem to see marriage as the solution to all their problems. "If only I could just get married and settle down"; "If I just had somebody to be there and care for me when I come home at night". This expectation is strengthened during the engagement period when people spend so much of their waking hours making plans for the future and ardently longing for the time when their marriage can commence. When they find that marriage itself does little to solve their existing problems and actually imposes a whole host of new ones, they may feel disappointed and betrayed.

It is frequently at this point that the marriage goes through its baptism of fire. Whatever happens the parties will be forced to accept the falsity of their illusions. The harsh realities of life will simply sweep them aside. It is how they react to that process which is crucial.

There is no point in having unrealistic expectations of yourself either. Even the best husband or wife will be tempted to wallow in disappointment and resentment at times. We all sympathise with the young lady who bitterly exclaimed, "I took him for better or worse but he was worse than I took him for".

The sea of matrimony may be a trifle stormy at this point and from time to time you may feel the sting of the spray. Nonetheless, most survive. The price of doing so is to be willing to recognise the expectations as unrealistic, to accept that the person you find yourself married to may be different from the one you thought you were marrying, but to persevere. You may need to rethink your expectations of the marriage. You may need to accept that marriage is not going to be the solution to all your problems and that, in fact, you are going to have to work pretty hard at it to make the relationship work at all. Yet, if you can ride out the storm you will be left with a deeper and more mature relationship.

You may be surprised to find that you rediscover a love which is just as rich and deep as when you were first married but which is based upon reality and not illusion. This can be a nitty-gritty kind of relationship that is strengthened rather than diminished by trials; the sort of relationship in which each understands the other's faults but loves him anyway. Frequently, this will only occur when each accepts a role in the marriage based on contributing rather than taking. As time passes, mutual trust develops based not upon naive romanticism, but upon real knowledge of the other person.

How are you to work through this stage of disillusionment in a positive manner? Let me make a number of suggestions.

(a) Decide that you will make a go of the marriage.

(b) Accept that the solution to the problem does not lie in trying to change your husband or your wife to accord with your image. The only person you can change is you.

(c) Accept that marriage is a give and take relationship and for you, initially at least, that may mean giving ninety per cent of the time.

(d) Try to put yourself in your spouse's shoes and imagine how he or she might feel about particular situations, especially those causing friction between you.

(e) Take the time to perform little acts of kindness from time to time. If your partner is at all sensitive, that should help him or her realise that, whilst there may be some problems between you, you still care. Unilateral acts of love and affection may well prevent the relationship from becoming a cold war. You may even move your spouse to reciprocate, but take a long-term view. Make allowances for pride—on both sides. It takes time to build up trust again.

(f) Try to develop real communication between you. This does not mean telling your husband honestly and candidly what a terrible person you think he is, how much he keeps annoying or distressing you and how fervently you wish he would change. Talk to him about interests you share. Ask him for his views about things. Find out how he likes things done. Tell him of your own hopes, fears and aspirations. By all means speak openly of any differences that lie between you. Don't just bottle them up and brood about them. But, on the other hand, when you have made your position clear, let the subject rest. Don't keep raking over the coals.

(g) Don't just talk. Listen! Many arguments are based upon nothing more complicated than simple misunderstandings.

(h) Be willing to give a little. If it infuriates your wife that you left the top off the toothpaste it may reflect an unreasonable attitude on her part but it won't cause irreparable harm to your psyche to put the wretched thing on.

(i) Pray about the situation, and in particular, pray for your spouse and pray that God would help you meet each other's needs.

(j) If you seem unable to close the gap between you then consult a counsellor. Resist the temptation to consult your friends and relatives, as such people are often too loyal to offer helpful or even objective advice. You are likely to succeed only in marshalling a group of people so obviously "on your side" that any conciliatory gesture may be seen almost as "selling out to the enemy". If your husband (or wife) will go with you to see a counsellor, all the better, but even if your partner is unwilling to participate or you feel it would be counterproductive to suggest such a thing, it may still be of great assistance to see one. Such people can often help you to put your problems in perspective and assist you in understanding how the other person may feel. It is preferable to find some reasonably independent person in whom you and your spouse have confidence and who has experience in marriage counselling. Christian couples frequently find their minister helpful. However, some do not have the necessary experience and you may be better off consulting a marriage guidance organisation conducted by your denomination.

It should be emphasised that the happiest and most successful marriages in the world go through stages of disillusionment. The fact that the feelings which I have described are experienced does not mean that the marriage is on the rocks or even that it is in any serious danger. It may indicate merely a stage that has to be worked through and one which, if faced with determination and compassion, will lead to a healthy well-integrated relationship. Unhappily, some couples seem unable to work through this disillusionment stage. In such marriages the hapless participants may be unable to air and resolve their grievances. There may be constant brooding by one party about the faults of the other, characterised by hurt, self-pity and bitter resentment, or the relationship may be punctuated by violent quarrels or unpredictable behaviour. Yet even at this stage if both husband and wife are willing to get together, discuss the situation and work together to resolve their differences, the relationship can be easily restored.

CHAPTER TEN

The Stage of Erosion

If the stage of disillusionment is not positively resolved then it slides into the stage of erosion. This is a more serious stage in which the underlying love and concern of the parties for each other, the very basis of the marriage itself, is progressively eroded. The causes of underlying dissatisfaction between the parties may not be evident to either of them at this stage but each will be acutely aware that the relationship is not what it should be.

The decline in the relationship may be expressed in many ways. There may be long periods of sullen silence or violent screaming outbursts; there may be even outbursts of physical violence. More commonly, however, there will be more civilised expressions of bitterness and resentment. The husband may begin subtly to embarrass his wife on social occasions. She may begin to nail him to the wall with icy glances from across the room. There may be an increased focus on rights, with each party trying to make sure of getting a fair share. There may be bitter clashes about household jobs left undone. One or both may embark upon a wild spending spree.

At this point there may be a conscious or unconscious tendency to avoid further confrontation. During the disillusionment stage there may have been anxious discussions or bitter recriminations in an endeavour to resolve the differences. Now there is the feeling of having had enough.

113

The arguments have been too hurtful. The emotional climate has reached the point where one or both of the parties may recoil from further recriminations.

This may be reflected in various kinds of avoidance.

The first and most obvious kind is the avoidance of certain topics. The couple may be able to engage in free and even intimate conversations about most things but when an area of disagreement or a problem is raised, then various psychological walls are quickly flung into place. The conversation may be terminated by an angry outburst, by an abrupt change of the subject or by the sudden realisation of being late for an appointment or of having some pressing task to accomplish.

The price which has to be paid for having a list of taboo subjects is that the difficulties remain unresolved and the hurts find expression in other ways. Some may find external expression by repeated complaints to friends or relatives but much will be turned inwards and there will be a gradual build-up of frustration and resentment. From time to time this may cause a sudden and seemingly inexplicable outburst but, more importantly, it will inevitably cause further erosion of the underlying relationship.

As time goes on, it will not only be the taboo subjects that are avoided. There will be a more general reluctance to discuss anything of an intimate or personal nature with the other party. Conversation and emotional interaction between the parties will become more and more superficial. This may in turn lead to physical avoidance where one or both begin to find reasons for coming home late. There may be eminently reasonable explanations for such delays but they will frequently be expressions of one partner's reluctance to face the other.

As this trend develops, there may be a discovery of all manner of new business, social or educational commitments which require great slabs of time away from home. If the situation is not faced this process may culminate in a gradual redirection of emotional energy from the marital relationship to outside activities or some other person.

As the intimacy of the relationship is eroded the parties may become conscious of problems in other areas of their relationship. Sexual differences may develop. There may be a lack of responsiveness on the part of the husband or the wife because the emotional climate has become bitter and lacking in affection. There may be a feeling that it is no longer an expression of romantic love and tenderness and, consequently, has been cheapened. The emotional cause of the problem may not be perceived by the unresponsive partner who may simply be aware of frigidity or impotence. It may require a trained counsellor to assist in discovering the underlying emotional cause. At the other end of the spectrum one partner may withdraw from any sexual involvement with the other as a deliberate protest. This may be nothing more complicated than an endeavour to get even.

This stage also provides one of the most prolific breeding grounds for violence known to man. Aggression is frequently born of frustration and at this point in the marital relationship both parties may find that they are frustrated almost to screaming point. Women tend to be more subtle than men, and wives are more likely to express their aggression verbally or in a variety of subtle non-physical ways which might be described as bitchiness. Of course it is true that men also express frustration in that manner but, in general, they are less inclined to do so if only because they tend not to be as good at it.

Men are far more likely to find their frustration boiling over into a violent rage. Back in the days when life was less complicated, that kind of response was very useful because it produced the adrenalin necessary to enable them to thump a marauding bear or meet whatever danger threatened. Unhappily it offers a totally inappropriate means of resolving frustration arising from marital difficulties. Whilst the majority of men are able to restrain the violent impulses that well up it is true to say that most will at least be aware of them and many will be conscious of the strain involved in trying to hold the lid on.

As a judge who was a member of the board of a psychiatric hospital once told me, few people, including judges, have any real understanding of the causes of violence. It is not an infrequent occurrence for a thoroughly decent man to fly into a violent outburst which leaves him as shocked and bewildered as his victim. That is not to say that such acts are any the less wrong or that they should be condoned. It is true, however, that people who recoil in horror at what they have done can usually be helped to overcome their problems.

This stage is obviously more serious than the stage of disillusionment: negative emotions such as resentment, bitterness and anxiety have become more deeply engrained and it is no longer a matter of merely sorting out a few things. It has become obvious that the marriage itself is in danger. Furthermore, whilst the stage of disillusionment involves a deterioration in attitudes, the stage of erosion involves a deterioration in conduct. As time goes by destructive habits may be acquired. Some are merely hurtful whilst others not only hurt but also involve a transfer of emotional dependence. A brilliantly cutting remark may wound the other party and at the same time bring a feeling of smug satisfaction. Putting one's friends before one's spouse will not only prove hurtful to him or her but strengthen one's position in the social sphere. Flirting may make it plain that the other party is not the only fish in the sea but it can also be exhilarating to know that one is still attractive to the opposite sex. The message that "you are not the only fish in the sea" is not only conveyed to the other party but subconsciously filed away "just in case".

In this context the reformation of the relationship is obviously more difficult. It no longer involves simply changing attitudes and expectations. There are deep hurts that will require healing. Renewed intimacy will have to be built up over a period of time and if the destructive habits are not dealt with they will give rise to further hurtful episodes which may torpedo any progress made. Furthermore, by this stage it is likely that some friends and relatives will have begun to align themselves on one "side" or the other. As well-meaning as they may be, their alignments are likely to be more of a hindrance than a help in any attempt at reconciliation.

Nonetheless, if both partners are motivated to try then the relationship can be retrieved. It will be a lot of hard work and the parties may well require the assistance of a trained counsellor over an extended period of time. It will be neither quick nor easy to get to the root of the problems and help each understand how the other functions emotionally, and, in particular, how the other perceives and reacts to different kinds of situations. Yet if they persevere they can still mend the breach and, in time, establish deeper lines of communication.

The marriage, after all, is still quite viable. The very fact that the parties are so deeply wounded often indicates the amount of love they still have for each other. They may fight but in a very real sense there is something worth fighting for. A lot of the anger may be engendered by the risk to the relationship perceived in the other person's conduct. Bewildered exclamations like, "Doesn't he see what he is doing to us?" convey not only anger and bewilderment but a subtle reminder that there is still an "us".

At this stage then one can, at least, know that there is a base to build on. Whether or not a new relationship can be built on that base depends upon the attitudes of the participants. For Christians it may depend in large measure upon the nature and quality of their faith. If they perceive their Christian commitment largely in terms of a rigid standard of morality then it may be very difficult for them to put aside the hurts of the past. Such people are fond of statements like, "I forgive you but I'll never be able to forget what you have done". It is hardly surprising if the other party sees that as Pharisaic double-talk which may be paraphrased as, "My moral code obliges me to forgive you so I'm paying lip service to the concept—but don't count on it, Buster!"

On the other hand if there is genuine forgiveness, a sincere acknowledgement that there have been faults on both sides and genuine seeking of each other's forgiveness then there will be a strong chance that the marriage can be retrieved. Both parties need to come together and acknowledge that the state of the marriage is "their" problem rather than "his" or "her" problem. If they can seek to solve it together with faith, determination and a hunger to understand each other's needs and hurts then they will have already advanced well down the track towards a more solid and mature marriage.

CHAPTER ELEVEN

The Stage of Detachment

If the erosion of the marriage is allowed to continue unchecked it inevitably results in a stage of detachment.

This stage really involves the death of that special kind of relationship which characterises a genuine marriage. The parties may continue to live under the same roof and may have a certain degree of involvement with each other but the emotional bonds have been broken and the relationship has become an empty shell. Whilst in the erosion stage there may have been bitter fights born of distress at the state of the relationship, conflict of that kind is unlikely to occur in the stage of detachment. Ironically enough, the marriage may become superficially more respectable. Neighbours and relatives may be heartened by what they perceive as the progress which has been made in the relationship. But, in reality, they have ceased to fight because the relationship doesn't seem worth fighting about any more. Of course, there may be fights. Constant exposure to each other in an atmosphere of sullen bitterness may well generate angry outbursts or even violence but they will no longer be fuelled by anger at the risk to the relationship.

The death of the relationship will frequently poison the atmosphere in the home, stifling expressions of joy, enthusiasm or optimism. At this stage the walls are well and truly up. Communication is likely to be both tense and stilted. The attitude to the relationship is not merely one of pessimism. The dominant issue is not, "How far should one go to achieve a reconciliation?" but rather, "How far should one go for the sake of preserving appearances or for the sake of other people?" They may attend social functions together, but not because they enjoy each other's company. They may be reluctant to separate because of the children and may even make desultory attempts to get on better with each other for their sake, but such attempts to rekindle the relationship will tend only to confirm the feeling that even the embers are dead.

This stage is reached when one partner no longer feels love and affection for the other or any real emotional involvement in the relationship.

One party to the marriage almost always arrives at this point earlier than the other. In many cases one party will have been desperately trying to revive the relationship right up until the very moment when the other walks out. One party may have felt that things were starting to improve and be quite unable to recognise that the other party regards the relationship as hopelessly irretrievable.

A lasting reconciliation is difficult to achieve once the relationship has reached this stage. If the stage of detachment has been longstanding and the resultant attitudes are deeply ingrained then even an experienced marriage guidance counsellor may be of little assistance. The residual love and mutual concern which underlies much of the conflict in the erosive stage is not available as a platform to build upon once this stage of detachment has been reached.

We Christians echo Christ's words in Matthew 19:26, "...with God all things are possible." and there are certainly cases where parties are wonderfully reconciled even after they have long moved through the state of detachment and been physically separated for months or even years. Yet at the same time it should be recognised that reconciliation is much more difficult. Praying for a reconciliation when the marriage is in the stage of erosion is rather like praying for a healing. Praying for a reconciliation where one or both of the parties have been in a state of detachment for some time is more like praying for a resurrection.

As the detachment is confirmed by the passage of time there comes a degree of resignation about the fate of the relationship. With time, that resignation inevitably colours a person's hopes and aspirations for the future. Memories are full of the pain of a relationship seen as "past". A rosy future with the present spouse is no longer imaginable. There comes a feeling that one has to face facts: things are not going to get any better. The future with that partner is bleak indeed. With these thoughts come the first subtle stirrings of the idea of making a new life. Most people will be initially reluctant to contemplate at a conscious level actually leaving the other party and totally abandoning the marriage. Yet at a subconscious level at least, there will be the awareness that in that direction lies the path of hope for the future.

The dilemma posed by this subconscious longing and conscious reluctance may lead to plans for the future which do not necessarily involve separation but which would be of assistance if separation occurred. The person will frequently answer his own disquiet at such plans by telling himself, "It's just in case," or "It's just a fall-back position". These fall-back positions may include resuming secondary or tertiary studies or taking other steps to foster financial self-sufficiency. They may involve establishing a separate bank account to which the other party does not have access. They may involve endeavouring to bolster one's social base by going out with friends more frequently or becoming involved in sporting or social clubs. Whatever the form there will be a subtle but significant move towards a reassertion of independence or, to put it another way, a weaning from the mutual dependence involved in a marital relationship.

During this stage the person may well find that he or she is flirting with members of the opposite sex. Initially it may be a cause of embarrassment or shock but it is likely to recur because there is an underlying need to be reassured that one is still attractive. In this stage one is acutely aware of standing amidst the wreckage of a failed marriage. Self-esteem is frequently at a very low ebb and any response to flirtatious signals will be gratefully received and savoured like a cup of water to a parched throat. It is small wonder that people going through this stage are so vulnerable to new emotional entanglements. An attentive suitor may be seen in stark contrast to the detached husband. He may represent excitement, tenderness, understanding and sympathy. He may be seen as a resurgence of romantic love long thought extinguished. Thus idealised, probably quite unrealistically, he becomes virtually irresistible.

A further drive underlying this flirtation is the need to be reassured that one could start again if separation did occur. It is one thing to leave a cold and sterile relationship to make a new life. It is altogether another to face the prospect of remaining forever unwanted like some kind of discarded pet taken out to the rubbish tip and left to fend for itself.

The development of fall-back positions and the increasing sense of independence which they bring inevitably lead to a confrontation and the prospect of leaving. At first, this too may be thought of as a fall-back position. It may be explored by thoughts such as, ''Well, if I did leave, what would I do, where would I go?'' There may be a great deal of thought given to the financial implications of separation. If there are children they will be a major area of concern. There may be some anxiety that the other party will seek custody and there may be lengthy legal battles. In extreme cases there may even be the nagging fear that the other spouse might suddenly disappear with them overseas or interstate and that they may never be seen again. More commonly there will be a great deal of anxiety about the effect that the separation may have on their emotional well-being. Further reflection may bring some apprehension about future conflict of loyalties. Perhaps the children might come to align themselves with the other party. If it has been a long marriage there may be considerable anxiety simply about the prospect of living as a single and independent person again. A great deal of time might be spent on wondering what life after separation might be like. Particular fantasies may vary from the abysmally pessimistic to the most wildly optimistic.

At this stage a person is bound to have a bad time with his conscience. The decision to separate will almost inevitably be followed by pangs of guilt. There may also be all kinds of remorse about the past. There may be enormous guilt over the prospect of the effect on the children of a broken home.

These feelings of guilt will be intermingled with anxiety, uncertainty and growing feelings of despair. The situation may seem intolerable. There may be a feeling of taking a great leap into the unknown, risking not only one's own future but the future of the children. The decision may evoke criticism from friends and fellow-Christians and will certainly involve a great deal of self-criticism and guilt. Yet, on the other hand, one may feel that to stay would be intolerable.

In the circumstances there may be wild mood swings and frequent vacillation. Accommodation may be booked but then cancelled. Sometimes a particularly angry scene will be the decisive factor. There may be almost a feeling of relief when a particular incident triggers a walk-out. In other cases a "temporary" separation may be arranged as a sop to conscience.

Friends and relatives may be told that, "We are just separating for a short time to sort things out and see if we can make a go of it" or, "I'm just leaving him for a week or two to see if I can shock him into coming to his senses".

Christians may experience a particularly heartrending kind of anguish. After all, isn't there something particularly sinful about leaving your husband or wife? "Haven't I got a duty to forgive?" "Can I really face my Christian friends or, worse, my minister and try to justify breaking my marriage vows?'' "But I just can't stand it! When I think of enduring the situation for another thirty years, something inside me shrivels up. Have I really got to choose between God and my sanity?''

As this kind of anguish grows, many people will find themselves staying away from church. They may also find themselves unable to pray. In a very real sense they have reached a point where they are unable to face God. At the time in their lives when they most need to be aware of God's support and forgiveness, they feel alienated from him. Their thoughts of him at this stage are characterised by guilt and, though it may never be consciously articulated, there is a deep underlying fear that if they go through with this terrible act of leaving a husband or wife, God may turn his back on them. It is in this stark climate that the decision to separate or not will be made.

PART THREE

TO STAY OR TO GO?

CHAPTER TWELVE

Clearing the Decks

The decision to separate or remain in the marriage is obviously a very important one with widespread implications, not only for the person making it but for the lives of other people, including the children. The seriousness of the decision demands sound judgement. Yet how can you exercise sound judgement when you are caught in a maelstrom of competing emotions and when what seems right one minute seems hopelessly wrong the next?

Let me suggest that an appropriate starting point is to clear the decks by re-establishing a proper relationship with God. He isn't glaring down on you with stern disapproval. Whether you have been conscious of it or not, he has watched over you and shared your anguish like a loving parent forced to watch his child suffer. He loves you in such a deep and profound manner that it is beyond the capacity of your intellect to grasp. His heartfelt desire is not to punish but to comfort. His attitude towards you is the same as that expresed by Jesus to the people of Jerusalem when he said, "How often would I have gathered your children together as a hen gathers her brood under her wings, and you would not".[23] He earnestly desires to be reconciled with you and to offer you comfort and support in this most trying time.

Furthermore, God is not in the business of making

people endure the unendurable. One of my favourite
passages in the New Testament is 1 Corinthians 10:13
which reads, "No temptation has overtaken you that is not
common to man. God is faithful, and he will not let you
be tempted beyond your strength, but with the temptation
will also provide the way of escape, that you may be able
to endure it". The word translated in the Revised Standard
Version as "temptation" has a wider meaning in the
original Greek which extends to trials of various kinds. The
verse could therefore be rewritten to read, "No trial or
problem has overtaken you that is not common to man.
God is faithful and he will not let you be tried beyond your
strength but with the trial or problem will also provide the
way of escape that you may be able to endure it". To me
that has always been a very precious promise.

It is, of course, true that Christians sometimes have to
endure severe trials but I do not believe God permits that
to happen unless there are compelling reasons for doing
so. Even then he may be counted upon to provide the
strength to endure them. If you come to God with faith
and sincerity and commit to him the seemingly intolerable
dilemma in which you find yourself, you will find that he
will provide the solution. Something will change. Either
the situation will change in some manner or he will lead
you out of it.

The price that must be paid, however, is to put yourself
in a right relationship with God and be willing to do things
his way.

The reason that most of us don't experience this kind
of release is that we become so panic-stricken at our plight
that we seize whatever straw is most obvious and pray that
God will strengthen it so that it may become the means
of our survival. He simply does not work that way. If we
want God to resolve any situation for us then we have to
be willing to do things his way. Ironically enough, if we
take all of our courage in our hands and decide to trust
him, we find that he is so much wiser than we are. In time,
and with the benefit of hindsight, we will realise that he

has led us out of the morass along the only path that
remained open.

There is yet another reason why you will need to re-
establish your relationship with God and to accept his
guidance. It provides a platform of security. Whether the
ultimate decision is to leave or to remain, it will have a
profound effect on your future and the future of your
family. From time to time you will be beset by nagging
doubts as to whether you have done the right thing. Those
doubts can cause great insecurity and undermine your faith
with devastating effect. You may find yourself plagued by
questions such as, "But what if I did the wrong thing? How
can I expect God to sustain me or help me if I've broken
his law and ventured out from under his protection?" When
those doubts come, and come they will, it can be a source
of very great comfort to be able to dismiss them with the
firm affirmation, "That's not true! I went back to God
and made it plain that however it hurt I would do things
his way. When I made the decision I sincerely believed
that it was the right thing to do. I was not being bull-headed
about the situation and I am confident that I did God's
will as I understood it."

When then do you need to do to put yourself in that
position of confidence?

The first and most important answer is that you need
to clear the decks of all those clamouring emotions which
buffet you in all directions, twist your stomach into knots
and make it almost impossible to make a reasoned decision.
To do this you will need to take the following steps.

1 Seek forgiveness

I appreciate that many people will promptly recoil and say,
"Now hang on a minute, it's all his fault". If by that
assertion you mean that the other person has been more
at fault or even far more at fault than you have then what
you say may well be true. On the other hand, if what you
mean is that you have been entirely blameless throughout

the entire relationship then let me say, as inoffensively as possible, that it is highly unlikely. If you accept what the Bible says about humanity then you will realise that only one sinless person ever lived and he did not marry. Accordingly, if you have managed to survive married life and remain sinless then you are the first person in the history of mankind to have done so.

Make a sober appraisal of the situation. If you conclude that your partner has been ninety-five per cent to blame and you have been only five per cent to blame then acknowledge that five per cent and ask God's forgiveness for it.

You need to take that step for two reasons. In the first place, the Christian position is that two wrongs don't make a right. That which is wrong is still wrong even if it was prompted by provocative or even outrageous conduct by someone else. While you insist on trying to justify it you will never be rid of the burden of it. The Christian remedy for sin has always been the same: to confess it, ask God's forgiveness, accept that he has forgiven you and then forget it.

In the second place whatever decision is made there will be some difficult emotional times ahead. It is almost inevitable that there will come a time when you are assailed by feelings of guilt. Those feelings may be put on to you by other people with a sanctimonious and judgemental attitude to anyone experiencing marital difficulties or they may arise from your own insecurity.

This can be a crippling time in which every waking thought seems to be prefaced by the words, "If only". People torture themselves by thinking up all kinds of fanciful things that they might have done or left undone and persuade themselves that but for that everything might have turned out differently. Of course, guilt and self-justification coexist and when the pendulum swings back all manner of arguments may be marshalled to justify every conceivable act or attitude and to place all the blame on the other spouse. These see-sawing mood swings are destructive and you must break the cycle if you are going to be free to make any sort of fresh start. If you have confessed your own part, however small, in the breakdown of the marriage and obtained forgiveness for it then you won't need to respond to suggestions of guilt either by wallowing in it or by commencing convoluted exercises in self-justification. You will be able to say to yourself quietly but firmly, "Yes, I know that I was partly to blame but God has forgiven me for that and I have put that behind me now. I don't have to worry about that any more. All I have to do now is get on with the task at hand".

You may also need to ask God to forgive you for the estrangement between you and him. If the cycle of distress, anger and anxiety has caused the loss of intimacy and trust in your relationship with God then it may be helpful simply to acknowledge that fact, ask him to forgive you and to restore and strengthen that relationship.

2 Forgive your spouse

People who are confronting this decision frequently share a common confusion. I don't know how many times someone has asked me, "Am I free to leave him or do I have to forgive him?" They usually look a little bewildered when I tell them that they have asked two totally separate questions. I usually then explain that they will have to answer the first, though I can offer some advice, but that the answer to the second is completely without doubt. No matter what the other party has done, you must forgive him. If you are married to a man prone to flying into violent rages that actually endanger the lives of your young children then the right thing to do is to leave him and remove your children to a place of safety. Yet you still have to forgive him for what he has done. Jesus said that we are to forgive our enemies and pray for those who despitefully use us. He put that principle into practice himself by praying for the tormentors who drove the nails into his hands. If you are a Christian then you are one of his followers and he requires you to have the same attitude.

The failure to forgive can also undermine your confidence in the decision you have made if you later feel it right to leave. When you experience doubt over that decision it will be helpful to be able to look back at the manner in which it was made and to be assured that you have followed the right path. If you are left with lingering doubts as to whether your decision was the right one in the circumstances or merely a reaction to your own anger and resentment then you may find that you have left open a chink through which insecurity and anxiety may pour with distressing force. If you know that you forgave your spouse you will be more confident that your decision was made with a clear head and a clear conscience.

3 Commit the situation to God

Suggestions like this are frequently made so glibly that one could be excused for thinking that those who make them have no understanding of what they ask. This is a forbidding prospect. Your whole future is involved in this decision and quite possibly the future of your children as well. Yet, despite the momentous implications of such a commitment, it remains indispensable.

God loves you and he cares about everything that is happening to you. He fully understands your situation. He knows all of the competing considerations that confront you. He sees straight through any façade you may adopt to conceal the emotional turmoil beneath. He grieves for your distress. He longs to bring comfort to you, to assure you that with him all things are possible. Whether you can perceive it or not he has a plan for you and he already knows the way to lead you out of this morass. Yet there is a price to be paid and the price is trust. As James put it, "But when you pray, you must believe and not doubt at all. Whoever doubts is like a wave in the sea that is driven and blown about by the wind. A person like that, unable to make up his mind and undecided in all he does, must not think that he will receive anything from the Lord".[2]

Imagine that you are out at sea when your yacht catches fire. You radio for help and as the heat becomes more and more intense you notice with great relief the welcome sight of a rescue launch. The launch draws up alongside and the captain yells, "Step across on to my deck". You only have two alternatives. You may stay with the burning yacht or you may trust the captain and jump wholly into his boat. If you procrastinate too long you may burn to death. If you try to rely upon the buoyancy of both boats by having a foot on each deck then you will inevitably wind up in the water. The only solution is to trust the captain immediately and to place all of your weight in his boat.

Your present position is the same. You may be concerned that if you agree to do things God's way then he may lock you into a situation that you will find intolerable. Yet you know that you haven't been doing brilliantly without him. Let me remind you what God said to the children of Israel, "I know the plans I have for you... They are plans for good and not for evil, to give you a future and a hope".[3] God is saying the same thing to you now.

All that is required is that you say to God, "Lord, I'm in a real mess. I commit this whole situation to you. I place it in your hands and I ask you to sort it out and show me what to do. I can't see any solution but I trust you with my life from this moment on. Whatever you tell me to do I will do. Please help me to maintain this attitude of trust and obedience. Amen".

You may not be aware of a fanfare of trumpets after praying this sort of prayer but something very significant will have happened. God will have taken over and in time you will become aware of a kind of peace known only to those who have relinquished the struggle to run their own lives. You will know that the ship is not rudderless because God is at the helm and he knows the way. As time passes the way ahead will become clear and you will realise that he is interested in more than just resolving a thorny question. He is interested in renewing every part of your life.

4 Maintain a continuing relationship with God

Having jumped into the boat you should get to know the captain. You can do this by reading the Bible, by prayer and by contact with other Christians.

When you pray, for heaven's sake be honest! If you feel miserable, tell God that you feel miserable and ask him to help you. Don't play parts. Don't try to sound like Thomas à Becket when he was sworn in as Archbishop of Canterbury. Richard Burton may have impressed the critics with his wonderful command of medieval English but God is not likely to be impressed by yours. If your prayer is to be of any value at all, it must be sincere.

5 Resolutely reject guilt and fear

They will blind you to the truths and push you into ill-considered decisions. Remember that you have been forgiven and that guilt consequently has no hold on you. Equally, remember that you have chosen to place your trust in God. If he holds your future then you need not worry about it.

6 Make a rational decision

If you have forgiven your spouse there can be no question of leaving to get even with him. Neither, if you trust God for your future, can there be any question of remaining with your spouse because you cannot face the future alone. As surprising as it may seem to many people, the question which a Christian must ask himself is simply this, Has the marriage irretrievably broken down? No, I am not recoiling from what I said earlier about the need for *porneia* or *ervath dabhar*. Whilst those concepts may be less narrowly defined than the English translations would lead one to suspect, it is clear that serious misconduct is intended. However, it seems to me that a Christian should be willing to forgive and to seek reconciliation even when adultery has occurred or there has been other serious misconduct. Yet, whilst it is always possible to forgive it is not always possible to effect a reconciliation. Your spouse may be bent on continuing a course of conduct which makes that virtually impossible. In these circumstances one must ask whether the marriage might not yet be retrieved if you persevere in an attitude of faith and patience or whether the harsh reality is that the intransigence of your partner has made resumption of a proper marital relationship virtually impossible.

Please note that I have chosen the phrase "resumption of a proper marital relationship" with care. It is that relationship to which God has called you. If you think you may be able to work towards such a relationship with your spouse then give it everything you've got. If after sober reflection and prayerful consideration you are convinced that your spouse will not or cannot participate in such a relationship then you may feel obliged to separate. The Bible refers to only one kind of marriage and that is one in which a man leaves his mother and father and cleaves unto his wife and the two become one flesh. It says nothing about any supposed obligation to remain under the same roof with a violent, malicious or adulterous spouse. To put it another way, it does not suggest that a person should remain bound to a spouse who has repudiated the marital relationship.

Do not decide in haste or anger. Take your time. Consider the position carefully and even when you have made a tentative decision make sure you commit it to God. Ask God to show you if you have decided upon the wrong course. If at the end of a week you feel that the decision is the right one then go ahead with confidence.

At the same time it is necessary to adopt an attitude of faith. In part, this means praying with the knowledge that you are talking to God and that he is listening to you just as if he were sitting on the other side of the room nodding in understanding of various things you are saying. It also means that when you bring problems to him you should do so with an air of expectancy. Many prayers are simply

litanies of complaints about the present and worries about
the future.

If you are feeling miserable and anxious and don't think
you can muster any real faith, then tell God that. Ask him
to give you faith and to strengthen you. Then begin to think
about those positive things which you can acknowledge and
thank God for them. If you do this conscientiously you will
find that your pessimism will begin to lift.

Faith, after all, has nothing to do with feelings, it is
simply a reliance upon what you know to be the truth. The
little boy who described faith as "believing what you know
isn't really true" had it backwards. Faith is believing what
you know is true, despite your fear or insecurity. A man
may exercise his faith in an aeroplane by travelling in it
from one city to another even though he is afraid of flying.
When he does so he is relying upon what he knows to be
true: namely that air travel is comparatively safe. The truth
of that fact is not negated by his fear but if he continues
to fly in faith then he may find that his fear is gradually
overcome. That is the kind of concept which Christians
have in mind when they speak about living by faith.

There are all kinds of situations in life which evoke great
anxiety. They may be confronted by faith though not in
the sense in which that word was understood by the little
boy. Faith does not lie in pretending that things are not
as bad as they really are but in reliance upon the fact of
God's love and protection. The risk is real and so is the
anxiety but God's love and protection are also real and,
when they are relied upon, the Christian finds that he is
kept safe and, in time, his anxieties are overcome.

Fellow Christians can be of great assistance or of great
hindrance. Ideally, you need one or two close Christian
friends who have a positive attitude and will support you
in prayer. They should be people in whom you can confide.
Unhappily, there are so many Christians who have a rigid
and dogmatic attitude toward marital breakdown that you
can't automatically assume that the nice sympathetic person
you have just met will be supportive. It pays to ask one

or two pointed questions about their attitude to separation and divorce before becoming too involved with people. Small groups are also excellent environments in which to get to know people and to obtain support during trying times.

If you really feel isolated within your church then talk to your minister or elder about the problem candidly and see if he can offer some constructive advice. If he can't you may have to think about changing churches. When you are going through a very trying time Christian support really is important, although, ultimately, your reliance must be upon God himself.

CHAPTER THIRTEEN

Making a Sober Evaluation

Having cleared the decks of guilt, resentment and anxiety
as best you can, the next step is to make a sober evaluation
of the situation. When you are emotionally involved, and
everyone in your situation is, this is not an easy task.

It may be of great assistance to discuss your position
with a trained counsellor or some objective person who
knows both you and your spouse but is in neither camp.
An outsider may frequently see something even from a
distance which those intimately involved in the relationship
miss. In any event, ask God to help you evaluate your
position. Take your time and expect that He will assist you
to understand it more clearly.

The first task is to determine the root cause or causes
of the marital difficulties. By this I don't mean listing all
of the other person's faults. There may be a plethora of
things to complain about but many of them will be
symptoms of deeper underlying problems. It is important
to try to distinguish cause from effect.

The more common Christian view and the earlier legal
grounds for divorce both emphasised matrimonial fault and
implicitly conveyed the idea that divorce was permissible
if one party could pin some sufficiently serious misconduct
on the other party to justify the action. Let me say as bluntly
as I can that that concept is unforgiving and un-Christian.
If you have truly forgiven your spouse for what he or she

has done then you will not be trying to pin things on him or her. That does not mean that you should not be looking at your spouse's conduct but rather that you should look at it as, possibly, a symptom of a continuing problem in the relationship. The task which now confronts you is to make a thorough evaluation of the root causes of the problem and to decide whether the conduct of the other person and, more importantly, the attitudes which underly it are so grave that they undermine the marital relationship and make any proper marriage virtually impossible.

To go through the exercise properly you will require scrupulous honesty and a willingness to confront and think about painful episodes that you would probably rather forget or at least try to ignore.

In many cases of course, the root cause of the problem will be fairly obvious but in others both parties may be bewildered by continuing conflict. In yet other cases there may be quite serious violent, or peculiar, behaviour which may present as a major problem in itself yet in reality be a symptom of a deeper unrest.

Take the case where one partner commits adultery. In such circumstances ecclesiastical counsellors have frequently been quite preoccupied with the fact that such behaviour fell within the so-called exceptive clause in Matthew 19 and thereby "freed" the "innocent" party to divorce and remarry. This unfortunate preoccupation tended to obscure the need to grapple with the underlying problem. Adultery is a serious matter but it by no means invariably signals the end of a marriage. There are many Christian couples who are still happily married despite adultery by one or both parties. No doubt it caused acute distress to the innocent party and, usually, to the guilty one as well. Nonetheless, a reconciliation was achieved in an atmosphere of forgiveness and the relationship was gradually restored. In many cases, the marriages are now stronger than they were before. Lest I give the wrong impression, let me hasten to add that I am not suggesting that a little adultery is a good thing as has been advocated in a number of trendy but totally unrealistic articles published recently. What I am suggesting is that if both parties try to turn back to God and bring their lives more into line with his will, they find that neither harsh judgementalism nor patronising condescension is required, but compassionate under-standing and forgiveness.

Once you have forgiven your partner and the person with whom the adultery was committed you are free to come to grips with two crucial questions: Firstly, what was the underlying cause, and secondly to what extent does that cause undermine your marital relationship?

Let us consider three examples:

(a) Allan is sent overseas for an extended assignment. His wife has to remain home because his company won't pay for her fare or provide accommodation for her and in any event, she has school-age children to care for. Overseas, he is lonely and at a loose end. The overseas branch of his company allocates a personal secretary to help him fulfil his assignment. She is warm, personable and attractive and they are constantly thrust into each other's company. The situation is fraught with temptation and he eventually succumbs. It is a brief but passionate affair born more of loneliness than anything else. It is not long before Allan returns home to his wife and children where he finds himself constantly troubled by guilt over what has occurred and finally tells his wife.

In those circumstances his wife will no doubt be distressed and angry. She remained faithful to him while he was away. She may feel that she will never be able to trust him again. In reality, however, all that has occurred is that her husband succumbed to temptation at a time when he was particularly vulnerable. He may be a decent and loving husband who, in normal circumstances, would have remained faithful to his wife. What he did was wrong but it does not indicate any deep-seated problem which is likely to make any future marital relationship between them impossible. All of us have feet of clay, all of us are prone to temptation and, from time to time, all of us succumb to it. An appropriate Christian response for Allan's wife to adopt is to forgive him, ask God to help her overcome the emotional reaction to the revelation of his unfaithfulness and work hard at rebuilding the intimacy they formerly enjoyed.

(b) Susan is married to David, a man some ten years her senior. He is a man of very rigid views with no patience for those who do not measure up to his standards. In his view a man is the head of the house and it is his responsibility to make all of the decisions. When she was younger Susan was attracted to him because of his maturity and confidence. He seemed to be the sort of man who always knew what to do, a born leader. Yet after twelve years of marriage the decisive leadership now seems merely dictatorial. He brushes aside her suggestions with a patronising smile that is clearly intended to convey that, ''You need not worry your pretty little head about these things. You just leave them all to me''. She feels that all her initiative has been stifled, that she has become a mere appendage. In her frustration and dissatisfaction she begins to drink during the daytime when her husband is away. At first she is able to conceal it from him but when he finds out he smashes the bottles and tells her not to be stupid. The drinking continues and there are repeated arguments until, after a particular scene she flees the house and seeks refuge in a local bar. The next morning she wakes up in bed with a strange man.

When asked for an explanation, Susan is quite unable to say whether it was just the alcohol, whether it involved fleeing into the arms of some sympathetic and available male or whether she was motived by the desire to get even with her husband. Whatever the true position may have been, it is apparent that the problem is much deeper than the simple act of adultery. In this case the marriage is under serious threat, not so much because of the adultery, but because of the underlying difficulties in the relationship. If the marriage is to be saved, those problems will need to be addressed.

(c) Meg's husband, John, had an affair with his secretary. When Meg found out about it she forgave him and tried to make a go of the marriage. Some months later she found that he was still involved with the secretary. There was a further confrontation and he promised never to see her again. Yet shortly thereafter Meg found them in bed together. There have been lots of promises, but Meg knows he is still seeing the other woman. She stays with him only for the sake of the children.

In this case the problem is the adulterous relationship itself and, in particular, the fact that its persistence indicates a serious conflict of loyalties. Unless John is genuinely prepared to renounce the other relationship there will be no hope for the marriage.

In each of the three cases that I have mentioned adultery was committed. Yet the prognosis for the marriages varied tremendously.

In the first example there was no deep-seated problem; with forgiveness and time to heal the hurts and permit trust to be re-established there was no reason why the marriage should not be saved. In the second example there were serious problems in the relationship itself and the adultery was merely a symptom of it. In those circumstances the future of the marriage was dependent primarily upon whether the underlying problems in the relationship could be resolved. Clearly that was not a situation which could be adequately dealt with simply by forgiveness and the passing of time to heal wounds. Specialised counselling may have been effective if both parties had been willing to make honest attempts to resolve their differences. In the third case the adulterous relationship itself constituted a serious problem.

I have chosen adultery merely as an example. The same kind of evaluation needs to be made in respect of other kinds of behaviour which imperil the marital relationship. A man may be violent because an extraordinary combination of circumstances has simply driven him to a point where he has lost control. Another man might be violent because it is the only way in which he can express his continued frustration. Another might be violent because he grew up in a tough neighbourhood, always admired tough men and has tried to solve his problems with violence all his life. Yet another man might be violent because of some underlying psychological maladjustment.

To understand the root cause of the problem is half the battle. When you have reached a point of understanding you will then have some indication of whether anything can be done to overcome the problem. If your spouse genuinely wants to change, then generally speaking you should make an effort to stick with him and help him. That is, I believe, the sort of obligation which one undertakes when one promises to take somebody for better or worse. On the other hand, I do not believe that means that anyone has to spend the next thirty years living with a drunken brute who has no intention of changing.

If you put your heart and soul into helping to overcome your spouse's problems one of two things will happen. Either you'll see your efforts crowned with success and your marriage rebuilt or it will become obvious that, in spite of promising the world, your spouse has no real intention of changing. In either event you'll be able to see more clearly what is likely to lie ahead for your marriage.

This process is not limited to making a sober evaluation of your partner's shortcomings. It involves an evaluation of the whole relationship, both positive and negative, and that includes your own contribution. It is worth bearing in mind Jesus' suggestion to remove the beam from your eye before trying to pluck the splinter out of your brother's—or your spouse's.[24] That principle holds true even if the blame is almost entirely that of the other partner. It is only commonsense to realise that a question such as, "What are you going to do about your problem?" evokes little more than resentment and a thoroughly defensive attitude. On the other hand questions such as, "Look, can't we face this together? What can I do to help?" are more likely to enlist a positive response.

Remember too, that a sober evaluation is not merely a matter of identifying problems but of evaluating their seriousness. All of us are, to a degree, a product of our backgrounds and temperaments. Language is a very clumsy medium of expression. When people are irritated or upset it is easy to misunderstand what another person is saying. If you have been brought up in a convent and absolutely abhor vulgar language then you may become deeply distressed by things let slip by your husband after a hard day's work in his panel beating workshop. From your point of view he is being unspeakably crude and offensive. From his point of view the problem is very simple. He works with panel beaters, not clergymen. The language may be blue enough to blister the paintwork on the ceiling, but it doesn't mean anything. The men at work don't even think about it. If the odd thing does slip out at home, so what? It's unintentional. You can't change everything just like that. Surely she should see that and not make a state trial out of every minor slip.

The same kind of differences can arise about a whole host of things. Sometimes tension is caused by different cultural backgrounds. Whatever the issue it is important to remember that no two people ever enter a marital relationship with the same set of presuppositions and expectations. It is an axiom of human nature that it is the small things which frequently cause the greatest distress. Yet, in making any kind of evaluation, it is important to distinguish this kind of tension from the really serious problems which undermine the basis of a marriage.

Ironically enough, one of the causes of marital

breakdown among Christians may be the faith and commitment of one party. If a person who has been a Christian
for some years loses his faith then the continued commitment of the other party may become a constant reproach.
This may be quite unintentional and usually is. The other
person is concerned about him and wants only to help him
regain his faith but the efforts provoke nothing but anger
and bitterness. Consequently, one frequently finds that
when a husband abandons his faith, it is not long before
he abandons his Christian wife as well. She may blame
herself and constantly wonder how she failed him but, in
reality, the criticisms of her attitudes or behaviour were
only excuses. The real problem was not that her behaviour
was bad but that it was good. Her husband, like Hymenaus
and Alexander in 1 Timothy 1, who "made shipwreck"
of their faith through bad conscience, was uncomfortable
with her. In these cases the prospects of obtaining a
reconciliation are quite poor. Unless he comes back to God,
he is not likely to come back to his wife.

CHAPTER FOURTEEN

The Decision

By the time you have cleared the deck and made a sober
evaluation the decision you should make may already be
clear to you. You may have realised that the presenting
problem is symptomatic of an underlying emotional
difficulty which you and your spouse should try to
overcome. In many cases it will have become evident that
the decision is not merely should I go or stay? Further
questions may arise. Can this problem be resolved? What
can I do to help? Should we consult a trained counsellor?
If the problem is sufficiently serious to threaten your
marriage it must be confronted. There is no point in simply
gritting your teeth and enduring the situation. You will
simply be postponing the inevitable.

Just how you go about resolving problems will depend
upon their nature. An appropriate first step may be to
approach someone with experience in marriage guidance
counselling. Most of the mainstream Christian denominations provide such services. Alternatively, your partner may
be willing to speak to some other person, possibly a member
of your church, who has a more generalised counselling
experience and the advantage of already knowing you both.

Non-Christian counsellors may also be of great assistance because of insights gained from their training and
experience. Your situation is by no means unique. Nearly
forty thousand Australian couples were divorced last year,

whilst in England and Wales there were nearly 154,000 divorces in 1986. There are countless thousands more who live apart and more still who live separately under the one roof. Counsellors who spend thirty to forty hours each week dealing with such people are obviously in a position to see the problem arising again and again, to note various attempts to deal with it and to see which methods work and which don't. A non-Christian counsellor, however, will pay no regard to the ability of Christians to overcome problems through prayer, forgiveness and faith. Consequently, his advice may be more pessimistic than the circumstances really warrant. On the other hand, there are many Christians including, I regret to say, pastors and other people involved in leadership who cause untold grief by asserting that, if you would only believe, God will transform your partner whether he wants to be transformed or not. It is not always easy to steer a balanced path between the kind of professional pessimism which denies God any role in the matter and the kind of presumptuous optimism which ignores our God-given free will and our commonsense.

If you are determined to straighten out your own attitudes and covenant to pray in faith that God will help you do so then he will. It may be a struggle but there is no doubt that he will hear your prayer and respond to it. Even the really knotty problems such as alcoholism or drug addiction can be overcome provided there is an attitude of what we Christians call repentance. However, repentance is not a mere matter of remorse. Many alcoholics are maudlin drunks who spend hours crying over what they have done and the effect it has had on their family. It might evoke sympathy but remorse of that kind, even accompanied by a good intention, is not what is required to provide any hope of rehabilitation. The repentance that is required is a wholehearted determination to change.

Perhaps the biggest single frustration experienced by people who work with alcoholics and those who are drug dependent is that so much of their time is wasted by trying to help people who have not really reached that point. Some have been referred by courts and, for them, it is a choice of a rehabilitation program or prison. Some may be concerned that their habit is getting out of hand and want to whittle it back to more manageable proportions. Others may genuinely wish to overcome their dependence but their resolve falls short of that kind of teeth-gritted determination which seems to be required. Once that point is reached a lot can be done to help the person concerned. Until then it is so much wasted effort.

I remember being deeply moved some years ago by an incident that occurred at King Cross in Sydney. I was chatting to our church social worker, a great woman of prayer who had spent some years working among drug dependent persons, particularly heroin addicts, both in Australia and overseas. We were suddenly interrupted by someone who introduced to us a young girl whom I'll call Monique—though that was not her name. Monique was slender almost to the point of emaciation and had a marked tremor which was evident not only in her hands but in the quaver in her voice. At the ripe old age of seventeen, Monique had just been discharged from hospital where she had been treated for serious complications as a result of her heroin addiction. She had been told that if she couldn't get off it then she had only months to live. Like most people who had had to find the hundreds or even thousands of dollars a week necessary to support a sizeable drug habit Monique had tried everything. At the time we spoke she was singing in a strip club for a man who paid most of her wages in heroin and she was living in a lesbian relationship with another heroin user. She was an attractive girl with elfin features and big, doe-like eyes. The pallor and thinness added a waif-like quality to her appearance and everyone's heart went out to her.

When the problem had been explained my social worker friend looked directly into her eyes and said to her, "Look I know you feel that there is no hope, but there is. I have seen girls like you in this kind of situation before. If you don't believe me I can introduce you to some of them. If you really want to overcome the problem I'll take you home with me. I'll stay with you twenty-four hours a day while you complete the withdrawal process then I'll arrange to get you into a flat with some Christian girls who will support you emotionally as you get back on your feet. One or two of them have overcome a similar addiction so they'll know exactly what you are going through and we won't let up on you until you have completely overcome it". Then as the first glimmerings of hope began to appear in those troubled eyes she added, "But it will cost you. If you want to do that you will have to turn your back on drugs and decide that you'll never go back to them. No fall-back position. You know as well as I do that if you say, 'I'll never take drugs again unless...' you'll go back to them the first time things get tough. You'll also have to give away your job and terminate your relationship with the girl you live with. You'll have to cut off all contact with any of your friends who are on drugs and form a whole new set of supportive relationships". The girl's face fell, her eyes darted desperately from face to face seeking some compromise. Then she dropped her gaze, shook her head sadly and in the tiniest and most forlorn voice I think I have ever heard simply said, "I can't".

She stayed with our group most of the evening and sang some hymns she had obviously learnt as a little girl in a fine and surprisingly strong voice. Later in the evening my social worker friend approached her again, gave her a card and told her that the offer would remain open and that she should ring her if she changed her mind. Monique thanked her and then left.

When she had gone I took the social worker aside and remonstrated with her about allowing the girl to leave. Surely, I thought, the important thing was to overcome the drug addiction. At least that way her life might be saved. Couldn't the other things be dealt with later? She wasn't angry at my presumptuousness but with deep sorrow explained, "Look, I know how you feel. I've known so many Moniques. Everytime I nurse a girl through withdrawal I wonder how many I've turned away to die but it just doesn't work unless there's the determination to cut off everything that is likely to pull them back into the old life and to start afresh. I know. I've tried it again and again. All that happens is that you give them false hope then when it fails, they think that they've tried everything and even God couldn't save them. There's just no hope left after that!''

So far as your own problems are concerned, it's up to you whether you make the decision to approach your problems with that kind of repentance. That is the part that God expects of you. I can remember another Christian counsellor saying to a close friend of mine who was an alcoholic, "If you do what's possible you can trust God to do what you find impossible. If you won't do what's possible, you're just wasting your time".

I have dealt with this at some length because it is imperative that you have a proper understanding of what you can expect God to do in your marriage and what he will not do. If you are determined to change your own attitudes and conduct you may depend upon God to help you and, in time, you will find that the transformation of your life has exceeded your expectations.

When it comes to praying for your husband or wife, however, you must recognise that only he can make the decision to repent in the sense of a determined effort to change. You may and should pray for him. Pray earnestly and with great faith that God will bring conviction of his need to change. Pray that he will be encouraged and strengthened. Pray that any hurts caused by previous misunderstandings will be healed, that all subterfuge will be stripped away and that he will be confronted by the truth with stark clarity. That can achieve wonderful results. The Bible abounds with examples of people like Saul on the road to Damascus whose lives were changed by a confrontation with God. Few of us are blinded or hear voices from heaven but most of us can recall times when we were challenged by God in one way or another. If we are concerned for someone else then we may pray that God will challenge him in the same manner. Yet, ultimately, the decision remains his. God has entrusted each of us with the gift of free will, so precious as to be almost incomprehensible. Many people assume that if God were real he would have ended all wars. The concept of God trusting men with free will knowing that many will choose evil is a proposition so startling that it never enters their heads. Yet that is what God has done and, having given that gift he will not withdraw it. Even Jesus would not overrule the free will of the rich young ruler when he turned away.

Among many Christians this concept seems to be overlooked. There is a recognition that God will not simply reprogram people into becoming Christians against their will but there is a feeling that God will reprogram people to make them return to a marital relationship which they have forsaken or to make them into better husbands or wives. This is simply untrue. Of course, few would assert the proposition in such bald terms. It is usually implicit in some absolutely spiritual statement about God's attitude to marriage. Marriage is spoken about not as a relationship between two people but as something with a tangible existence of its own. Thus conceptualised we speak of marriages as being "sick" and pray for their "healing", sidestepping any knotty problems about free will. Yet when you speak about a marriage being sick all that you can mean is that one or both the people involved are failing to honour their vows. Consequently any healing of the marriage is dependent upon a change in the attitudes and behaviour of that person or persons. At any given time there are thousands of Christians living on false hopes engendered by simplistic statements such as, "If you only believe, God will heal your marriage". Such a statement may be paraphrased as, "If you only believe, brother, God will take hold of your wife, amputate her free will and reprogram her as a fully compliant little robot who will be a wonderful wife from now on". One hardly needs to add that God will do no such thing.

For these reasons, the prospects of a lasting reconciliation are dependent largely upon decisions that are not yours
to make. It is that factor of unpredictability which may
leave you uncertain as to whether it will be possible to
maintain any real marital relationship in the future.

In many cases a sober evaluation will be sufficient to
resolve that question. You may decide that the problem,
whilst distressing, is one which can be overcome because
it consists of a single incident, or series of incidents, and
is not symptomatic of any deeper or more lasting condition.
Alternatively, you may realise that there is a serious underlying problem but, now you can see what it is, you may
be confident that the two of you can overcome it together.
There may be evidence that your spouse has a strong desire
to overcome the difficulty between you and you may be
able to agree upon a plan of action. At the other extreme
there will be cases where one party has persevered and
forgiven the other, prayed, sought advice, tried to persuade
the other party to attend marriage counselling and done
his best to remove the beam from his own eye. Yet despite all
those efforts, the other party remains totally unmoved. He
has made it abundantly clear that he has no interest in
changing and no interest in retrieving the marriage.
Between these relatively clear-cut extremes will lie a whole
range of cases in which the decision will be more
complicated.

It would be difficult if not impossible for anybody who
is not intimately acquainted with both you and your partner
to offer any real advice as to whether or not the marriage
can be retrieved but the following pointers may be of some
assistance:

(a) If you are the predominantly innocent party your duty
    is to forgive the guilty and try to save the marriage.
        If you are the guilty party your duty is to forgive
    yourself and try to save the marriage. No matter what
    the circumstances might be your first priority should
    be to seek to retrieve the marital relationship.

(b) Consequently any reasonable prospects of reconciliation should be thoroughly explored.

You are not concerned with a court case to be decided on the balance of probabilities. If there is even a ten per cent chance of retrieving a viable marital relationship, then take that chance.

(c) Do not give up on that first priority until all reasonable hope of achieving a reconciliation has failed.

(d) If you feel that you may be approaching that point but are not sure then set yourself a particular period of time and pray persistently that God will show you what to do within that time.

Whilst you may not notice anything dramatic, you should find that there is at least some significant change of heart in that period or, alternatively, a growing awareness in you that the marriage is over.

(e) Beware of rosy prophecies especially from people you don't know.

Our churches contain a smattering of good-hearted people who seem pathologically incapable of distinguishing their own desires from God's will. If one of them forms the view that you're a nice young man and your wife should come back to you, you're likely to hear the immortal words, "Thus saith the Lord", followed by an indication that precisely that is about to occur. Many seem able to shrug off any responsibility for such prophecies when they are not fulfilled. They have a seemingly infinite capacity for persuading themselves that what they would like to happen will happen and are heedless of the disappointment caused by the false expectations they arouse.

(f) If your husband is repeatedly violent then leave.

It will rarely be the right thing to expose yourself to the risk of serious harm and it will never be the right thing to expose your children to such a risk. You may not feel it right to close the door on the relationship but you should, at the very least, make it plain that you will not return to him until he has sought help for his problem.

(g) Once you have come to the conclusion that the marriage has broken down irretrievably, then leave.

Many people remain under the same roof with a former spouse for months or years after it has become apparent to them that their marriages have ceased to exist in any real sense. People may fall into this error through a misunderstanding of the biblical position, through unresolved guilt, through a misunderstanding of the implications of forgiveness or simply through insecurity. If the relationship has actually been terminated then continuing to live together under the one roof is likely to produce nothing but bitterness and, perhaps, more serious problems.

A friend of mine had that last point demonstrated rather vividly. He was a quiet and sensitive man with seemingly inexhaustible patience and I had never seen him display any sign of annoyance let alone serious anger. His wife had been involved in a series of adulterous relationships over a period of several years. He had constantly forgiven her and sought to rekindle their relationship, but she had made it plain that she had no intention of remaining faithful to him. As time went on things continued to deteriorate and ultimately reached the point where men were coming round to the house while he was at home. While it had long been evident to him that the marriage was effectively over he continued to live with her for the sake of the two small children. She resented him being there and taunted him about her relationships with other men. Yet he felt that, in the interests of the children, he should keep his temper and make no response. Consequently, although I didn't know it at the time, he was bottling up an enormous accumulation of pent-up emotions.

One night he had a particularly offensive telephone call

from one of his wife's lovers and, as he told me later, something "suddenly snapped". He scooped up a kitchen knife and ran out of his house to attack the man who had rung. Fortunately, he came to his senses after running the first two or three hundred metres. When he came to see me he was absolutely aghast at what he had done. I sought to console him by pointing out that he had, after all, come to his senses before any harm was done. He replied in a shaken voice, "Yes, but what if I'd met him coming up my driveway?" I pointed out to him that he was living in an intolerable situation which was generating pressures of a kind that he simply could not handle.

Your particular situation may not produce reactions as drastic as that, but if you have come to the conclusion that you and your partner no longer have a viable marriage then there is no point in living together. If you have tried everything else and nothing has produced any change of heart then there is one remaining possibility. The shock of actual separation may jolt him into reconsidering his position and discussing the situation with you in a more serious fashion. It seems to work in a surprising number of cases. There are many marriages where the parties separate but are reconciled after a comparatively short period. In any event the relationship reaches a point where you simply have nothing to lose by bringing the situation to a head. The separation will either precipitate some breakthrough in the other party's attitude or his failure to make any significant response will confirm that the marriage is, indeed, at an end.

(h) In the period immediately following separation I believe there should be a willingness to consider a reconciliation if there are any sort of overtures from the other party.

It seems to me that it was this period immediately following the separation that St Paul had in mind in 1 Corinthians 7:11 when he spoke of, a wife remaining single or being reconciled to her husband. As I

mentioned earlier, this principle could not apply to
women who had been divorced if only because Paul
could not have considered them wives, but he did seem
to feel that there should be a period of time after
separation in which the separating party should regard
herself as still married and remain willing to be
reconciled to her husband, should the opportunity
present itself. Obviously that does not involve a lifelong
commitment. I don't believe that there can be any
hard-and-fast rule about the length of time involved.
There will be some cases where a reconciliation is
simply out of the question. There may be, for example,
a situation where the husband has just been sentenced
to life imprisonment for murder or where the wife has
moved in with another man and has already become
pregnant to him. Even in cases where the circumstances
are not so extreme one would expect to see some
indication of a desire for reconciliation within a
relatively short period after the separation if it is to
occur at all.

(i) While it grieves me to have to say it, if you are in doubt
about your position don't seek advice from your
minister or other Christian friends unless you are sure
that they do not espouse some rigid dogma which will
prevent them from offering any constructive assistance
or guidance.

Often people are merely "pelted with texts". Your
denomination will probably have a marriage guidance
organisation which will be better equipped to advise
you.

If you are really troubled about what you should do then
wait some further period and continue to pray. It is better
to move with confidence a month later than to rush out
the door and spend the next few years contending with
niggling doubts about whether you should have stayed.
However you need to remember that God expects you to

use your commonsense and to face the facts. You also need to ask yourself whether your qualms really reflect uncertainty about whether or not the marriage can be retrieved or simply doubt and confusion associated with the emotional climate in which you are living. If despite some further period you still feel uncertain then the only suggestion I can make is that you fix a date for departure some weeks ahead and ask God to give you some clear indication prior to that date if he wants you to stay. If you are honestly willing to be corrected then God will not let you wander off the track. If at the end of that time there is no indication that you should stay and the other party shows no sign of a change of attitude or wanting to re-establish the marriage, then you should feel free to leave.

PART FOUR

THE AFTERMATH

CHAPTER FIFTEEN

Is There Life After Separation?

People arrive at the point of separation in so many different ways. Few follow the steps which I suggested in Part III. Some simply wake up one morning and find that they are alone. A curt note on the dressing-table tells them that it is all over. Others flounce out at the climax of a spectacular argument leaving only the slam of the door as the exclamation mark at the end of their marital sentence. Some leave almost by tacit agreement, whilst a few leave sadly, having tried their best only to conclude that the marriage could not be saved.

The emotions experienced immediately following separation will depend very much upon the nature of the marital relationship and the circumstances in which it broke up. Perhaps the most devastated are those who loved and trusted their partners and were completely surprised by the separation. Such hapless people can be left in a state of shock, unable to credit that it has really happened and sadly bewildered as to the reason.

At the other extreme are people who have spent years trying to salvage their marriages and in the process endured all kinds of violence and depravity. Such people may find that although the separation brings some tinges of regret they are overshadowed by the relief that a particularly trying chapter in their lives has come to an end. Between those extremes lies an enormous range of human experiences.

161

If the other party has taken the children and disappeared there may be a reaction of near panic at the thought of never seeing them again. In other cases there may be outrage at the discovery that the departing spouse has cleaned out the joint account and taken everything not nailed down. Yet, despite the diversity, the emotional reactions experienced after separation are characterised by a number of common features.

There will be some initial confusion. No matter how intolerable the marital relationship may have been there will have been at least some degree of predictability about it, settled patterns of familiarity and security. There will have been a familiar place to live, a predictable income and, to some degree, an established routine. Life is steeped in a myriad of habit forming activities essential to a person's lifestyle. You may think that the only thing you have come to expect is the unexpected but there will be routine things like the provision of meals, the running of a household and a dozen other things that you do every day which form an unobtrusive but important background and continuity. Upon separation all of that is instantly stripped away. You have to start again. Furthermore, that sudden change of lifestyle occurs at a time when most people are distraught and preoccupied with the severance of the relationship. Few will have made any concrete plans for coping with the practical details of a new life. Consequently there may be a pervading sense of insecurity punctuated by confusion about particular needs.

The confusion is invariably accompanied by anxiety. The uncertainty itself generates anxiety. The situation before separation may have been intolerable but at least it was familiar. Now there is the feeling of being launched into the unknown. Where will I live? How will I cope financially? Will I cope with the children by myself? How will the children react to a broken home? Can I really cope with living alone? What will my parents think? What will my friends say? A constant barrage of questions to which there is no ready answer. Beyond those specific questions is a more generalised anxiety about facing the future alone. Perhaps the most intimidating question is simply, "What will become of me?"

As time goes by and one begins to establish a more settled lifestyle, some of these worries abate. Yet the passage of time may bring new anxieties to replace them. One may look to friends for encouragement and support only to find many of them don't want to become involved. Many couples may feel a conflict of loyalty between their affection for you and their affection for your former spouse. They may try to resolve that by simply drawing back and refusing to take sides. That is, of course, a perfectly natural reaction but a sensitive person seeking comfort can easily perceive it as a callous rejection. Invitations to friends' homes may dwindle. Evenings shared by two married couples can be a lot of fun but when one couple splits up it can be very difficult for the remaining couple to carry on concurrent friendships with both the estranged husband and wife. Even if they try, every dinner party for three is likely to provoke inescapable memories of happier times. This can prove distressing for your hosts as well as for you. Parties are easier but even then your hosts may rack their brains to find someone with whom they can pair you off. If it seems impolite to invite both you and your former spouse, they may agonise about whether to invite one in preference to the other or duck the issue by simply failing to mention the party at all.

Further complications may occur because of your new-found availability. Newly separated women are frequently appalled at the manner in which male friends and acquaintances treat news of the separation as an announcement that they are now available for amorous adventures. Some are equally appalled when their female friends suddenly become very possessive of their husbands and seem to fear exposing them to a predatory female. The resultant social deprivation coming, as it does, at a time when a person feels the greatest need for support can strengthen feelings of isolation and vulnerability.

The anxieties generated by the reaction of old friends may be accompanied by anxieties about meeting new people.

A new place of residence will involve meeting new neighbours. It may also involve new schools, new shops, a new doctor and a whole host of other people with whom one will have to establish some kind of acquaintanceship. The attitudes of old friends and inhibitions about being the only single person in your old group may impel you to try to establish friendships with other people in similar circumstances. This may be done on an individual basis or it may involve joining organisations such as Parents Without Partners but no matter what course is pursued it will involve new people and new situations.

There may be particular anxieties about contacts with the opposite sex. Will they still find you attractive? Will you be able to relate to them naturally after years of marriage? Will you ever be able to establish a lasting relationship again? Could you trust anybody again? How would the children react to a new romance?

Separation also brings with it an uncertainty generated by the abandonment of long-term goals. In most marriages people look forward to annual holidays, home renovation, replacing the family car and a whole host of other things which may not be very important in themselves but which subtly colour the future with pleasant anticipation. Those goals are suddenly replaced by a new and unsettled existence which has so many immediate problems that long-term goals cannot be even considered let alone established. Life may suddenly become a question of survival: a matter of solving the present problems and getting through the day. Any thoughts of the future are likely to be vague and uncertain and the clamour of competing demands will probably ensure that they are at least temporarily consigned to the too-hard basket.

A further problem is loneliness. Marriage usually provides some sort of companionship. Even if there are constant fights there is still another person living in the same house and the fights themselves may be a sufficient distraction from boredom and loneliness. When one has to live alone for the first time in many years an empty house can seem like a hollow aching void. You may find yourself fabricating excuses to ring people or running down to the shop at the slightest pretext. This kind of problem is aggravated by the kind of lifestyle to which those of us who live in western cities have become accustomed. Self-esteem is frequently dependent upon fulfilling the expectations of others and earning their approval and acceptance.

Most people can't bear to be alone with themselves. If you doubt that, go to some place where people are frequently kept waiting. It may be a railway station or a doctor's surgery. A barrister's waiting room would probably be ideal. You will see that most people display a strange need for newspapers, magazines or small talk, anything to deliver them from the plight of being alone with their thoughts.

With the ache of loneliness comes a renewal of anxiety. "Is it always going to be like this?" "Am I going to be a lonely old man?" "How am I going to cope with this?" "How can I bear to face my mother?" "What will I do about...?"

Another major problem is guilt. Even a person who has spent years trying to salvage a hopeless marriage and long regarded separation as inevitable may find himself besieged by doubts and recriminations when he has taken the step of actually leaving. Human nature is a funny thing. People who have endured an intolerable situation for years may suddenly find themselves recalling the good times before things began to deteriorate. Memory after memory may come back touching every raw sensitive nerve and bringing regret and doubt. "Did I really do the right thing?" "Would things have come good if I'd only persevered?" "It wasn't all bad; he used to be so kind!" "If only I'd stood by her a bit longer".

It is perfectly natural that these thoughts should come but you must be very careful about giving them too much

credence. It is not uncommon for people to go through a
phase where they adopt an unrealistically charitable attitude
towards their former spouse and take all of the blame for
the separation upon their own shoulders. This tendency
is frequently reinforced by vague feelings that a Christian
should always be able to make a success of his marriage.
If he hasn't then it must be due to some kind of sin or
failing. This guilt may tempt him to place punitive
connotations on various difficulties, which in reality, are
simply an inevitable consequence of the need to start again
in a single lifestyle. When things go wrong he may find
himself asking himself, ''Did God let that happen to show
me how wrong I've been? Is God trying to punish me?
Am I no longer under God's protection?''

Thoughts about the future invariably raise new spectres
of guilt. One has to confront questions about divorce and,
probably, remarriage. Those questions, in turn, send one
crashing headlong into the theological pitfalls I have already
described. You may feel that it is all so unfair. You may
even smell a rat. ''Is God really so harsh as to require me
to remain single for the rest of my life or return to that
drunken thug who made my life a misery for so long?''
Yet there will always be a well-meaning minister or
Christian friend to thrust a text under your nose, and say,
with a sad shake of the head, ''Well there you are!''

At church the sermons will suddenly seem to be alive
with the evils of divorce and the guilt which people rightly
bear for breaking up families. Christian friends may also
offer all kinds of ''helpful'' advice about the need for
forgiveness and reconciliation with your former spouse.
They may do so in a compassionate and courteous manner
but if you are sensitive, you will probably discern an underlying desire to save you from the consequences of your sinful
conduct.

Ultimately, you may find yourself feeling more and more
estranged from God. In a very real sense you just can't
bear the thought of facing him.

You have turned to members of the church for understanding and support in a time of great distress but have found that the dominant attitude is one of reproach. They sympathise with you but feel unable to become involved in binding up your wounds because of the theological problems involved. They had hoped to be able to squeeze you into a comfortable pigeonhole, one that would have enabled you to feel forgiven and free to start a new life, secure in the knowledge of God's love for you. Unhappily, you just did not fit. It was all really regrettable but, in the end result, the only thing which could be done was to point out to you the error of your ways and the hopelessness of your position.

If this has happened to you, you can console yourself with the fact that at least you are not the first. Many people have thought that they have been cut off from God by an enormous chasm which could never be bridged, except by returning to the completely intolerable situation from which they have fled.

This can be a heartbreaking period. It can feel as though one is caught in a vortex of destructive emotions. Confusion leads to anxiety which leads to anger and then to guilt, loneliness, despair and more confusion, more anxiety and so the vicious cycle continues. You ask God to restore your marriage, to make your wife behave more reasonably, to give you custody of your children or a hundred and one other things that seem absolutely imperative, but those things don't happen. You get angry with God and wind up screaming at him, "Don't you care that I hurt? Don't you care about my kids? How can you say you love me and leave me in this mess?" Then when you cool off, there is more guilt. Not only do you have a broken marriage to feel guilty about but you have presumed to get angry with God himself. You have even shouted at him! Do you expect him to forgive you now? Do you expect him to answer your prayers now? Maybe he will just give up on you and leave you to your own devices. Maybe he already has. Lurking beneath the surface may be a question too frightening to articulate, "Have you divorced me too, God?"

The reality of the pain cannot be denied. No matter how strong a Christian you may be, no matter how correct your attitudes may be, it still hurts. Most Christian teaching these days seems to emphasise the victory of Jesus in such a manner that the agony of the battle is overlooked entirely. Christians glibly promise that if you have faith you will know the peace of the Lord and you won't even have to strive or struggle to attain the right result.

Those assertions can convey a very real truth if they are understood in the context of the overall biblical picture of the struggle between good and evil. If they are understood to mean that God promises Christians a panacea which instantly kills the pain and provides an idyllic solution to every problem, then they are dangerously misleading. Any parents who have lost a child can tell you that, although they have no doubt of the truth of God's promise of eternal life, rejoice in his victory over death and look forward to that great day when they will be reunited with her, they are left with an ache like a knife through the chest. They loved their child and she has been torn away from them. For the rest of their lives they will be without her.

When there is a divorce it is just as important to re-establish a proper relationship with God as it is when there is a bereavement. Yet, again, no matter how strong the commitment and how full of faith the Christian there will still be considerable distress which will not be swept aside instantly but which will have to be worked through over a period of time.

CHAPTER SIXTEEN

The Way Out

The first thing to deal with is guilt. Few people ever come to terms with it as quickly as they should. Even when they do, it immediately springs up again like a weed that has been snipped off at the surface.

There is no need to carry a great burden of guilt. In fact, you have no right to carry it! If you are a Christian then there is one precept that is at the very heart of your faith and that is that Christ died so that you might be forgiven. You either believe that or you don't. If you don't believe that, then why do you call yourself a Christian? If you do believe that, then how can you permit guilt to maintain its hold on you? To do so is to negate the meaning of Christ's death.

Many people need to be confronted with the fact that preoccupation with guilt is a denial of their faith. When that happens, some adopt a pained look, shake their heads sadly and complain that you just don't understand. They don't usually say it explicitly but there is an implicit suggestion that their sins are in some unstated way so grave as to be beyond even the grace of God. That is preposterous nonsense! Jesus forgave the men who were nailing his hands to the cross. Have you done anything more serious than to murder the Son of God? God says, so simply, that if we confess our sins he ''is faithful and just to forgive us our sins and to cleanse us from all unrighteousness''.[25] There is no conceivable basis for any suggestion that this principle does not apply to sins committed within marriage or related to a separation and divorce.

The way to cope with guilt is to simply take God's word literally. Confess your sin, ask for God's forgiveness and you will have it. That is what God has promised. Isn't he trustworthy? Then thank God that he has forgiven you and that you don't need to feel guilty any more. There may not be any immediate feeling of relief but you will have been forgiven.

Feelings of guilt may still come and you will be tempted to wallow in such thoughts as: ''If only I hadn't . . .'' You can confront those negative feelings with an affirmation of the truth. You may need to develop a conditioned reflex by constantly responding to such thoughts with a simple prayer such as, ''Well, thank God I'm forgiven and I don't have to feel guilty any more!''

The second thing to face is grief. You may have been confident of your marriage, and convinced that you and your spouse would face life together no matter what happened. You may have committed the marriage to God and prayed frequently that God would bless your union. You may have looked forward to growing old together. Now all of those dreams are in tatters: the marriage has been torn apart leaving you feeling as though you have a gaping wound in your chest. You may feel that everything worth living for has been destroyed. Yet the end of one chapter of your life will give way to the beginning of another.

Psalm 30 says that weeping may endure for a night but joy comes in the morning. For some people the night passes quickly whilst for others it seems to drag on almost interminably. For some the darkness will be relieved by early settlement of disputes, a reasonable approach by the spouse, understanding friends and other forms of comfort and support. For others there will be a nightmare of tortured emotions and a future full of hopelessness and despair. There may not be even the faintest glimmer of light to offer any hope of the morning. Yet though some nights may be longer or darker than others, all give way to the light of the morning.

You must look forward to the morning and refuse to give way to despair. Even if you are still at the stage where you can see nothing but unresolved questions you can take heart because there will come a time when you have sorted out the problems, put the whole situation behind you and made a fresh start. To weather the storm of these devastating emotions can be quite an ordeal. Yet you will come through it. Thousands of people experience that kind of ordeal each year. They not only survive but come out of it with greater strength and maturity.

You may feel absolutely shattered. No matter how bad the relationship became your marriage will have been, at one stage, a very precious thing. The destruction of that relationship will inevitably carry with it the kind of grief experienced when a spouse dies. The similarity may not be immediately obvious. When someone dies there is usually a sense of shock coupled with some denial, a feeling that it has not happened. That reaction quickly gives way to profound feelings of grief. On the other hand, when a marriage breaks up the grief reaction is far less straightforward and far less predictable.

That is partly because there is no precise point at which a relationship can be said to have died. Even when a person has been terminally ill for a long time death still comes as a definite and final event. The destruction of a marital relationship, however, is a process that drags on over months or years. Even when separation has occurred and there is no apparent sign of life in the relationship, the parties will still find themselves plagued by odd doubts. "Is it really over?" "What would I do if he suggested a reconciliaton?"

However there will have been milestones marking stages of deterioration and indicating increasing degrees of probability that the marriage has died. There will frequently have been a "final" act of separation, sometimes in dramatic circumstances. Yet many people still harbour some hopes of a reconciliation even after the marriage has been formally dissolved by a court. One occasionally meets people who nurture hopes of a reconciliation for the rest of their lives. The other party may have divorced them, remarried and even had children from a subsequent marriage yet, despite all, hope lingers on.

In these circumstances the grief reaction which one would normally expect is inhibited. To some extent hope and grief are mutually exclusive emotions. How can you grieve for the passing of a friend when you hope that he will recover? At least at a subliminal level, grief and hope may fight a running battle with each other.

Another factor which complicates the grief reaction experienced following a marital breakdown is the clamour of other strong emotions and competing demands. At the very time when one would normally expect to begin working through grief one may find oneself thrust into new and frightening situations. There may be a bitter fight over custody of the children. There may be constant recriminations about the past punctuated by angry scenes. There may be the feeling that one has been thrust out of a warm nest into a cold and hostile environment and left to fend for oneself. There may be great anxiety about financial issues and about facing the future alone. There may simply be the feeling that it has all proved to be too much and that if one does not exert iron self-control one is likely to come apart at the seams. All of these things tend to crowd out grief or, at least, greatly inhibit it at the conscious level. Unhappily that does not mean that it has been resolved. All that has happened is that it has been repressed. It may then simmer away under the surface and boil over at some unexpected stage in the future.

As in the case of a bereavement, one deals with grief for a marriage by a period of mourning. Mourning involves an acknowledgement of the loss which one has sustained. It involves facing the fact that even if one cherishes some hope of a reconciliation, the reality of the situation is that the marriage is over. There is a sense of relinquishment of the struggle to hold the marriage together or to rekindle it.

This is a crucial period, and unfortunately Christians, in particular, tend to handle it very badly. Even the normal grief which follows the death of a husband or wife is frequently handled badly by Christians. Since "death is swallowed up in victory" it is seen as a denial of faith to give in to grief. With marital breakdown the situation is worse. Christians who believe in life after death do not necessarily believe in life after divorce. Yet, ultimately, a similar problem emerges. What Christians tend to do in this situation is to look at the breakdown in their marriage as being so completely against God's will that it cannot be accepted as final. Grief is accordingly repressed by a subconscious pretence that the marriage is still alive.

This is unfortunate because the mourning process is very important. It involves permitting oneself to experience and work through the emotional loss. The emotion most commonly associated with grief is sadness. But whilst one may experience quite profound sorrow it will be accompanied by other such strong emotions as anger, resentment, a feeling of having been hurt, a feeling of helplessness and perhaps the odd tinge of relief. It is not pleasant to have to face these emotions and the time of mourning will certainly be part of your night of weeping.

These things will not vanish spontaneously. If they are not worked through they will inevitably re-emerge at some later stage, usually when least expected. When they do, if they are not recognised for what they are, they may be confused with other kinds of feelings attributed to other problems. For example, a person may have remarried and be in that somewhat difficult stage of working through the stage of disillusionment into a more mature relationship when strong feelings of depression and other negative emotions begin to break through. The person concerned may easily assume that this is an emotional reaction to the state of the second marriage. It may give rise to serious doubts about his feelings for his new spouse. Consequently it may begin to undermine the second marriage and, in turn, precipitate a whole series of emotional reactions which genuinely do relate to that second marital relationship. Yet in reality what has surfaced is unresolved grief. If one is to lay a solid foundation for the future one must first put to rest the ghosts of the past.

While marital breakdown is, of course, a process rather than a instantaneous event there will frequently be one decisive moment when a person acknowledges that the marriage really is at an end and by that acknowledgement becomes free to commence the mourning process. This moment may be reached as a result of some cathartic experience, as a result of a long hard talk with a counsellor or trusted friend or simply by sober reflection. However, when that acknowledgement is made it will frequently involve more than a mere relinquishment of the struggle to retrieve the marriage. There will usually be a very definite decision to knit together the tattered threads of life and start afresh. There is frequently an instinctive feeling that this kind of decision constitutes a significant landmark. The decision may be confirmed by some act which may seem insignificant to an onlooker but which really constitutes a declaration of independence from the former spouse. The wedding ring may be removed. A person may suddenly abandon his previous determination to hang on to the former home. He may take a long-term lease to a flat, move away to another city or simply instruct his solicitors to apply formally for a dissolution of the marriage. What is important is not the manner in which the decision is made or even the manner in which it is implemented. The really important thing is that it marks a change of attitude from one of constantly trying to retrieve that which is past to one of confronting the future albeit with appre-hension and uncertainty.

Ironically enough that positive step frequently has the effect of unleashing strong negative emotions. One of the most common is anger. This is only to be expected. Anger is a normal part of the mourning process whether that process relates to a death or to the breakdown of a marriage and the consequent destruction of a familiar lifestyle. In the former situation the anger may be directed at anyone who could conceivably be blamed for the death. It may be directed at the survivors or at the doctors and nurses who should have done more. It may be directed at the deceased himself or even turned inward at the person mourning. If all else fails it will frequently be directed at God for "taking him" or "permitting it to happen". In the latter situation there may be a similar process of casting around for someone to blame. There may be the other woman, the interfering mother-in-law, the courts, or the whole rotten system. More frequently, however, it will be directed at the spouse.

Furthermore, to some extent at least, it will be a justified anger because there will always be some genuine grievances against the conduct of a spouse. These grievances may be brooded over and, perhaps, in time subconsciously embellished. The anger will also colour expectations for the future. Sometimes a cynicism develops, a willingness to find fault. Phrases such as "it's just what I expected him to do" may spring readily to mind. Future conduct is judged harshly with any ambiguity resolved against the spouse. A siege mentality may develop, a feeling of being constantly ripped off. This, in turn, may lead to an increasingly rigid approach, a stubborn refusal to give an inch. It may also lead to increased demands. Violent outbursts and bitter accusations may be directed at the spouse.

The anger may also creep into conversation with friends and relatives who may be swayed by this litany of denunciations and rally to your support. In doing so, they may become, to some degree, infected by your anger towards your spouse. This may, in turn, produce a cross-fertilisation of anger. Expressions of sympathy may fuel your anger by vindicating the burning sense of injustice that you feel at the manner in which you have been treated.

Sometimes the anger may be directed not at your spouse

but inwards. You may blame yourself for the marital breakdown and each new incident may add to your self-anger. This may produce or contribute to a profound feeling of depression. Depression may, of course, be a reaction to the collapse of your lifestyle and of your hopes and dreams for the future.

Anger tends to be very selfcentred or at least centred upon the person who has suffered the injustice. To be able to experience the injustice but endeavour to put yourself in the shoes of the perpetrator requires considerable maturity. The other party may well be going through a similar stage of mourning and be contending with a similar outburst of anger. This can lead to a vicious circle in which there is an over-reaction to an initially minor provocation followed by a succession of actions and reactions—each more serious than the last—until the situation has escalated to a near feud. This can create a climate of bitterness which may endure for many years. It may also create an attitude toward the other party which is subtly conveyed to the children.

Ironically, although the anger may, in a sense, be justified the person who has behaved in a provocative manner may not be revealing his true colours as you might think but simply the depths of his inner turmoil at the breakdown of his marriage. People frequently react to this kind of stress by behaving in a manner which is completely out of character.

A fellow lawyer who had extensive experience with divorced clients once told me he had always found it incomprehensible that apparently normal and decent people could behave like lunatics when their marriages terminated. Then his own marriage broke up and he found to his horror that he was behaving in a similar fashion. I can still remember him saying, "If you had told me in advance how I would behave I would never have believed you! Even now when I look back I can scarcely believe that I could have done some of the things that I did. I can actually remember crawling through a hedge at three o'clock in the

morning with a pair of field glasses to spy on her. Can you
imagine it! Forty years old, a degree in law, years of
experience with people going through similar experiences
and I find myself acting like a lunatic!''

Don't be too hard on yourself. You will be angry. It
is a normal reaction to the other even more negative
emotions such as confusion, reaction, guilt and anxiety.
Anger seems to somehow draw emotional energy away from
these things and lessen their effect. It seems to be a kind
of defence mechanism, a kind of shield against being
completely alone. It also makes it easier to accept the
termination of the relationship. There is no need to feel
guilty about the fact that you experience anger. This is a
common misconception among Christians. The moral
question involved is not whether or not one should
experience anger but how one should deal with it. It is no
more sinful to experience anger than it is to experience
temptation. Unless you choose to feed it, you need not fear
that you have been forever cast in the role of an angry
person. It is a stage which will normally run its course and
in time subside.

During this angry stage you may find it very difficult
actually to feel any real forgiveness for your spouse. That
can also become a bind. God does not ask more than we
are capable of offering. What you can do at this stage is
simply tell God that you do forgive the person and ask him
to bring you to the point where that forgiveness is not
merely a question of will but is reflected in your feelings
and attitudes. If you are serious about that, you will come
in time to view your spouse with a degree of understanding
and compassion. You may come to realise that he, in
common with my lawyer friend, has acted in an outrageous
fashion, not out of any deep-seated vindictiveness, but
because of emotions which he was ill-equipped to handle.

Unhappily, there are people who feed their anger. They
brood over real or imagined wrongs reliving each detail
in their minds again and again. Their conversation is full
of derogatory remarks about the former spouse and lurid

descriptions of that spouse's misconduct. Whilst they may not actually plan revenge they harbour and even nurture constantly smouldering resentment. If this course is maintained they can reach such a degree of bitterness that it cripples their outlook on life.

The former spouse is seen not merely as having behaved unreasonably, but as all bad. Adolf Hiter may have some redeeming qualities, but not this person. This attitude is inevitably perceived by the children. In some cases their attitude to their mother or father will be poisoned by it. In others, they will simply be left distressed and confused: unable to understand why one parent reacts to any display of affection for the other as an act of betrayal. I do sympathise with people who find themselves locked into such a prison of bitterness. Some people are so badly hurt by the destruction of their marriages and by the conduct of an errant spouse that it seems impossible to react in any other way. Glib suggestions to forgive and forget merely underline how little people understand. Yet as justified as the anger may be, you must break the cycle of bitterness.

In the first place no Christian can be justified in harbouring resentment. Jesus made it very plain that if you do not forgive others then "neither will your Heavenly Father forgive you". He did not add, "unless, of course, you're justified in hating them". That may seem hard but when you become a Christian you agreed to accept Jesus' standards rather than your own.

In the second place, none of this bitterness hurts the person who is the object of your resentment. It hurts you. It eats away like a cancer, stopping your emotional development and depriving you of the opportunity to put the past behind you and make a fresh start. If also hurts any children you may have. Don't delude yourself. You can't harbour bitter resentment towards the other parent of your children without having them affected by it. Your former spouse may have done terrible things but your children are innocent victims. They are entitled to the best emotional nurture you can provide: even if it means forgiving a spouse who doesn't deserve forgiveness.

If you are on the other side of the fence, confronted by an implacably antagonistic spouse, don't panic and above all don't succumb to the temptation to respond in kind. Keep contact between you to a minimum. Remember that Rome was not built in a day. Be prepared to give a little and be patient. Finally pray for the embittered spouse and be thankful you are not locked into a similar emotional bind.

Another common element in this stage of mourning is anxiety. This can be caused in a variety of ways.

The marital breakdown may erode the image a person has of his role in life and hence of his worth. A man who has devoted himself to providing a home and security for his wife and children may have been dependant upon his success in achieving those things for his sense of purpose and for the feeling that he was a successful human being. When his marriage breaks down, his wife obtains custody of the children and the home has to be sold so that the proceeds may be divided, he may be inclined to feel that he has lost more than his relationship and his house. He may feel that, in a very real sense, he has lost a part of himself. Similarly, a woman who derives her self-esteem from her ability to run a home, care for her family and who sees herself as the force behind her successful husband may be devastated when her husband clears out taking the children with him. Christian women may be particularly vulnerable to such feelings because they have frequently been encouraged to see their primary roles as wives, mothers and homemakers and to depend for their status upon the positions their husbands have enjoyed in the community. These kinds of experiences may lead to an intense fear that there may be nothing left to live for.

A person may also become generally more fearful and anxious simply because the secure pattern of life has been shattered. People who have been recently bereaved sometimes experience this kind of anxiety. One terrible thing has happened, why not another? All kinds of irrational fears may intrude. This kind of anxiety reaction is even more prevalent after marital breakdown. It may be due, in part, to uncertainty over the division of the marital property and, perhaps, the obligation to pay maintenance. These matters frequently give rise to the spectre of continuing financial difficulties. The threat of litigation hanging over a person's head like the sword of Damocles for as long as two or three years may add to this uncertainty.

Like the rest of the community we do not always do well when it comes to dealing with fear. We feel that we are castaways on some turbulent ocean blown in one direction or another at the whim of a blind and unreasoning fate. Yet we are children of a kind and wise Father who directs our course. We may still encounter storms upon that turbulent sea but he will sustain us and see us through them. This knowledge should bring at least a measure of security.

Christians who face life-threatening operations frequently possess a degree of calmness which marks them out from other patients. Unhappily, when it comes to marital breakdown, Christians are frequently more anxious than those who do not share their faith. How can this be so?

The answer lies in our perception of divorce and in the enormous sense of guilt involved in even considering it. There is something terribly wrong when the attitude of the church subtly conveys this message. Even if your husband was a drunken thug and treated the marriage vows with contempt right from the beginning of the marriage you may feel this terrible guilt. After all doesn't Paul talk about the believing party consecrating the unbeliever?

If you'd been a better wife, if you had tried harder, if you had exercised more faith, if you hadn't provoked him, if you hadn't been guilty of a hundred other foibles of human nature, then it might all have been different. Perhaps he would have become a Christian and you could have had a rich marriage together. Perhaps his contact with you was his last hope. Perhaps he has lost the chance of salvation now and it's all your fault.

What of the marriage itself? If it is always God's will to keep marriages together as everyone keeps telling you,

why did yours come apart? Others in the church are
married to non-Christians. They have stayed together.
Where have you failed? How are you going to justify to
God what you have done. What about the way you feel
now? The church says that you can never marry again
because your first marriage still continues beyond divorce.
Can you face the thought of a celibate and lonely existence
for the next thirty or forty years? Will you sooner or later
be drawn into a temptation which you won't be able to
resist? What about all that anger and resentment that you
can't seem to suppress? How can you approach God when
you feel like that? Doesn't the Bible say that you should
leave your gift at the altar, go and make peace with your
brother and only then return and offer it to God? You can't
do that, you know you can't, you've tried. The anger and
resentment are still there like some inoperable cancer.

These doubts may be confirmed by your own part in
the marital breakdown or by an awareness of other attitudes
and longings which seem terribly wrong and sinful. You
may have been almost overpoweringly attracted to someone
else. It may never have progressed beyond your own
imaginings and desires. Yet it may have produced a great
deal of guilt, and probably, a great degree of anxiety about
the state of your relationship with God.

The situation is so filled with anxiety because lurking
deep beneath the emotional turmoil is the fear that it is
not only the relationship with your spouse that has come
to an end but your relationship with God. Sometimes this
fear may be recognised. You may say, ''I can't seem to
pray anymore, I'm afraid that God has given me away''.

The fear may be reflected either in a feverish burst of
Christian activity or in a complete withdrawal. In the latter
case the person may find that he is unable to find God and
seek to cope with the situation by withdrawing from his
normal church activities and seeking to distract himself from
his plight. In many cases the person concerned will not
really understand the underlying reason for his actions. The
fear of the destruction of his relationship with God and the

risk of losing his eternal life may lurk deep in his sub-conscious but his mind simply refuses to face such a horrifying prospect.

This particular kind of fear opens the door for other fears by undermining faith. Our faith comes from our relation-ship with God and from our confidence that he will protect and sustain us in every circumstance. When we reach a point where we feel that our guilt is so great that God will cast us adrift and leave us unprotected, it becomes very difficult to exercise any real faith. Furthermore, the prayer life through which our faith usually finds its expression will abruptly seem dry and sterile. If God has withdrawn from the relationship then what is the point in trying to pray? It's like shouting at the receding back of someone who has turned away and made it plain that he does not want to listen.

This loss of faith does not merely shunt a Christian into the same position as a non-Christian might occupy in similar circumstances but into a position infinitely more vulnerable. Everyone builds up a particular set of emotional responses to cope with the problems of life. At times of great stress or danger a non-Christian may be accustomed to relying upon many things. He may depend upon financial stability, his education, his standing in the community, the support of his family or simply upon a confidence in his own ability derived from his experience of life. It is true, of course, that many Christians also fall back upon such things but for many a firm trust in God will have been the source of their security in any crisis. Such people have frequently come to depend upon God in that manner because at some stage in their lives they have found the more common emotional props inadequate. For a Christian, in a position of extraordinary stress and anxiety as a result of the break down of marriage, to feel that God has turned his back is a frightening experience, resulting in a gnawing anxiety that, from time to time, erupts into near panic.

Because the root cause of this anxiety is really guilt, that problem must be tackled first. Guilt must be met head on in the manner previously described. Once the guilt has been dealt with and a proper relationship established with God then the anxiety may be confronted with confidence. In some cases simply accepting forgiveness may almost automatically resolve the problem of anxiety. In other cases there may be a need to claim the biblical promises of God's protection and to stand upon them each time a threatening situation arises or anxiety is experienced. Where the anxiety is really deep-seated there may be a need for specific counselling and deeper ministry.

The stage of mourning may also be characterised by depression born of self-pity. This is perfectly understandable. You have been through a heartbreaking process. You may have lost not only your spouse but your children and your dreams for the future. In these circumstances anyone might be excused for feeling sorry for himself. Yet in the long run self-pity can become crippling. It can become chronic when a person cannot bear the thought of relinquishing a relationship and continues to clutch at straws. If your whole attention is focused on the former relationship and vain hopes of a reconciliation, then self-pity is inevitable.

Relinquishment of the former relationship usually frees a person to begin thinking about the future in a more positive manner. There may still be an acute sense of loss but a start can be made on plans for a new life. Reaching this point of relinquishment can be in itself an agonising process. Feelings of regret for the termination of the relationship may virtually force you to pursue any chance of a reconciliation. At times false hopes are fostered by the other party's reluctance to hurt. In other cases there may be a feeling that the spouse does not want a divorce either, but has simply been influenced by the family.

This dilemma may sometimes be resolved by frank discussion with your minister, mutual friend or some other person who may be willing to act as an intermediary. If even that is refused then overtures of reconciliation may be conveyed by letter. If they too are ignored then your only course may be to fix a particular period in which you will pray for and be open to the prospect of a reconciliation. If nothing occurs within that period you may decide to accept that the marriage is at an end.

Certainly, to endeavour to cling to a relationship when one party is adamant that it is finished is a heartbreaking exercise in futility. Christians particularly seem to be prone to refusing to face the facts, probably because of a confused understanding of God's attitude to their situation and the resulting emotional overtones. Yet marriage is the voluntary union of two people and it subsists only as long as both seek to maintain it. When one partner resolutely abandons it, the marriage is over. It does not matter how reluctant the other may be to see it end or what views he may have about the morality of the situation, he simply does not have a choice.

Some people go to extraordinary lengths to endeavour to force the departing spouse to return. A great many custody cases are fought because one party feels that the other will return rather than live apart from the children. Some people even seem to be able to persuade themselves that it is their duty to engage in this kind of emotional blackmail; but in the long run it can only harm the children and intensify the bitterness and alienation between the parties.

If you find yourself clinging to hopes of a reconciliation with a sense of desperation even though all overtures have been spurned then you may need to take two further steps:

(a) Pray, preferably with the support of Christian friends, that God will enable you to relinquish the future to him and to trust him even if it is a future without your spouse.

(b) Consult a qualified counsellor with experience in separation counselling.

Yes, it is important to consult a counsellor. Some of them

will have seen hundreds of people experiencing the same kind of difficulty as you. They can tell you what is productive and what isn't.

Once the point of relinquishment has been reached a person may become conscious that a great struggle has been won. The tension between the realisation that the marriage is over and a steadfast refusal to face that fact may have contributed to much of the fear and anger evident during the earlier part of the separation. With acceptance of the fact that the marriage is irretrievable the struggle can give way to a more positive kind of mourning in which there is deep sorrow related to happy memories of the relationship and profound regret at its termination. It still hurts but it may fairly be regarded as a positive experience because it facilitates healing and permits a person to start afresh uninhibited by the ghost of the former spouse and their shared relationship.

Because acceptance may occur at different levels, it is common for people to feel they have reached this point and worked through the mourning process only to find that when a court formally dissolves the marriage the finality of that step triggers further periods of depression and sorrow.

CHAPTER SEVENTEEN

The 35-Year-Old Adolescent

When people say that their marriage is on the rocks, it is not difficult to grasp their meaning. When the marriage breaks down the participants will sometimes feel as though they are perched precariously on a rubber raft desperately trying to prevent it from capsizing as it sweeps inexorably downstream towards the rapids. The craft is buffeted from side to side as it picks up speed and hurtles through the spray just missing jagged rocks projecting from the spume. At last comes a time when the marital conflicts are finished, the person has accepted that his marriage has irretrievably come to an end and the emotional turmoil has begun to subside. At this point there may be a feeling of having survived the rapids and emerged, perhaps a trifle shaken and battered, into a wide and relatively tranquil pool. The prominent emotion may initially be one of relief and of "Thank God it's over!"

With this relief comes a gradual release of the emotional load. The person begins to relax, to become less uptight.

Oddly enough this feeling of relief may also evoke more feelings of guilt. There is a feeling, "I should care more". The need to feel guilty about marital breakdown has been so firmly ingrained that many Christians feel guilty about not feeling guilty. They may even wonder whether the feeling of relief may be due to their attitudes having become so profoundly sinful that their consciences have become deadened. Normally such fears are unjustified. They spring, in part, from an oversensitive conscience rather than a deadened one.

The relief is associated with a growing sense of freedom. As one emerges from the emotional turmoil and as the legal rights and obligations of the parties are untangled there is the freedom to start again, albeit with less money than the parties shared when they were still married. Perhaps most importantly there is a freedom from the feeling of "being locked in" to an intolerable situation, being bound in some indefinable way to the former spouse. At times this new-found sense of freedom can seem almost too good to be true. There may be a vague apprehension that the other spouse is likely to bring further applications to court for more money, less access or some other purpose which will embroil you in further conflict. Some years ago there was a cartoon pinned to the notice board in the legal practitioners' room at the Family Court building in Parramatta. It depicted a nervous little man peeping over the edge of his solicitor's expansive desk and enquiring in a quavering voice, "Tell me ... um ... if I get behind in my maintenance payments can she repossess me?"

With this new-found relief may come a more calm and rational approach to life. The person may find that he can be more objective with his former spouse. In retrospect, he may begin to realise that many of the hurtful things were not actuated by malice but were simply an expression of her own hurt. There may be a sense of resignation and regret tinged, perhaps, with a measure of sympathy. This is one of the reasons why bitterly contested disputes over access to children sometimes evaporate in the course of time.

At this stage a person may also begin to reorientate himself from brooding about the past to looking hopefully to the future. He may become preoccupied, not with marital conflict, but with his own personal development. He may be concerned to get back on his feet. As he begins to see things more objectively he may begin to realise that there are a whole range of opportunities available to him. As he considers them he may find himself exploring various alternatives and trying to imagine where they might lead. It may seem as though the world is suddenly full of adventure. His new-found freedom may become an acute reality bringing the kind of boyish exhuberance he had left long behind. This attitude was vividly expressed by a young man at a party celebrating his recently granted divorce who kept shaking one fist above his head triumphantly and shouting, "I'm free! I'm free!" Even if you don't find it necessary to express your new-found freedom in such a childish manner, you will probably find that you reach a stage when you are acutely conscious of it.

At this stage people often find themselves over-reacting to their former restrictions. Marriage entails responsibilities which permeate virtually the whole of a person's life style. One doesn't have to be either henpecked or browbeaten by a dominating husband to have one's attitudes, emotional responses and expectations of life conditioned by marital and family responsibilities. Most people marry at a relatively young age when their attitudes are reasonably malleable. During the years of marriage they not only mature but develop well-entrenched attitudes and expectations which implicitly accept the constraints of marriage. When the marriage is swept aside a person may find himself acutely aware of his new-found freedom but totally confused as to what to do with it. The last time he possessed such freedom he was little more than a boy. Now he is a mature man. When he was single his conduct was, to some extent at least, inhibited by consideration for his parents. Now he has neither parents nor spouse to look disapprovingly over his shoulder. He may, for a time, throw himself headlong into the pursuit of happiness. There may be a feeling that, "I owe it to myself".

This may be characterised by the resurrection of old forsaken dreams. It may involve the pursuit of activities forsaken due to financial constraints or family responsibilities. The precise nature of these pursuits will vary tremendously from one person to another. One man may begin to chase every female in sight, another may embark upon a wild spree of parties and fun, whilst yet another might take up some new and exciting sport such as sky-diving or kayacking.

Mercifully this stage doesn't last. The euphoria of taking out two different girls at once and the excitement of keeping each in ignorance of the other usually give way to a feeling that such behaviour is really somewhat juvenile. A person may also find that the initial enthusiasm for his wild spree is overcome by simple exhaustion. More than one forty-year-old divorcee has ruefully reflected that youth is such a wonderful thing, it's a shame God chose to waste it on teenagers. In time the pendulum will swing back and there will be a strong tendency to slip into a more comfortable and better balanced lifestyle. An introspective person may be surprised to realise that some of the habits which he thought had been imposed upon him by marriage were really attributable to his own personality.

In many respects the inital stage of reacting to new-found freedom resembles a second adolescent period. There's a perception of limitations and restrictions falling away; of new vistas unfolding. A dazzling variety of new challenges, new adventures and new possibilities clamour for attention. Many experience a new drive, a feeling that the restrictions of the past have been shaken off. ''Now I can really go places!'' It's true that greater experience and maturity should make a difference but sometimes they seem to be almost deliberately suppressed. There may be a feeling of having come through an ordeal and being entitled to a time of happiness as compensation for past sufferings. In some cases the reaction may be more extreme than it was in the first adolescence not only because parental constraints are no longer applicable but because the insecurity which characterises the teenage years has been largely overcome and one is less inhibited by the need to conform. There is a degree of confidence in one's ability to cope with life which few teenagers possess. That confidence may have taken something of a battering but it will now be re-emerging.

While many people go off the rails during this period, it is, of course, by no means a universal reaction. Many may experience the temptation to do so but resist it. That resistance may stem from a sense of morality. The glitter of a profligate lifestyle may be tempered by the concern that to embrace it like the prodigal son may be to grieve the Father and, ultimately, to create a new set of problems. Others may resist the temptation simply because of their maturity and common sense. A person may feel, instinctively, that this is an important time in his life; a time for a fresh beginning; and that it would be a shame to squander his opportunities by injecting large amounts of time, money and emotional energy into mere trivia. Others may bypass this stage altogether and emerge from the divorce with the feeling of having weathered a storm and having grown in the process. Such a person may be conscious of a new maturity and may look to the future with a more sober and reserved attitude. He is likely to want to get on with the business of re-establishing his life and be unwilling to have his attention diverted by what he regards as purely juvenile pursuits.

It would be unfair, however, to say that all those who do over-react in this period of second adolescence are lacking in maturity or commonsense. What has occurred is that their emotional reactions to what they have been through have, for a time, emerged as the dominant factor. Underneath they may be mature people with a great deal of common sense and in the long run those qualities will bring them back to a more stable lifestyle.

Those who emerge from the divorce process with a deep feeling of insecurity may experience a different kind of adolescent reaction. They may experience a return to that terrible stage where one is torn between an overwhelming desire to be loved and accepted by one's peers and a terrible anxiety that one might be rejected or betrayed. Teenagers can be like chameleon lizards; they change their colour according to their background. When jeans are "in" any other kind of garment is simply not to be contemplated. If "everybody" is interested in a particular sport, then it must be avidly followed even if it really is an intolerable bore.

In the second adolescence the same kind of ambivalence to other people may be evident. On the one hand one may be acutely conscious of the emptiness of life. There may be a great aching not only for companionship but for relationships at a deeply personal and intimate level. On the other hand, there may be an awareness of emotional wreckage and concern that what recovery has occurred is still very precarious. Phrases such as: "I just couldn't take any more" have a continuing echo which may be reflected in a pattern of keeping other people at bay. The threatening aspect of personal relationships may be avoided by preventing people from getting too close. This attitude may be perceived by friends and acquaintances as aloof or even cold but it will usually be quite the reverse. From time to time longing may become stronger than apprehension, and there may be an apparently uncharacteristic overture of friendship or warmth of response. This process may tend to produce one or two really close relationships as islands in a sea of isolation. Sometimes the intensity of such a response may produce an apparent rejection. The other person may have offered friendship but have been quite unprepared to sustain the emotional dependence involved in the extremity of the response. Of course, any apparent rejection at this stage will be traumatic and may intensify the apprehension towards new relationships.

Even a person who feels relatively secure is likely to encounter some of this kind of reaction when he begins dating. When you feel fifteen or sixteen years old again all the misgivings and insecurities may come flooding back. How do you know whether a person is really busy or whether that is just an excuse? How on earth do you behave on a date these days? Unlike a teenager encountering these traumas for the first time, an adult may be acutely conscious of his age. He may feel that he has reached that stage in life where someone going out with him will expect him to be self-confident and to know how to treat her. But the last time he went out on a date seems so long ago and he may wonder whether the particular code of ethics and courtesy he learnt still applies. Relationships between men and women have changed so much during the past ten or fifteen years. Is it gentlemanly or chauvinistic to open a door for a lady these days? Is it the done thing to take her arm or hold her hand? Do they expect you to kiss them goodnight at the end of the evening? Patterns of behaviour that were acceptable in a twenty-year-old in 1968 may be of dubious guidance to a forty-year-old in 1988.

If the woman is newly divorced she may be equally insecure. She may appreciate the freedom from the social conventions of earlier years but, paradoxically, find herself groping for some guidelines as to what is acceptable. In this age of liberation and equality is it still polite to wait to be asked or could you invite him around for dinner without being thought to be forward? What on earth do people talk about these days? Fifteen years of marriage and a bitterly contested divorce seems inappropriate for an opening topic. Should I invite him in for coffee at the end of the evening? If I do, will he take that as an invitation to try to seduce me?

The first few dates are likely to prove thrilling but you are likely to be acutely conscious of your nervousness. There may be a pervading sense of strangeness or even wrongness. If you were married for a number of years, it can be difficult to adjust to the thought that you are free to become romantically involved with another person.

Some very straightforward steps can help you over this difficult stage. It may be helpful to discuss your misgivings with a single or divorced friend of the same sex as yourself. He or she may be able to answer your specific questions and, more importantly, offer general reassurance. They may also be able to help you re-establish yourself socially by inviting you to parties or other functions or, perhaps, by arranging for a double date. If they have any sense they will also remind you that you are really worrying over nothing. If you are friendly, courteous and interested in the other person then you have done all that could be reasonably expected of you. Minor social gaffes will be readily overlooked by any reasonable adult.

Once the uncertainty has been overcome, you will begin to get to know the other person better. At this stage it is not uncommon to become very deeply involved. When that happens it is imperative to pause and analyse your feelings. Your divorce may have left you with a great and an unfulfilled longing for a really close personal relationship. It is a wonderful thing to have someone to laugh with again, someone whose company dispels the loneliness. The thought of having someone who cares about you again can be heady wine. A relationship in which you can share a deep longing and intimate feelings may assuage much of the aching emptiness. It is easy to confuse those feelings with love. No doubt that is why so many people marry on the rebound. Yet frequently what has happened has been a simple transferrance of emotional dependence to a sympathetic and available person. The resulting warm glow may not be the kind of genuine love that is likely to lead to a lasting marriage. There may be a mixture of relief from loneliness and anxiety, a sense of having needs fulfilled, gratitude and, perhaps if you had been praying for God to send someone special along, the feeling that this person must be the answer to your prayers. Yet, unhappily, many rebound marriages fail because the relationship was based upon mere emotional dependence and the qualities necessary for a long-term relationship were lacking.

One factor that should make you think very seriously about the nature of your new relationship is any strong similarity between your former spouse and the person with whom you have now become involved. A transfer of emotional dependence will frequently be made to a person whose appearance or characteristics have a degree of familiarity about them. Familiarity may make people seem less strange and consequently less threatening. Of course, some familiar traits may evoke a flood of unpleasant memories and unfavourable comparisons. Yet it remains true that many people do form close attachments to people very similar to their former spouses. Some may fail to appreciate the similarity and their friends will often be aware of it before they are. Others will explain it to themselves by comments such as: "He's just like John was before...", "She's like Helen could have been if only...". This phenomenon may explain why a woman will divorce one alcoholic husband to marry another or why a man previously married to one domineering woman will immediately find himself involved with another.

The new relationship may, of course, develop into a strong and enduring marriage. There is no need to assume that every new romance is an expression of the rebound phenomenon or that a relationship which starts in that fashion may not ripen into a full and lasting union. But if you have been badly hurt once it is prudent to take the time to analyse your feelings and to be sure that you are sowing the seeds of future happiness. Apart from anything else, it is only fair to the other person that you ask yourself whether you are able to offer the depth of commitment necessary for a satisfying long-term relationship.

As you begin to get back on your feet you will find that experience has brought a new level of maturity which may permit you to gauge your own feelings with a degree of perception that would not have been possible prior to your first marriage. Again dominant emotions such as bitterness and cynicism on the one hand or anxiety and a sense of desperation on the other tend to cloud the issue and make it difficult for you to make a sober evaluation. If it is the first close relationship since the divorce then gratitude and loyalty may also make it very difficult for you to look at the situation objectively. To overcome these problems it may be necessary to take a step back or even withdraw from the relationship completely for a time. You may be able to see the situation more clearly when away on holidays by yourself or if, in some other way, you are able to distance yourself from it.

A further problem often experienced at this stage is the barrage of criticism or helpful advice from a great variety of people concerned about the divorce. The parents of your new-found girlfriend may see you as a lecherous and evil Svengali seeking to debauch their innocent Trilby. The sister of the new man in your life may treat you as a brazen Jezebel seeking to seduce her brother from the paths of righteousness. Friends may be aghast to see you expressing interest in the opposite sex when "as we all know" you are still married in the sight of God. Sometimes the censure may be unspoken but no less obvious. There may be a new protectiveness towards husbands or wives. You may simply find it incredibly difficult ever to be alone with unattached members of the opposite sex.

That these attitudes are as prevalent in the church as elsewhere is a cause for regret but there is no point in railing against them. They are not likely to change overnight. The only way to deal with this kind of problem is to ignore it until you have come to a point where you are confident in your own beliefs. If you then act in accordance with your conscience you'll be able to face others with confidence. There is no point in becoming involved in arguments with people who disagree with you at this stage. You are not likely to convert them to your manner of thinking and the exercise may well prove confusing and distressing.

Finally, let me suggest what some people might regard as a further heresy. St Paul referred to the three great virtues as faith, hope and love and said that of the three, love was the greatest. You might note that "being right" didn't even get a mention. In the long run genuine love will win over most of those who do not understand. You may leave them safely to God who loves them as he loves you. Remember too that God has not rejected you even if one or two of his "assistants" have. He has brought you through the heartache and wants you to understand that you have not only his acceptance, but his love.

CHAPTER EIGHTEEN

Coping Alone

From the moment of separation you will be in unfamiliar territory.

If you have left your former home then you will have an immediate need to find accommodation, but even when you do, initially it will seem an alien environment. After living in one home for some time you will have acquired habits based upon an instinctive knowledge of where things are. Now not only are they not in those familiar places, but many of them will have been left in the old home. The new accommodation will usually be smaller and you may find quarters cramped, especially if you have brought children with you. Many mothers find that it is one thing to cope with three young children in a suburban house with grassy lawns, swings, cubby houses and the other paraphernalia of childhood. It is altogether another to cope with them in a two-bedroom flat on the sixth floor of a building which towers above a cement car park.

The children are likely to be particularly difficult to manage because they will be upset by the separation. There may be tearful demands to know where the other parent is, why they have been moved to the new place and what is going to happen about all sorts of arrangements that you may not have even considered. The usual techniques of distracting children may be of little use because the strange surroundings will be a constant reminder of the recent upheaval. You may find that you are not handling the situation very well. It is by no means easy to handle distressed children in a confined space, specially when you have to complete moving in at the same time and your own mind is reeling with self-doubt and confused anxiety about the repercussions of your decision.

When Monday morning comes the children will be due at school. That fact will mean that a decision will have to be made as to whether the children are to continue at the same school or be moved to another one closer to their new home. If they are to stay at their old school they may have to travel long distances each way. If they are moved to a new one there will be a further disruption in their lives. They will have to come to grips with new teachers and, possibly, new curricula. They will also have to make new friendships at a time when their classmates may have been attending the school for two or three years and have already sorted out their cliques. They may, for a time, be treated as interlopers. Even if they are wholeheartedly accepted, their very newness will evoke questions about their family including, of course, questions about Mum and Dad.

If you have remained in the former home then you may be better organised. In this situation, however, there will be a different set of problems. The house will suddenly seem very lonely. If the children are still there the familiarity of their surroundings will make them easier to manage but there will still be the same clamour of tearful questions. Furthermore, the very familiarity of the home will evoke painful memories and associations not only for you but for them. There may be some half-finished project begun with the aid of the absent parent which lies in silent reproach in one of the bedrooms. There may be a routine of games or simply being tucked into bed which has now been disrupted.

The children will not be the only people who demand explanations. There will be a constant barrage of telephone calls from family and friends. All of them will be well-meaning but most of them will manage to put their foot in it in one way or another. Some may tell you that you're acting like an idiot, others that you should have done it years ago. Some will relate a series of anecdotes about your spouse which "you ought to know". Most will feel compelled to inflict good or bad advice upon you.

If you are not working, there will be an urgent need to arrange for a social security pension or, failing that, for some kind of emergency relief. If you are working there may be an urgent need to arrange for someone to care for the children before and after school or, if there are pre-school children, throughout the day. There are many arrangements to make. You'll need to arrange for electricity and telephone services to be connected. If you don't have your own car you'll need to sort out what public transport facilities are available to get to and from work, the children's school, the shopping centre and all kinds of medical, sporting and social facilities.

You will also need to come to terms with your former spouse about custody of the children and access arrangements and it is not something that can be ignored. Your former spouse is not likely simply to permit the children to pass forever out of his or her life. Nor would that be in their best interests. No matter how you feel, that person is the father or mother of your children. If the departure followed a violent quarrel or you simply rounded up the children and left whilst your spouse was away then you may find yourself with a fight on your hands. If you send the children off to school on Monday morning then you may find that they are collected by the other parent at the end of the day. If you seek to avoid that by refusing to disclose your address and sending the children to a new school, your spouse may make an *ex parte* application to the Divorce Court for interim custody. The court may be reluctant to entertain such an application in your absence but if your spouse proves that you have taken steps to conceal your whereabouts a judge may feel that you have forfeited the right to notice and grant custody to your spouse until the merits of the case can be determined.

There are really only two ways of avoiding these risks. The first and most logical alternative is to broach the matter directly with your former spouse. If the quarrel has been a particularly violent one and you are nervous of a confrontation, then you could always use the telephone. If even that prospect is too daunting, then you can make an urgent appointment to see a solicitor and ask him to do it on your behalf. If, during the course of that initial approach it becomes apparent that there will be a dispute about custody then your spouse should be made to understand that whilst you accept that his or her rights will be pursued through the courts, the children will still need to live with one parent or the other till the hearing of that dispute and that it is that question which you need to discuss. Clearly the children cannot be subjected to the process of being snatched backwards and forwards like relay batons. If you cannot reach any agreement even on that basis then you will have to approach the court for appropriate orders.

All these factors combine to produce enormous pressure and anxiety and it is small wonder that people sometimes behave in an irrational or provocative manner at this stage.

No matter how amicable or acrimonious the relationship between you and your former spouse may be you will need to exercise considerable care in determining what you tell the children. Whatever you do, resist the temptation to tell them that their father or mother is a heartless monster who doesn't love them any more. Such comments may hurt the former spouse but they will be devastating to your children.

Unless the situation is desperate, take the time to make at least some tentative arrangements before you leave. Planning will minimise the disruption and, more importantly, the emotional strain involved. Remember that you can't walk down the street and rent a flat instantly. It usually takes at least a couple of days to organise a lease. If you can't secure one before you leave you will need to find temporary accommodation until you can make long-term arrangements. You may also need to make some hard

decisions about what to take with you. That decision will
be influenced not only by such factors as the size of the
anticipated accommodation and the availability of some
means of shifting heavy items but also by the impact it is
likely to have on your former spouse. This is also the time
when you will need good friends. Do not hesitate to ask
for help from a member of the family and/or a close friend.
Even if they can't do anything to assist you physically they
can provide moral support and that is likely to prove more
valuable than anything else at this troubled time.

If it is at all practicable do try to talk to your spouse
before leaving. Sometimes the climate of hostility will not
permit it, but if there is any chance at all you really should
take it. The marriage may now be "on the rocks" but there
will have been happy times and you really do owe the other
party the courtesy of telling him or her that it is over and
you are leaving. To simply come home and find the house
ransacked and your spouse gone can be a very distressing
experience. From a purely selfish point of view it will be
of great assistance if you can maintain some semblance of
a civil communication with your former spouse.

There will undoubtedly be financial questions to resolve.
In this respect simple prudence would suggest that it would
be wise to take legal advice. Nonetheless if you can sit down,
discuss the situation amicably and come to some agreement
between yourselves you are likely to save a great deal of
money, a great deal of time and a great deal of heartache.
I am not suggesting that you should renounce your rights
or ignore your legal advice. However it is far better to take
a little less than to waste two years and then spend
three thousand pounds in legal costs securing your full
entitlement.

If you have children you will have to resign yourself to
the fact that despite the contemplated divorce you will be
obliged to have at least some degree of continuing contact
with your former spouse for many years.

There will inevitably be an order for access. Many
parents who have formed a great dislike for their former

spouse imagine that they can persuade the court to deny access. That will not occur unless there are very strong grounds. The other person may be an alcoholic, a womaniser, a person of violent or erratic behaviour but no matter what you may think about the strength of those grounds, you will almost certainly find that the court will decide that there should be access. The reasons for their reluctance to deny access will be discussed a little more fully later. For the moment it is sufficient to say that access is denied only in exceptional circumstances.

That means that once every fortnight, perhaps once every week, you are going to come into contact with your former husband or wife. If there is constant wrangling and bitterness between you that will inevitably cause greater emotional stress to your children. There may also be the need to discuss questions involving your childrens' future: matters such as the choice of schools, the opportunity of overseas travel, their illnesses, operations and a host of other things. For the children's sake you should try to prevent an all out war of the kind which might prevent such a limited relationship from working successfully in the future or at least make it very difficult.

CHAPTER NINETEEN

Blessed are the Children

Parents have widely divergent expectations as to the effect their divorce is likely to have upon their children. At the one extreme are those blithe souls who assume that the children will be completely impervious to it. Their attitudes can be expressed by the proposition that this is a matter between the parents; it has nothing to do with the children. "They'll still see both of us so what's the hassle?" Mercifully, people in that extreme category are rare. At the other extreme are those who look at their children with a deep sense of foreboding. Even in these enlightened times most criminals come from broken homes. It is usually accepted that when a marriage breaks up the children are emotionally shattered and likely to end up with psychological problems. If you're lucky and they don't commit suicide they get involved with drugs. If by some miracle, they escape all that, they are sure to lose their faith and grow up to be heathens. Many Christians actually feel this latter view has scriptural support. After all, doesn't the Bible talk about, training "a child in the way he should go, and when he is old he will not depart from it?"[25]

There are many Christians who may not accept all of these wild assumptions but whose level of anxiety for their children has assumed dimensions out of all proportion to the gravity of the risk. Christians in fact seem particularly prone to worry about the future lives of their children following their divorce. Of course they are right to be concerned about their children. Children are particularly vulnerable following their parents' separation. A child is dependent upon his parents, not only for the provision of food, clothing and shelter, but for the provision of love and emotional security. When parents separate the secure environment that the child has so far enjoyed may be split down the middle. The child will usually have had no advance warning of this step. Even if there have been violent parental quarrels or other signs of discord, the full extent of the rift will rarely have been evident to the child. Most people try to avoid arguing in front of the children and if there are odd lapses the child is usually too un-sophisticated to realise its significance. This is like the clashes that he has with a brother or sister which do not involve any conceivable risk to the family's cohesion. When the marital rift comes he is left in a state of bewilderment with no criteria by which he can assess the uncertainty of his new lifestyle. The separation may also mean that children have to face new schools, new friends, new neigh-bours. Only a person totally lacking in sensitivity would pretend that these events are unlikely to cause considerable distress and anxiety. Yet whilst these things are undoubtedly true the fact remains that most children prove to be remarkably resilient to pressures of this kind and most survive and grow to adulthood without the catastrophies commonly predicted. There are, in fact, some cases in which the children emerge from an atmosphere of violence or tension with almost audible sighs of relief.

This devastating mixture of parental anxiety and guilt is perfectly understandable but it is nonetheless an attitude which falls far short of a proper Christian approach to the situation. If you have fallen into this destructive cycle of fear and self-flagellation, let me ask you to stop splutter-ing and consider the matter afresh.

Custody

The question of custody will have to be faced. Increasingly joint custody orders are being used. Here the formal legal custody of the child is given to both parents, with day to day care and control only to one. The purpose of such orders is to increase the involvement of the parent without care and control in the child's upbringing. However, one parent is inevitably going to see more of the child than the other, so whether the issue is one of straight custody, or one of care and control, the issues and the ultimate outcome are much the same. Unhappily, many Christians approach this question with an attitude of frantic desperation particularly if it seems likely that they may lose custody. They may fully believe their lawyers when they are advised that they are unable to succeed. At some level such a parent may acknowledge that, for purely practical purposes, the children would be better off with the other parent. He may be forced to accept that the children wish to remain with that parent and may even be obliged to concede that he himself does not have the time or resources to care for them on a full-time basis. The harsh reality of the situation may be that a fully contested custody case would achieve nothing but needless acrimony and a depletion of funds resulting, ultimately, in a poorer level of accommodation for the children.

Despite all, there will often be a stubborn determination to persevere in the face of all odds. This attitude may be misunderstood by both the non-Christian spouse and the judge who ultimately hears the case. It can be construed as a stubborn refusal to face the truth, an insensitivity to the children's needs, a vindictive attempt to hurt the other parent or a self-centredness that simply will not brook any consideration of the needs of others. The truth of the matter, of course, is that this desperate striving after custody is not dependent upon any of those things. It usually springs from a Christian's belief that it is imperative that the children be brought up in the "nurture and admonition of the Lord".[27] If the other parent does not share this belief then the Christian parent assumes that the only way in which the child can receive a Christian upbringing is by obtaining custody.

Frantic desperation is induced because of the perceived

risk to the children's spiritual development and, ultimately, to their eternal souls. Such issues as accommodation, schools or even the emotional nurture of the children fade into insignificance compared to the need to ensure that the child grows up in a Christian home where he is likely to accept Christ and receive eternal life.

Many judges and counsellors underrate the importance of this kind of issue to Christians. To say that Christians regard the issue as a matter of life and death would not be to exaggerate but rather to under-estimate the serious- ness of the situation.

Whilst no person of sensitivity, whatever his faith, could fail to sympathise with a Christian parent in this agonising situation, the underlying attitude is completely indefensi- ble. This statement may shock many Christian parents but I believe that it is true.

The question that has to be asked by every Christian parent whether divorced or not is simply this, "What am I going to depend upon for my children's future and for their salvation?" This question is really nothing more than an application of an even more blunt question which we all have to face, namely, "In what do I trust?"

Parents who find that their attitude toward an impending custody case has gone beyond the level of normal concern and become an almost all-consuming passion may find that, subconsciously at least, they have answered that question already. The answer reflected in the attitude which I have described is, "I depend upon myself. It all hinges on me. If I can have them in my care constantly then I might be able to persuade them to become Christians. I might be able to bring them up the right way and save them. If I don't get the chance they will be lost".

This attitude does not reflect a proper understanding of our Christian faith. Certainly Christian parents are expected to act responsibly towards their children but they must never allow themselves to forget that their funda- mental trust is in God. The biblical position is quite clear. All of us are exhorted to trust God rather than ourselves.

We are told, in the first epistle of Peter, to cast all our cares upon him because he cares for us. We are given the example of Job who suffered the loss of his wife, children, possessions and suffered various physical afflictions yet still declared that though God slayed him, yet would he trust in him.[28] The Bible also teaches us that God has a particular care and concern for children. It was Jesus himself who took a small child and told his disciples, "Let the children come to me, and do not hinder them, for to such belongs the kingdom of heaven".[29] The Bible describes God as the father of the fatherless and Psalm 27 says that, "If my father and my mother forsake me then the Lord will take me up" (AV). If you believe these promises then you need not approach any questions of custody or access in an attitude of desperation.

The proper Christian attitude towards your children's future may be expressed in a simple resolution, "I will do what I can to provide for my children's future and to give them a proper Christian upbringing but, ultimately, I will put my faith in God and not in myself. I acknowledge that I have a duty to do what I can but, ultimately, the overall responsibility is God's and he will provide for them with my help, without it or even in spite of it."

Children are not little computers whose future is dependent upon parental programming. They ultimately must decide for themselves. This is true for all children whether their parents are divorced or not.

Whilst I am not denigrating the value of a Christian upbringing it is totally unrealistic and lacking in faith to assume that your child will inevitably go to the dogs if he lives in a different household from you. God is quite capable of looking after him. You may entrust your child to God and be confident that God will overcome the adverse effects of separation and divorce. Your children may experience difficulties but God will not abandon them and as they grow older he will bring conviction to them. They may find that wherever they turn they are confronted by people whom he has brought across their path to point them back to him. God would care for your children even if you were unable to contact them at all.

In fact, with access you will have some contact with them and you may pray with faith that God will use you as a tower of strength in their lives. Desperation about custody is not only based upon failure to trust God, it is also based upon the implicit assumption that a Christian parent can only be an important influence in a child's life if he has custody rather than access. This proposition is also untrue.

It is true that a custodial parent may have the children for twelve days out of fourteen but the fact remains that for most of that period the children will be at school and that contact with them will be limited to a couple of hours during the day. There is also a sense in which the custodial parent tends to become taken for granted. Custodial parents themselves perceive this and become very distressed about it. There is a feeling that they do all the hard work, impose all the discipline, hear all the children's complaints and then at the end of the week see the other parent greeted as a long-lost friend come to give them a good time. It is true that children usually look forward to access visits and I suspect that there is frequently a tendency to talk to the non-custodial parent more freely.

The truth of the matter is that your influence is much more dependent upon the relationship which you have with your children than upon the amount of time you are able to spend with them. Many men who work long hours see their children only at weekends even if they are not divorced. Some actually spend more time with them when alternate weekends are specifically set aside for the purpose of access. Children readily perceive that the roles of mother and father are different and they will have an interest in the views of both. Furthermore, when you look back on your own life you will realise, perhaps, that the critical moments which influenced the course of your future life were brief indeed—frequently just a chance conversation in which two or three sentences were crucial.

Your attitude to the contact you have with your children

should be one of faith in every circumstance. If you truly trust God to make the contact with your child fruitful you can afford to relax about it. There is no need for anxiety or strain. The future of your children is in the Lord's hands and you don't need to engineer it. You should feel free to enjoy their company and to trust that, in time, God will create between you a strong and loving bond which will endure into adulthood.

The Christian parent who obtains custody is often led by this kind of anxiety about bringing up the child in a Christian environment to adopt an obstructive attitude to access. The Christian parent may feel that the non-Christian one is not a fit and proper person to have a continuing influence on the children. The non-custodial parent may have a history of alcoholism, promiscuity, violence, dishonesty or anything else which falls into the catalogue of human frailties. The custodial parent's reaction to his or her former spouse may include an element of outrage, "Why should I have to send my children into the hands of that beast?'' was a question asked by one distraught mother. No matter how you may feel about access, the court will almost invariably grant it.

In this area also the proper attitude to adopt is one of faith. A Christian with custody of his children should be grateful for the opportunity to care for them and should trust God to ensure that they are not adversely influenced by contact with the other parent however personally unacceptable that parent's behaviour may be.

Yet that is by no means the only consideration which should influence your attitude. Whether you agree with your former spouse's lifestyle and habits or not, the fact remains that he or she is a person for whom Jesus died. You may have been hurt very badly and any resentment you still harbour may be perfectly justified. Yet despite all that, God still loves that person. The attitude you should have therefore, is one of forgiveness. Jesus said that his followers were to love their enemies, to pray for those who despitefully used them. Even if all your complaints were justified and your spouse was totally in the wrong the commandment remains. You must not only forgive but pray for your former spouse.

Now let me hasten to add, if I have not already made it clear, that I am not talking about forgiveness in the sense of taking the person back. That is a totally different question. For the purposes of this discussion I have assumed that the marital relationship is at an end and that the only question is the attitude which a Christian should have to a former spouse rather than to a current one.

As you pray, you should also pray that God will enable you to come to some understanding of the causes of the other person's behaviour. Even Christians who are normally very understanding and sympathetic may have a blind spot where their former spouses are concerned because they have been badly hurt. Yet the fact is that few people who behave in a thoroughly outrageous fashion do so out of sheer malice or perversity. Most people behave in such a manner as a reaction to deep hurts or frustrations or as a result of some deep-seated emotional imbalance or psychological disturbance. It may be wise to be afraid of them but that fear should be tempered with pity.

You should also remember that if you no longer regard yourself as that person's spouse then you no longer have the right to expect a particular standard of behaviour from him. If your ex-husband chooses to spend his money on an expensive car and an extravagant lifestyle that is his business. If he chooses to drink heavily or to have a succession of flatmates all of whom prove to be attractive females then that, too, is none of your business. His behaviour is your concern only to the extent that it poses a substantial threat to the physical, emotional or spiritual wellbeing of your children or, alternatively, to the extent that it indicates that he may be in need of more prayer.

Another misconception common to Christians is that the views of the other parent are worthless. Even if the other parent is also a Christian there will usually be a feeling that ''He can't be much of a one or he wouldn't have broken up the marriage'' or some similarly "charitable" sentiment. More commonly the other parent will not be a Christian and his views will simply be swept aside on the basis that he does not accept the same standards as the Christian does and you are determined that a proper Christian standard is going to be applied to anything concerning the children. Any attempt by the other parent to discuss the matter may seem vaguely threatening. One does not wish to be inveigled into something contrary to the will of God simply to be courteous or tolerant. After all, as St Paul asks, "Can light consort with darkness?"

This attitude is not only infuriating to the other parent, it is also presumptuous and unfair. A Christian father may be perfectly justified in deciding that in the event of any irreconcilable conflict concerning a matter of morality he will follow the Christian standard in preference to that urged upon him by the other parent. He will never be justified in refusing to discuss the children's welfare with their mother or in peremptorily dismissing her views and *vice versa*. Whether you like it or not that other person is the father or mother of your children. That relationship involves certain rights which you should respect.

There are many parents who may not share your faith but who are intelligent, sensitive and articulate people who have a great concern for the physical and emotional well-being of their children. The other parent sees the children when they are out of your care and in situations with which you may not be familiar. He may have a great deal to contribute. He may be genuinely concerned about some aspect of your care of the children or, more commonly, the manner in which the children perceive your attitude to him. These things can cause a great deal of unnecessary hurt. If your attitude is dogmatic and inflexible the rejection implicit in that action will itself cause unnecessary hurt.

If, as the parent with custody, you are genuinely concerned about the welfare of your children then that concern should normally extend to fostering a proper relationship between them and their other parent. They will almost certainly maintain such a relationship but the degree to which it becomes a positive factor in their lives rather than a negative one is, at least to some extent, dependent upon your attitude. Yet the extremity of your distress may make it impossible to assess the situation objectively.

You may feel so hurt and distressed that you cannot imagine contact with your former spouse being anything but destructive. One father summed up his feelings in these words, "I feel like I've had to throw my children on the altar like Abraham did with Isaac and sometimes I feel like there was no ram with its horns caught in the bush and I have been obliged to plunge the knife home!"

Try to remember that although your children will undoubtedly be upset by the separation they will almost certainly settle down in time. Because children display their feelings so much more effectively than adults do it is easy to over-emphasise the degree of emotional disturbance which they have suffered. Parents who are themselves hurt and distressed, as virtually everyone is immediately after separation, are particularly likely to overestimate the degree of distress suffered by their children. Frequently, the first set of tears will produce a feeling that, like Job, "The thing which I have greatly feared is come upon me".[31] The distress of the children may be very real but it will subside if the parents themselves resolve their differences and reach a stage at which they can maintain the limited contact required by their joint parenthood with some semblance of courtesy and tolerance.

It is also important to realise that most children really wish their parents were living together again and many dream about some day in the future when that will happen. Most children also have a desire to please both parents. These attitudes, ironically enough, often cause confusion and disputes between the parents. It is not by any means uncommon for a child to tell his mother that he loves her very much and wants to remain with her and immediately thereafter tells his father that he loves him and would like to live with him. The mother construes the child's statement to her as a clear-cut indication that the child wishes to remain in her custody. The father, on the other hand, construes the child's statement to him as a clear indication that he is fed up with mother and wants to see Dad win a custody case. For that reason it is not uncommon to see a bitterly contested custody case in which each side strenuously asserts that the children concerned wish to live with him or her as the case may be. These general assertions are frequently supported by all kinds of other statements rightly or wrongly attributed to the child in which he has either complained about the other parent or made statements supportive of the case of the parent seeking custody.

Sometimes the child may be simply playing both ends against the middle. I can remember one case some years ago in which a thirteen-year-old boy was the subject of a custody dispute. The mother claimed that he had been repeatedly beaten by the father and the father vigorously denied those allegations and claimed that the boy had constantly told him that he was being bashed by the mother's new husband. A rather perceptive welfare officer interviewed the boy and finally established that he had in fact told each parent that he was being beaten in the other household and that neither claim was true. When pressed for an explanation he finally confided that if he told his mother that his father was beating him she made it up to him by taking him out and buying him presents. Unfortunately, father sought to console him in the same way when he told him that his stepfather was beating him. It turned out that the mother, father and stepfather were all thoroughly decent people who treated the child better than he deserved. When the counsellor finally asked the boy who he really wanted to live with the lad mused about the problem for a while and then said thoughtfully, ''I don't really know. I guess it depends on who makes me the best offer!''

Most children are not quite so manipulative as the young

scoundrel just mentioned. Frequently when a child tells both parents that he wishes to live with them all he is really doing is expressing his heartfelt desire that the family be reunited. Even if a child realises that that is impossible, he may nonetheless express his deep need to hold on to both mother and father by telling each what he believes they would like to hear.

There may be an element of manipulation in these cases but it will usually be motivated not by the desire to obtain some tangible benefit such as an extra night out but by insecurity and a longing for the love of both parents. The potential for misunderstanding in this kind of situation is obvious. If the estranged parents can display the maturity to put aside their differences in order to be able to discuss any concern about the children then misunderstandings will be minimised.

A further area of misunderstanding is sometimes created by the negative attitude displayed by a child towards the non-custodial parent. That parent may readily assume that the child has been turned against him by constant propaganda on the part of the other parent. In some cases, of course, that is precisely what has occurred. On the other hand, there are many cases in which the custodial parent genuinely realises that it is in the child's interests to maintain contact with both father and mother and does the best that he can to encourage access. Despite encouragement from the custodial parent, however, a child will frequently display anger and hostility to a parent whom he feels has deserted him and who still refuses to come back to the family. This attitude usually subsides as time passes if the non-custodial parent is patient and continues to display an attitude of love and affection towards the child. Sometimes a parent may have to accept that he will be able to take out only two of the three children. He may be tempted to insist upon his rights and demand that the third child be produced. There are circumstances in which that course may be required.

If the custodial parent is endeavouring to frustrate access

by seizing upon the slightest excuse to withold the children
the non-custodial parent may have to take a hard line about
the matter. More commonly, however, to take a hard line
in the face of genuine reluctance by the child will simply
exacerbate the problem. The parent would be much better
advised to take a long-term view of the situation, tell the
child that he respects his wishes and will be happy to take
him out another time when he is ready to go. If he then
takes out the other children and ensures they have a good
time then they will undoubtedly come home bubbling with
enthusiasm about their adventures and during the course
of the next week will be his advocates to the child left
behind. If the problem persists then it may be prudent to
arrange for a counsellor to discuss the situation with the
custodial parent and the child in question.

The Divorce Court employs counsellors who are happy
to assist in that way and, if the custodial parent proves
reluctant to co-operate in that respect then the other parent
may seek an order requiring counselling.

Whilst individual children vary both in the nature and
the extremity of the reaction to parental separation it is
possible to offer some indication about the type of response
which may be expected at varying ages.

(a) Up to the age of three children may react to the breakup
     of their parents' marriage by fretting, having disturbed
     sleep patterns and by throwing tantrums.

     They may cry and cling to the custodial parent at
     the commencement of a period of access. That does
     not necessarily indicate a lack of affection for the other
     parent but simply a degree of insecurity. At the end
     of the period of access there may be a similar time of
     clinging to that parent. The best means of coping with
     access is to provide frequent short periods so that the
     child will not become too insecure at being away from
     the custodial parent for too long but, equally, will see
     the other parent sufficiently regularly to maintain a
     relationship.

The understanding of children in this age-range is very limited and there may be a need to constantly repeat simple explanations.

(b) Children aged four to five years may react by being tearful and complaining on the one hand or irritable and overly aggressive on the other.

Such children are frequently anxious and, even at that early age, may actually blame themselves for their parents' separation. If their distress is at all severe they may regress in terms of language and toilet training and, as with younger children, may exhibit disrupted sleep patterns.

As with the younger age group there may be a need constantly to repeat simple explanations and for constant reassurance to overcome the basic feelings of insecurity. They may ask a lot of questions and these should be answered as simply as possible. At this age it is usually possible to increase the periods of access. They are, however, very vulnerable to any continuing conflict between the parents and if such conflict cannot be overcome then periods of access may involve a distressing conflict of loyalty.

(c) Children aged five to six years can also be very moody. They may be very aggressive or they may become withdrawn and spend a lot of time fantasising about the absent parent returning home.

They are a little more autonomous than younger children and may seek comfort from a teacher or some other supportive person. At that age they may also be developing activities which provide some distraction from the distress of the separation. They may need to discuss the situation with their parents and they should be given a straightforward explanation of the situation. It is important that they understand that they are loved and cared for but this should be balanced with normal firm discipline. There may be initial distress during access visits but this will usually settle down.

(d) Children aged seven to eight years seem to be particularly threatened by parental separation.

They are prone to anxiety about being abandoned by one or both parents and, for a time, may be constantly worried about how particular needs will be met or whether there will be anyone to care for them in particular circumstances. There may be an almost desperate need to please the custodial parent who is perceived as being immensely important now that he or she is in sole control of the family. Their anxiety and the desire to please that parent may inhibit them from asking questions or even participating in a discussion about the situation.

Such children need warmth and comfort from parents and preferably from teachers and other important adult figures in their lives. It may also allay their anxiety if the custodial parent takes the time to provide unsolicited explanations of anything likely to cause confusion or uncertainty. In this age range it is also fairly important that access be frequent.

(e) Children in the nine to twelve years age range have a greater degree of understanding.

Unhappily, they frequently seem to have enough understanding to grasp the seriousness and permanency of the situation but lack the emotional maturity to cope with what they perceive. This is one of the difficult ages in which their distress may be reflected in bad behaviour such as angry outbursts, lying or even running away from home. Children in this age range may see the situation as demanding that they choose sides. They may scathingly blame one parent for "breaking up the family" and may perceive that parent's conduct in leaving the family home not only as a rejection of the other spouse but a rejection of them. There may be a fierce loyalty to the custodial parent and a feeling that this loyalty demands a rejection of the other parent.

Children in this age group need the help and support

not only of both parents but of friends and other family members. It may help them to discuss the situation with a trusted adult who is not regarded as being in either one camp or the other. It can also be helpful for them to pursue social and sporting activities because such activities tend to divert at least some attention and emotional involvement from the family situation.

(f) Children aged thirteen to sixteen years fall within what may fairly be described as a problem age.

One authority has suggested that on his thirteenth birthday a teenager should be nailed into a barrel and fed through the bung hole. On his fifteenth birthday the parent should nail up the bung hole. Even at the best of times this is an age of great insecurity and anxiety. It is a time of rapid physical, emotional and social change. The settled and relatively secure patterns of childhood are shattered and there is a need to forge a new self image. It can be a time of great insecurity about the degree of acceptance one is likely to receive from peers, about physical attributes, sex and all manner of educational and social aspirations. The parental separation can aggravate these anxieties and add a whole list of new ones.

This can also be an age of passionate loyalties to friends, football teams, rock groups and other things which, temporarily at least, spark an almost patriotic fever. When Mum and Dad separate there may be a conflict of loyalties involving significant emotional distress. This conflict may be resolved by aligning with one parent ''against'' the other but the young person may vacillate between support of one parent and the other. At this stage of adolescence it is almost inevitable that the separation will cause emotional upheaval characterised by anger which may, from time to time, boil over into rage and a feeling of betrayal. There may even be a feeling that both parents have betrayed the child by failing to keep the family together.

Children at this age have virtually full adult intelligence and are able to understand far more than their parents frequently assume. On the other hand, their emotional upheaval and small experience of life make it almost impossible for them to make an accurate assessment of the situation without assistance. As with the slightly younger age group it may be a source of great encouragement to talk it over with a mature and perceptive adult. Unhappily, this is also the age at which virtually everything seems embarrassing. Even things common to their peers may cause much blushing or macho bravado as the case may be. Assistance by teachers, counsellors or family friends is frequently refused because of a, perhaps repressed but nonetheless profound, sense of shame and the feeling that the conversation would be just too embarrassing to contemplate.

Again, these children need to be able to withdraw, to some degree at least, from the family conflict and that may be facilitated by the pursuit of social and sporting interests. The emotional upheaval and, in particular, the conflict of loyalties is not something that can be cured instantly but something which will need to be resolved over a period of time.

It is obviously of great importance that parental expectations be defined in the light of the new family structure. At the most elementery level this should involve explaining to the child that although the relationship between the mother and father didn't work out it was not the child's fault and need have no bearing upon his relationship with either parent. The child should never be made to feel that he is obliged or expected to choose between one parent and the other. It should normally be explained that the differences between the parents are purely personal ones and that they will not be canvassed with the child. If it is at all possible the child should be informed that the arrangements for custody and access have been agreed upon

by both parents as being the best arrangement that could
be made for him. Whatever the feelings of the custodial
parent the child should be encouraged to maintain a close
relationship with the other parent. He should be encouraged
to enjoy periods of access and to contact the other parent
from time to time by telephone even if additional face to
face contact is not possible. At the same time, both parents
should understand the importance of the child forging his
own life and arrangements for access should take into
account any regular commitments the child has.

It may also be advisable to discuss with children the
manner in which the family unit will function and in
particular, the role which they are expected to play.
Constraints of time and money may mean that there are
certain changes which have to be made to their routine.
You may not be able to do certain things for them that
the parents of their peers do. They may also have to
shoulder more of the household chores than they have been
accustomed to doing. The need for these things should be
explained clearly but firmly. Other children may display
a great interest in entitlements.

A child may discover that a court is likely to let children
live with whichever parent they choose. In some cases this
has led to children answering any threat of discipline or
restrictions with the threat to pack up and go to live with
the other parent. If you give in under the compulsion of
such a threat then any effective discipline will become
impossible. The only way to treat such a threat is to call
the child's bluff. If there is not too much residual
antagonism between you and your former spouse you may
be able to discuss the situation openly and seek to enlist
his help. One of my closest friends had been denied access
to his sons for three years and would have given almost
anything to have more time with them when access was
finally resumed. In the midst of that yearning his former
wife approached him and explained that the boys, who were
then aged thirteen and fifteen, were constantly threatening
that if she didn't let them go out at night they would go

to live with Dad. He was a man who wanted his children but also wanted to prevent them from becoming devious and manipulative. During the next period of access he explained to them that he was not going to provide a home for them just so they could escape their mother's discipline and that if they ever came to live with him they would find that he was more strict than she was.

If you love your children you have to make sure that they are disciplined. Equally, of course, you have to make sure that they know that they are loved. One of the difficulties about this age is that children frequently seem to behave so badly that life seems to be a constant battle to keep them in line. In the struggle to maintain control it is sometimes easy to overlook their need for warmth and affection.

Parenting After Divorce

One thing that can be said with absolute confidence about being a single parent—or a divorced parent with custody of the children—is that it isn't easy. After years of marriage you may be thrust into it quite unprepared for a host of problems you have never even considered. Those problems will have to be resolved at a time when you are perhaps still distraught from the break-up of your marriage and uncertain as to what the future may hold. You may have consoled yourself with the thought that ''at least you'll have the children—only to find that they are so upset and badly behaved that they feel more like a millstone than a life raft. Furthermore, you may see each outburst of distress or bad behaviour as a further indication of the harm done to them by your failure to keep the family together. You may look to the children's future with great uncertainty and anxiety.

The problems faced by single parents are many and varied and it would be impossible to canvass adequately every problem likely to arise. Despite this I would like to offer some advice:

(a) **Tell the truth in love.**

It should normally be better to tell a child the truth even if it is unpalatable than to permit him to cling to hopes or dreams which you know are not going to be realised. If the other parent is not likely to return then don't pretend that he is. The child may be upset to think that Dad is not coming home again but, in the long run, that distress cannot be avoided and your pretence may merely prolong the anguish and undermine the child's trust in you. If your child comes home and finds you in tears or obvious distress don't brush aside questions with a brave "Nothing!". Tell him truthfully that you are upset about the separation or about whatever specific thing has caused your distress. A child who is at all perceptive is not likely to believe that there is nothing wrong and a brusque dismissal of questions may simply provoke speculation about all kinds of terrible things which may be far worse than the truth.

This general principle may sometimes have to give way, however, when questions are asked about the cause of the separation or about the other spouse. If your twelve-year-old daughter wants to know why Daddy doesn't live at home any more, a reply implying that he would "rather live with that tart with the blonde dye in her hair than his children" will prove singularly unhelpful. It should be noted that the biblical injunction is not merely to tell the truth but to speak it with love. Normally this simply means when one tells the truth one must do so in an atmosphere of love and concern for the person to whom one is speaking. Sometimes, however, a divorced parent is obliged to walk a tightrope maintaining the most precarious balance between the dictates of truth and those of love and compassion.

(b) **Don't criticise your former spouse in front of the children.**

When you have been badly hurt it is natural that you should feel angry and upset and that you should talk to other people about the way you feel. It can be very important to get things off your chest. In these circumstances it is natural that a single parent should slip into the habit of complaining to his children about the other parent. There may be a subconscious desire to evoke their sympathy and support. If custody proceedings are still pending there may be a desire to win the children over to your side. This problem can become very serious. It sometimes blossoms into a tug-of-war in which each parent desperately tries to pull the children in his or her direction. Of course, it is the children who feel the strain, frequently suffering quite severe emotional or psychological problems and sometimes reaching the point where they have lost all respect for both parents. The merits of the marital conflict between you and your former spouse are not the business of the children. Furthermore, as mentioned earlier, it is almost invariably in the children's interest that they maintain a positive relationship with both parents. If you are wise you will foster that relationship no matter what your feelings may be for your former spouse. Consequently, even when the other parent fails to arrive at the appointed time for access, forgets a birthday or otherwise defaults in a manner which directly affects the children you should still be as positive as possible in your comments.

(c) **Don't pump your children concerning your former spouse's activities.**

Divorce Court proceedings are sprinkled with affidavits in which one parent or the other sets out comments which the children have made from time to time concerning various things that the other spouse has said or done. Such comments are usually inadmissable and when the matter is finally heard a judge usually disregards such matters. The practice is grossly unfair. It involves using a child to spy on his mother or father. Even if the information is elicited by subtle questioning, the purpose of which escapes the child, the fact remains that he has been used in a most unfair manner. To carry on in that fashion can only cause trouble in the long run. It may engender bitterness on the part of the former spouse. It may cause him to become suspicious of his child and to censor mentally everything he says in the child's presence. It may even evoke great resentment in the child himself if and when he realises that he has been used in this fashion.

Your children should be entitled to enjoy their relationship with you free from the fear that they are going to be cross-examined about everything which you have done together. Equally, they have the right to enjoy their relationship with their other parent without being cross-examined about that. There is nothing wrong with asking the children whether they had a good time when they return from a period of access. If they want to talk about an exciting outing then there is nothing wrong with listening and making positive comments to indicate that you are pleased that they had a good time. It is when a parent goes beyond that and starts prying about personal details that the difficulty arises.

(d) **Don't try to be more than a good mother or father.**
Remember that your children have two parents, notwithstanding the separation or divorce. Many single parents make the mistake of trying to crowd out the other parent. Sometimes that is done deliberately because of resentment and hostility, the feeling that the other parent forfeited the right to consideration. In other cases the parent slips into the practice of trying to fulfil the other parent's role because the other parent is not on the scene for most of the time. It is, of course, essential that a single parent assume some of the jobs formerly done by the other parent. Yet there is a fine line between carrying out some of the other parent's

jobs and taking over the other parent's role in all respects. A single mother does not need to become an expert on everything. If she has always coped with things like football or limited slip differentials then by all means let her go on doing so but she should not feel obliged to become involved in them merely because her son's father is not there to answer questions. Her ex-husband probably has a telephone connected and would be more than happy to give the benefit of his expertise. Equally, a single father should not feel obliged to become an authority on netball or the latest fashion in hairstyles.

Let me hasten to explain that what I am concerned about is simply that a single parent need not feel under any burden to take over the role of the other parent whatever that role may have been. To attempt to do so will produce nothing but frustration and exhaustion. It may also mean that the other parent is gradually squeezed out of a role which might otherwise have enriched and consolidated the relationship between that parent and the children.

(e) **Don't try to compensate for the separation by relaxing the normal parental restraints.**

This may be characterised by discussing everything rather than laying down rules and by persistently trying to participate in the games and activities which the children pursue—like a mate instead of a parent. In the long run this produces erosion of respect for the parent and, sometimes, resentment of the intrusion. Children have many friends. They have little need of one more. What they do need is the security of a parent who will stand firm like a rock in a storm and will set the parameters for their behaviour. When the children can only live with either their father or their mother it is doubly important that the custodial parent fulfil his or her parental role and refuse to be sidetracked from it by some trendy concept of mateship.

(f) **Don't promote any of your children to the role of co-parent.**

It is easy for a mother to slip into the habit of telling the young son that he will have to be ''the man of the house'' now that Daddy has gone. It is equally easy for a father to encourage a daughter who is helping him with the cleaning and cooking by telling her that she has taken over from her mother. Whilst these comments are well-intentioned and complimentary they sometimes impose an enormous weight of responsibility on the child. It is one thing for a child to take over particular jobs which he feels confident to handle. It is altogether another for him to feel that he has to fill the shoes of his father in terms of overall responsibility for the running of the family. Of course, the parent may have intended no such thing but children can be surprisingly literal and when one parent has gone it is only natural for a child to imagine that a replacement will be needed.

(g) **Don't be embarrassed about your children's nostalgia for times when you were all together.**

During the marriage there will have been happy times that the children may look back on with great affection. They may have photographs, souvenirs or mementos of those occasions which mean a great deal to them. Don't take those things from them or make them feel that they are unable to talk about them in your presence. At a time of distress a child needs to be able to look back on happy times. Furthermore memories of that kind add a note of cohesiveness to the child's life. Now that his parents are separated he may lead two separate existences. It may be important to him to be able to relate those existences to the time when you were all together. The fact that he is nostalgic for times shared with your former spouse does not mean that he doesn't love you or that he wishes to leave you and live with that parent.

(h) **Anything which your children may perceive as posing a threat to their future security should be discussed with them openly.**

Any man introduced to them by their mother, for example, may well be regarded as a potential surrogate father. The reactions of children may range from noisy and perhaps, embarrassing curiosity to overt hostility but whatever the reaction there will be an underlying question, "How is this going to affect me?" Unhappily, that question is rarely asked in a direct manner and, consequently, it is usually left unanswered. It is usually better to offer some explanation than to leave your children to speculate.

(i) **The position of your former spouse in relation to salvation calls for particular sensitivity.**

Children have a happy knack of asking questions which take your breath away, "Why isn't Daddy a Christian?"; "Does that mean that Daddy will go to hell when he dies?" If you are not careful you can provoke a sense of outrage and of bitter resentment not only against you but against God. You can also cause your children enormous anxiety and the sense of utter despair at the thought that the father whom they love so much being eternally dammed. Yet to lie about the matter may be equally dangerous because the children may then blithely raise the matter with your former spouse only to have everything that you have told them contradicted. Some Christian parents try to resolve this dilemma by telling the children that they don't know and that they will have to take it up with the spouse concerned. That inevitably leads to the other parent being asked whether he is a Christian and if the answer is "No," to a theological debate for which the child is ill-equipped either intellectually or emotionally.

There appears to be no perfect answer to this problem but the course which I would suggest as involving the least risk is to simply tell the child that all you can really say is that God loves the other parent very much. You can explain that you really don't know whether he has actually become a Christian or not because that is a matter between him and God. No matter what your private opinion may be, that much is literally true.

Which of the people in the crowd would have given the dying thief on the cross any chance of the salvation which Jesus promised him had they not heard the actual words spoken?

It is usually better if the child is encouraged not to speak to the other parent about a Christian commitment. Any number of reasons can be given for that request. For example, you might be able to say to a child, "Look, I don't want your father to think that you only want to see him because you want him to become a Christian. He wants you to see him because you love him". Whatever the explanation the child can usually be diverted by being encouraged to pray for his father (or mother) instead. Here, too, sensitivity is needed. Unless the child is particularly mature I would suggest a simple prayer along these lines, "Dear Jesus, thank you for my father. I know you love him very much. Please look after him, keep him well and strong and help him to get to know you more and more. Amen".

(j) **Ask for help if your children don't settle down after the divorce.**

Children vary in the extremity and duration of their emotional reactions to the separation and divorce of their parents. Like the adults they go through various emotional stages involving shock, adjustment and, ultimately, the establishment of a new lifestyle. During the initial period of emotional upheaval a whole host of behavioural problems may become apparent. Don't be concerned about that. It is perfectly normal. As the child adjusts to the new situation those behavioural problems usually evaporate. Most children seem to settle down reasonably well within the first year after the separation. If one of your children does not settle down in that time then there may be an underlying problem which is not evident to you.

Sometimes the problem is created by a single unresolved question. The question may be relatively straightforward. A child may feel that his father or mother doesn't love him any more. "If she did she would never have left." Another child may be plagued by something a little more complicated. He may ask for example, "How can I trust God when he lets this sort of thing happen?" Problems of that kind can frequently be resolved quickly and painlessly by an experienced counsellor. Occasionally a child exhibits some more serious kind of personality disorder. That is comparatively rare and when it does occur can usually be identified by a trained counsellor who can then offer advice as to the most appropriate course to pursue.

Parents without custody of their children have different but equally real problems to handle. Here are two suggestions which might help:

(a) **Don't try to buy your children with expensive presents and exotic outings.**

Often non-custodial parents seek to cement the relationship with their children by buying them trail bikes, video cassette recorders, computers and other expensive presents. Others seek to achieve the same thing by trying to make each access period the occasion of a visit to a circus, a lion park, aquatic carnival or some other place intended to produce great excitement or interest. Practices of this kind will often lead the custodial parent to believe you are trying to buy the affection of the children with a view to obtaining custody. In the long run it will also produce problems for you because you will be unable to sustain the initial burst of excitement and will be forced to cope with unrealistic expectations which you yourself have created. A good long-term relationship must be based upon mutual love and affection rather than the provision of exciting things.

(b) **Try to make them feel that your house is their other home.**

If you do not have custody of your children, you may find it adds some measure of security to your relationship with them if they can see you at your home and, preferably, if they can have some clothes or toys which remain there permanently. The presence of such things in your home will be a tangible promise of further visits. Unless the children are very young it will usually be helpful for them to stay overnight at regular intervals. If you have a spare room you might allocate it specifically to them. Don't ignore them but don't go out of your way to pamper them. There will be an air of artificiality about that kind of treatment which may prevent them from feeling at home. Let them help with chores or participate in whatever you are doing.

Whether you have custody or not, remind yourself frequently that your responsibility is simply to care for your children.

God does not expect you to carry them around on your back as a burden. He has not only forgiven you your mistakes, he has heard your prayers for your children and will nurture them in the years to come.

CHAPTER TWENTY

Once Bitten, Twice Shy

Few of those who have survived shipwreck on the sea of matrimony adhere to their initial resolutions to avoid further entanglements with the opposite sex. There may be a moment at which they are certain that they will live out their lives as recluses possibly in a monastery or convent, but sooner or later someone will turn up who will galvanise those jaded red corpuscles into a frenzy.

In evaluating a relationship it might be useful to bear in mind the amount of time which has passed since your marriage broke up. It takes time to wend one's way through the emotional morass that follows the termination of a marriage. Within that morass there are pitfalls including the risk of a rebound romance based upon one's need for support and general insecurity rather than those qualities which give rise to a lasting and mature relationship. A further problem is that it takes some time for it to sink in that the first marriage has finished. Until that point is finally reached it can be very difficult to establish the foundations for a lasting relationship with someone else.

Many people vacillate in their attitude to a former spouse. One day they may be angry about the way in which they have been treated. The next day there may be a feeling of resignation about that marriage and a desire to start again. The person may find himself making comments such as, "One door closes and another opens". The next day something may happen which triggers a memory of happy times together. Abruptly the resignation has given way to nostalgia and a real sense of loss. Hopes of a reconciliation may be kindled, dashed and then revived.

The essence of any marriage is commitment. The wedding ceremony includes as part of the vows the phrase "forsaking all others". You simply cannot make a commitment of that kind if you are not sure that you are no longer committed to your former spouse. If you are still emotionally entangled to the point where you are still hoping for a reconciliation then you should not contemplate remarriage. To do so would be completely unfair. The only vow you would be ready to make would be one professing undying commitment—unless your former spouse came back.

In the first few months after the termination of a marriage a great deal of time is usually spent on looking back to things that went wrong and to the marriage itself. That is not necessarily a bad thing. As discussed earlier there is a great need for people to work through a period of mourning. Nonetheless, it is very difficult for a person who is looking back to a former marriage and still working through the pain associated with its breakdown to bring to any new relationship the positive qualities that it demands. A new husband or wife is entitled to expect that his or her spouse will bring to the marriage an undivided love and a readiness to look forward to their future together with eagerness and determination. A person cannot do that if he is still at the stage where he is constantly looking back to the former marriage and is unable to offer the new relationship his full attention and involvement.

Conversation is frequently a good indicator. If you are still spending a great deal of time talking to the new man or woman in your life about your former marriage and everything that went wrong with it then you are probably not at the stage where you could make a wholehearted commitment. The other person may be very sympathetic but that will be beside the point. The problem is with you, not him or her. Anyone who has really reached the point of making a lifelong commitment should be living in the present and delighting in plans for the future, not living in the past.

The emotional investment which you have in the former marriage will make it very difficult for you to assess your own feelings in relation to someone else. If you have doubts it is better to resolve them before the marriage than afterwards. A little more time may enable you to resolve your feelings and assess whether what you feel for this person is the kind of love that you would expect to bring to a new marriage or mere gratitude, companionship, physical attraction or a host of other things. It may also be of assistance to go out with other people. If you have been married for a number of years then it may have been a very long time since you were involved with anyone else romantically. If you are measuring your feelings for someone by comparison with your former spouse then you may be seriously misled. It will be much easier if you have had the opportunity of going out with other people or, at least, have considerable contact with them.

If you are satisfied that sufficient time has elapsed to enable you to settle down emotionally, and that will not usually happen in less than twelve to eighteen months, then it may still be useful to pause and take stock of yourself. If the emotional aftermath has cleared you should be able to look back at least with some degree of objectivity and realise that you have not only grown in maturity but you have also learnt a great deal about yourself. Look at your strengths and weaknesses. Then look at your intended mate. What kind of a person is he or she? Are you making the same kind of mistake that you made before? If you take a step back and try to view the situation objectively does the relationship still look promising or are there red lights flashing? Can you see substantial areas of incompatibility?

The next question which should be asked is whether the relationship between you is a healthy one? A healthy relationship is one in which there is give and take: that is, one in which there is a significant degree of inter-dependence.

A friend of mine has suggested that in a really good relationship it is not so much a matter of give and take but rather a matter of giving on both sides so that the taking is in reality little more than receiving. Whilst there is a great element of truth in that I believe it is also true that a husband and wife should support each other. A healthy relationship is not one in which one person is predominantly a taker. There are obvious exceptions such as that which occurs when one party to a marriage becomes crippled or seriously ill, but in normal circumstances a marriage in which one person clings to the other and draws strength and support without reciprocating is likely to encounter difficulties. The person who has been hurt very badly by the breakup of his first marriage may well find that he has this kind of demanding attitude though he may never have thought about it. That may not be his fault, he may be so badly hurt that he is able to contribute very little. Furthermore, the person with whom he has now become involved may genuinely take delight in binding up his wounds and helping him get back on his feet. In a very real sense they may both be getting something out of the relationship. That kind of dependent relationship is perfectly valid. It may involve not only a romantic kind of involvement but also the kind of Christian love that makes one want to support a brother or sister in need. Yet if marriage is contemplated, it would be wise to look for a degree of healing which would permit the relationship to become more evenly balanced in terms of mutual dependence.

There are, of course, all kinds of issues which are important to a marital relationship and I will not attempt to canvas them all. For the present I am only concerned with the unique position in which divorced people contemplating remarriage find themselves.

One further area which is particularly important is that of the parties' own Christian beliefs. A good deal of attention has been rightly focused on the difficulties which may occur when a Christian marries a non-Christian. St Paul in his second letter to the Corinthians advised them not to be "unequally yoked together with unbelievers".[32] That is not a matter of rejecting a non-believer as unworthy but simply an acknowledgement that a Christian has made a commitment which has to be the first priority in his life. If he marries someone whose priorities and aspirations are incompatible with that there will inevitably be conflict. If you are to marry a non-Christian you will need to consider the likely areas of conflict and discuss them with your intended partner.

When one or both parties to an intended marriage have been divorced there is a need to go beyond the mere fact that both are Christians, as important as that is, and confront specifically their beliefs about divorce and remarriage. I have discussed this aspect earlier. If it is a particular problem to you please re-read what I have written in Part I, pray about it, and discuss it with the other person concerned. You must face up to the problem and try to thrash it out between you. If you simply ignore it, it may provide an undercurrent of guilt and insecurity which will undermine your marriage.

One of my clients whom I will call John had been married and divorced at a comparatively early age. He had then become a Christian and in due course met his second wife, Sarah. Sarah had been a Jewish girl who, after much soul-searching had been converted to Christianity. As time went by John became more involved in Christian work and was ultimately appointed a full-time pastor of his church. By this time he and Sarah had been blessed with three lovely young children. His wife helped him in his ministry and they gave every appearance of having a close, loving relationship. Then John was dismissed from his position by the elders of his church. They had found out that John was divorced and explained that since God did not recognise John's divorce his second marriage was not valid and the relationship was one of flagrant adultery. They told him that they could not permit anyone living in open immorality to minister in the church and they had no alternative but to sack him. That was a bitter blow to John and although he quickly found another job it was apparent that he had been deeply hurt. Unhappily, the hurt went deeper than he realised. Whilst he rejected the proposition that he was living in adultery and felt, deep in his heart, that his marriage was part of God's blessing, Sarah began to brood about it and from that moment on the relationship began to deteriorate. When she finally left John, taking the three children with her, she also left behind her Christian faith. It is easy to be critical of those men but they were no doubt sincere. The point that I wish to make is simply that Sarah had not worked through those issues before her marriage to John and, consequently, fell prey to guilt and doubt when this kind of criticism came.

Whilst it is wise to be cautious you need to remember that your experiences will inevitably throw up a whole series of fears which can sap your confidence in even the strongest relationship. You may find yourself asking questions such as, "How can I be sure that it will last this time?" The answer to that question is, of course, that husbands and wives are almost the only important acquisitions in life which come without a guarantee. Whether it is your first marriage or your third no one can assure you that you are going to live happily ever after. What can be said is that many divorced people are unduly pessimistic about marriage. Most of them do ultimately remarry and most of those marriages are successful. People frequently bring to subsequent marriages a degree of maturity and a determination to make things work which offers a greater chance of sucess than in first marriages.

Another fear is that the other person will betray them. That is, of course, conceivable but people are less likely to approach a subsequent marriage with rose-coloured glasses and less likely to miss the warning signs. The fact that you have been hurt once does not mean that you are going to be hurt again. To assume that one wife is going to let you down just because another has is as illogical as assuming that all men steal cars because some do. The answer to this kind of fear is to commit it to God and to permit time and continued contact to resolve any qualms that you have. A relationship of trust takes time to develop.

Many divorced people are terrified of making the same mistakes again. Whilst you may rest assured that you have not suddenly become infallible you are not likely to repeat the mistakes you have made if you are determined to learn from them. There are, of course, those who simply look back on the past marriage with no acknowledgement of error on their part and explain the divorce by blaming it entirely upon their former spouse. There is an old adage which says that those who fail to learn the lessons of history are doomed to repeat it. It is those who accept no responsibility for their own part in the breakdown of a former marriage who are likely to make the same mistakes again.

A question commonly asked is, "Can I really be happy again?" The answer to that question depends very much upon the attitude of the person asking it. There are those who go from one marriage to another constantly seeking someone who can confer happiness upon them. I remember chatting to a young man who had just finished his third short marriage expounding that hope with a note of near desperation. Some Christians approach God with the same kind of attitude. Most of their prayers really boil down to a single cry, "Lord make me happy!"

Yet happiness is not something which one catches like measles. There is a degree to which a person makes his own happiness and that is especially so within marriage. It has been truly said that "happiness is not so much a matter of what you have but what you enjoy". You can decide, almost cold-bloodedly, that you are going to enjoy things, that you are going to appreciate the good things of life. You can choose to turn your back on the things that have gone wrong and concentrate on what you do have. You can choose to exercise faith that God is bringing good out of disaster. You can learn to appreciate a spouse. You can learn to stop overlooking your children and rejoice in the little things that they do or, if they are older, in the things they refrain from doing.

Another great source of happiness is praise. Some Christians respond to trials by the most gloomy and pessimistic of prayers. "Dear Lord, you know how terrible my life is. I don't know where to turn. God, everything just seems hopeless. You have got to do something or I don't know how I will stand it..." Others approach the matter more positively. They look back and remember all those times in the past when they had been confronted by problems but when God provided the answers. When they pray their prayers are not only full of faith but full of thanksgiving. "Father, I just thank you that you love me. I am conscious of your unfailing goodness. You have looked after me all my life and done so much for me. Now I have this problem and I am so grateful that I don't have to bear it by myself. I thank you that you will see me through this difficult time and I don't have to let it weigh me down or become depressed. What a relief it is to know that you shoulder my burdens for me". If you work on your happiness then you will bring a real joy into your relationship. If you remarry with the attitude that it is up to your new husband or wife to make you happy you will inevitably be disappointed.

Ultimately, what you have to do is to trust God to guide you as to whether or not the relationship is the right one. I firmly believe that one of the reasons for the great proliferation of theological dogma concerning divorce and remarriage is a reluctance to trust God to provide guidance in particular concrete situations. There is no substitute. You simply have to pray it through. If you do so he will either confirm that it is right or show you that it is not. That is not to say that you throw your commonsense out the window. God expects you to exercise the intelligence and judgement he gave you. But if you do your part and you really are willing to be corrected then God will not permit you to blunder into disaster. If you feel it is right to remarry then go ahead with honest confidence. Do not permit yourself to be weighed down by crippling fears. Whatever you do, don't hold back from a wholehearted investment of love and devotion because of anxiety that things might go wrong. To do so is simply to court the very thing of which you are afraid. If God has led you into that situation then he will see you through it. Put the past behind you and your fears with it. You will have disagreements and, perhaps, fights. Married life is not an unending bouquet of roses or, if it is, it is one in which the thorns are still attached to the stems.

When difficulties come, don't panic. It may be natural for all your anxieties to rear up and for you to think, "Oh no, here we go again!" When that happens you really must take yourself aside and speak to yourself sternly. That is not fair either to your spouse or to yourself. How would you like to be judged on the basis of another person's past misconduct? Remember that this is a new situation. Your new commitment demands that you try to resolve any difficulties between you in an attitude of love, reconciliation and understanding and that you do not permit the hurts of the past to infect the present.

When you are contemplating remarriage remember that the purpose of the exercise is not to obtain another mother or father for your children. They already have two parents. The purpose of the exercise is to obtain a life-long mate, someone with whom you truly can become one flesh. Your children may resent that because they may see the person you intend marrying as someone who is seeking to supplant the other parent. You need to exercise a great deal of sensitivity about this. An unthinking introduction of someone as "your new Daddy" or someone who is going to be "your mother now" may cause enormous problems. The person you intend marrying may not have any intention of having the children accept him in place of the other parent but the children may nonetheless perceive his entry into the family unit as a very threatening event. Not only does it herald the possible displacement of the other parent, but it may mean that their relationship with you is relegated to second place.

The resultant climate of resentment and suspicion may cause misunderstanding and other difficulties. These problems may well take considerable time to resolve. It is simply not reasonable to expect children to adjust overnight to such a radical change in their family structure. It is equally unrealistic to expect that a strong and loving relationship will be forged between stepparent and stepchildren instantly. A relationship of that kind has to be built up and that will require both patience and sensitivity upon the part of the stepparent. Yet in the long run the problems can be overcome and if the stepparent in particular continues to offer the child unconditional love a strong relationship can be forged. It will not be the same as the relationship between the children and the other natural parent. That parent will continue to be their mother or father. But there will be a new relationship which will become a positive element in their lives.

Divorced people contemplating remarriage frequently experience near panic when their children express antipathy to their new partners. Christians in particular are likely to consider withdrawing from the proposed marriage. They frequently have an overdeveloped sense of guilt and anxiety concerning their children and may confront themselves with emotionally charged ultimatums such as, "Shouldn't I put the happiness of my children before my own?" Whilst it is perfectly understandable that Christian parents should be concerned about their children a question such as the one I have quoted implicitly assumes that the happiness of their children will be forever destroyed if the marriage proceeds. That is almost certainly untrue.

If you look at the situation objectively you will probably find that it is not the particular person to whom your children object but the simple fact that you are contemplating marrying anyone. That is a relatively sophisticated concept and one which children may not be able to grasp, much less articulate. Yet if you examine the situation carefully you may well come to realise that similar objections would be raised to any person no matter how patient, loving and kind he or she might be. That may be so even if the children express a strong personal dislike for your intended partner and even if they assure you that they would be quite happy to see you marry someone else. They may be quite sincere, but there is a sense in which they can feel secure in that assertion because marriage to anyone else is not contemplated.

I am not, of course, suggesting that Christians should simply ignore their children's interests. If you were to note that your children were actually being badly treated by your proposed partner then that should lead you to reconsider the proposed marriage. Would you really want to marry someone who was impatient, insensitive and generally behaved in a hurtful way towards children? More commonly, however, you will find that the problem stems from anxiety, misunderstanding and the fact that the children have not had sufficient time to come to terms with the new situation. If you form a close loving relationship with someone and are convinced that it is God's will you should marry, then you should go ahead.

If it is at all possible you should permit your children to have as much contact as possible with that other person so that they will already be on friendly terms with him when you inform them of your intended marriage. When you do break the news you should tell them that your new spouse will be their friend. The new spouse will not be trying to take the place of their mother or father. The children already have another parent and will continue to have the same degree of contact with him or her as they have done in the past. They will not be expected to call the new spouse "Mummy" or "Daddy" but "Aunty Sue" or "Uncle Bob" or whatever other form of address seems suitable. A mother will also need to explain to the children that whilst her surname will change as a result of the marriage theirs will not. In short, the children should be made to realise that this new relationship is essentially one between you and your new spouse which affects them indirectly because of their presence in your home even if that presence is limited to periods of access. They should be made to understand that the relationship is not some sort of catastrophic event which is likely to rupture the relationship with the other parent or put at risk the relationship with you.

It is also advisable to make these things equally clear to your former spouse. Notice of an intended remarriage sometimes seems to cause difficulties. Long-resolved differences over the custody and/or access may suddenly erupt again. Occasionally this is due to jealousy born of a lingering possessiveness. The other spouse may have failed to come to terms with the fact that the marriage is really over. More commonly, however, it is the product of apprehension concerning the relationship with their children. A mother may begin to wonder whether the woman who has taken her place as wife will endeavour to take her place as mother. Any reference to a new "Mum" will be seen as a confirmation of the worst of her fears. To a father the suggestion that the children adopt the surname of their mother's new husband may be seen as an endeavour to pass them off as the other man's children and to erase totally any tangible link with him. The custodial parent may regard these fears as fanciful and unreasonable but they are nonetheless real to the other parent. If you wish to allay your former spouse's fears and avoid the risk of future conflict then it is best to raise the matter directly and give assurances that none of those things are contemplated. That can be done either by letter or telephone but it should be done in a very matter-of-fact manner.

Many Christian parents who have custody seem to feel a strong desire to obtain a formal adoption order in favour of themselves and the new spouse specially if that spouse is a Christian. In law the other natural parent then ceases to be the mother or father of the child. The new spouse becomes the parent in his place. However, if the other natural parent declines to consent to such an order the court will not grant the application unless there are strong reasons for dispensing with his or her consent.

Most natural parents react to the very suggestion of such an order with a mixture of outrage and panic. That is perfectly understandable because what is contemplated is not a mere change of name with all of the perceived risks to the relationship which I have already mentioned but an actual termination of the relationship itself. Such a termination has far-reaching consequences. It means that never again will that parent be able to seek the court's assistance to obtain access to his child. The court will simply refuse to recognise him as a parent. It also means that, in the event of his death, the child will not receive any part of his estate unless specifically named in the will. The child may obtain a certain degree of perceived security from an adoption order particularly if he has come from a troubled family background but few non-custodial parents are willing to consent to such a course. In fact, even parents who have not seen their children for several years frequently refuse to consent to such an adoption. The finality of it and the fact that it has the effect of severing the bonds of parentage usually are too much to be faced.

The compromise of changing the child's surname is sometimes adopted when the mother has custody but that, too, has its problems. In the first place, whilst it may have some initial value in enabling the child to feel more secure as a member of the new family unit the child may ultimately wish to return to the former name. That is not merely a matter of petulance. It may be important for a child's sense of identity. Furthermore, it is also likely to produce a great deal of opposition and resentment on the part of the natural father whose feelings should be considered simply as a Christian duty. If you have the attitude of compassion which our Lord has commanded you to have even towards those who "despitefully use you" then why cause needless distress? Furthermore, even if you decide to ignore your former spouse's feelings, it by no means follows that a court will adopt the same attitude. It is quite likely that you will change the child's name only to find that he obtains a court order compelling you to change it back again. That may cause considerable confusion and distress for the child, and produce an atmosphere of confrontation between you and your former spouse which may take months to resolve.

Finally I believe that if you are contemplating any of these steps you should seriously question your motives. Certainly, I have met some very fine Christian couples who had the purest of motives and have been quite certain that God has led them to seek an order for adoption because that would foster a degree of security which was important to the child at its particular stage of development. Unhappily, I believe that the motive is more frequently a matter of simple insecurity on the part of the custodial parent and the new spouse. If you are merely trying to entrench your custodial position or further secure your relationship with the child then steps of this kind are not the way to do it. Your security in that relationship should depend upon nothing but your determination to be as loving and caring as you can and your trust in God that he will bind you all together and overcome any problems that may arise. Legal decrees and clever manoeuvres are a poor substitute for that kind of faith.

PART FIVE

THE LAW

CHAPTER TWENTY-ONE

Law and Morality

Christians hold widely varying attitudes towards the law.

At one extreme there are those who see the practice of law as being the very antithesis of Christian principles such as love, forgiveness and proper moral values. Some see it as little different from the work of the Devil himself. I have actually heard Christians assert that the practice of law is not a proper profession for a Christian to pursue. Some years ago I remember mentioning to a clergyman friend my involvement with the Lawyers Christian Fellowship. My friend chuckled, "Christian lawyers? That is a contradiction in terms!" He was only half-joking and my rejoinder, "You mean like practical theology?" did little to widen his grin.

At the other extreme are those who see the law as a great tool for the imposition of proper Christian standards. Some people tend to quote with relish St Paul's description in his letter to the Romans (13:6) of the authorities as "God's agents for punishment". (NEB) They sincerely feel that anything which is immoral should be illegal. Accordingly, it can fairly be asserted that law and morality are, or at least should be, co-extensive. Few would dispute that the Spanish inquisitors went too far, though many would feel that at least they were on the right track.

Between these extremes lie hosts of more moderate points of view.

These attitudes towards the law are also reflected to some

degree in the expectations that Christians have of the law and, more particularly, of the courts. This diversity of expectations is, of course, shared with the community at large. At one extreme there are people who are absolutely certain that any involvement they may have with a court will end in unmitigated disaster. Such people may have in mind Jesus' suggestion in Matthew 5:25 that you settle with your adversary before he brings you before a court. The implication which some seem to draw from that story is that they should settle because they'll never get justice once they get there. More commonly, however, one encounters a faith in the ability of the judges and magistrates to dispense justice which to a lawyer is bewilderingly naive. This kind of faith is by no means unique to Christians. Frequently people who have no religious faith of any kind display the most childlike trust in the judicial system. One may explain that a judge is merely a fallible human being like the rest of us and that he has only the demeanour of the witnesses and the plausibility or otherwise of their evidence to assist him in determining who is telling the truth. Consequently if one man says the light was red and another man says the light was green the judge may believe the man with the most convincing manner rather than the man who is telling the truth.

In other cases an experienced and competent lawyer may explain to his client that, however just he may feel his claim to be, it is doomed to failure because it is barred by a Statute of Limitations or some other insuperable legal barrier. In such circumstances it is not uncommon for the bewildered lawyer to be confronted by a client who smiles deprecatingly, shakes his head and says in a condescending fashion, "That can't be right. Don't you believe in justice?" When one explains that the case will be heard in a court of law and not necessarily in a court of justice the client is aghast at such "blasphemy". Some almost seem tempted to move their chair back from the desk in case they are struck by the inevitable lightning bolt.

These false expectations are so entrenched that they prevent some people from seeing that no decision a judge could give in their particular cases would solve the real problem because it is one which simply cannot be resolved by legal process. Let me explain by means of an example.

About twelve years ago I was involved in a case concerning the custody of a little girl, then aged nine. There was a great deal of animosity between the parents, both of whom desperately wanted the child. She had become the rope in a vicious tug-of-war between them. Each had told her that the other was the most depraved human being imaginable and they repeated that refrain in different ways at every opportunity. The little girl had been cajoled, bribed, threatened, and ultimately, kidnapped on no less than three occasions. By the time the matter finally came before a court she had regressed from a bright little girl who had usually been at the top of her class to a withdrawn and frightened child who was frequently incontinent and who communicated, if at all, by disjointed words interspersed with baby sounds. She had been examined by no less than four psychiatrists who all agreed that she was seriously disturbed and might never fully recover. The poor child had been dealt an appalling psychological blow by the mutual enmity which existed between her parents. She had been placed in a position where any display of affection for one parent was seen as a betrayal of the other. In these circumstances what could a judge do? The only power he had was to decide which of the two parents should have custody and since they were both equally afflicted by bitterness there was little to choose between them. Yet each parent seemed to have this faith that somehow what the judge did would provide a solution to the problem. He would wave his judicial wand and the little girl would be well and happy again. If only life were so simple! What was required was a decision by each parent to stop hurting the other and to join forces to create an atmosphere in which their daughter might be healed. But, of course, no judge can force people to change their attitudes in that manner.

The traditional view which Christians have taken concerning the role of law in society is that it is a gift of God to preserve the peace and maintain order. This role is fostered by recognising a series of rights and obligations, the vast preponderance of which owe their origin to the Judeo-Christian ethic which emerges from the Bible. Much of the law of negligence, for example, is derived from the old case of *Donoghue v Stevenson*[33] in which the court posed the question put to Jesus, "Who is my neighbour?" In answering that question the court laid down the rule that a person had a duty of care toward any other person whom he might reasonably expect to be affected by his actions. The laws established to implement these principles are influenced, of course, by other factors such as the practicability or otherwise of the particular measures and the need to prevent infringements of other rights recognised by the law. In addition, modern law reform is increasingly influenced by purely political considerations.

It is important to recognise that the law does not exist to impose a uniform code of morality upon the community. Nor should it seek to do so.

Whilst it is true to say that such laws as do exist should be morally right, that is, they should be humane and just, the converse is not true. Not all moral principles should be reflected in sanctions imposed by the law. Accordingly, one may hate one's brother without infringing the law but any attempt to kill or injure him will result in the imposition of the penalties prescribed for the particular offences committed. For the same reason immoral acts such as selfishness or gluttony are not crimes punishable by the state.

Nonetheless many Christians still assume that whatever is wrong should be unlawful. It is for this reason that one prominent Christian group in Australia felt constrained to campaign against a proposal to decriminalise attempted suicide. I doubt if those sincere people really saw any virtue in having a policeman drag a distraught woman from the edge of a cliff only to snarl at her, "We'll teach you to be so distressed as to attempt suicide. We'll throw you in a cell for a few months; that will fix you!" Yet they felt locked into adopting a position which they must have known would exacerbate rather than solve the problem.

Some assert that the more serious acts of immorality should be subject to criminal sanctions whilst the less serious acts could be left as matters of private conscience. Both these views gained considerable support from the "educative" theory of law. That theory holds that even if the law prohibiting a certain action is unenforceable or if its enforcement would actually be counterproductive the act in question should still be prohibited because the mere fact that conduct of a particular kind of illegal will "educate" people into realising that it is wrong.

There are serious objections to this theory despite the eminence of some of its adherents. In the first place, it simply does not work. The prohibition era in the United States is but one of many examples afforded by history of the speciousness of such an argument. In the long run the law does not impose community standards; it reflects them. In the second place, the question has to be asked, "By what criteria can we distinguish between more serious and less serious breaches of a moral code? Is there any scriptural support, for example, for the proposition that stealing is more serious than adultery to take two examples taken from the Ten Commandments?

In practice the law is usually confined to protecting people against the infringement of their rights by others and does not trespass into the area of morality unconnected with such rights. For this reason the criminal law does not prohibit adultery but it does prohibit rape. When this distinction is overlooked confusion results.

There have been few areas of law in which such confusion has been more evident than divorce. Lawyers have a saying, "hard cases make bad law", which refers to the manner in which difficult situations can sometimes induce the formulation of principles which fit those situations but produce injustice in others. The following passage from the report of the Committee on One Parent Families chaired by Sir Morris Finer suggests that this maxim also held true in earlier ages:

The practical realities of life in the Middle Ages demanded

a method of legitimate avoidance of the rigours of the doctrine of indissolubility. The church provided such a method by developing an elaborate theory of nullity. It was argued that only a valid, consummated, Christian marriage was indissoluble. If an impediment to the validity of a marriage had existed when it was contracted, then that marriage would be held by the ecclesiastical courts never to have taken place at all. Many impediments were soon established; the most important were the degrees of consanguinity and affinity within which marriage was prohibited. Before the Lateran Council of 1215, marriage was forbidden between persons to the seventh degree of blood relationship; afterwards the prohibition was narrowed to the fourth degree, that is, to third cousins. To the impediments of blood were added those of affinity. Since sexual union made man and woman one flesh, it followed that all the blood kinswomen of a man's wife or even of his mistress, were themselves connected to him by affinity. To the impediments of sexual affinity the church then added yet another series created by the spiritual relationships of godchildren. No wonder that Mr Joseph Jackson is moved to speak of the law of affinity as "a mixture of mathematics and mysticism", and that Pollack and Maitland write of "the incalculable harm done by a marriage law which was a maze of flighty fancies and misapplied logic". By such extravagant doctrines, the canonists enabled the church of Rome to square the matrimonial circle and to maintain the theory of indissoluble marriages whilst providing the practical freedom of divorce *a vinculo*. In a society in which most marriages took place within small and close-knit communities, it was far more likely than not that some grounds for nullity would be available; and the system may sometimes have been of benefit to an ill-matched pair. Its principal use, however, was as a "means of obliging the great ones of the earth" and augmenting papal revenues.[34]

The absurdity of such a law was obvious. "It was said . . . that marriage could be annulled because a person had stood

godfather to his wife's cousin. The marriage of Roger Don-
nington was declared null and void because before its cele-
bration he had had sexual intercourse with the third cousin
of his future wife".[35]

In England the questions of marriage and divorce were
regulated by the ecclesiastical courts from the time of
William the Conqueror until 1857. In the early years the
courts recognised decrees of nullity and separation and
decrees of the Pope. Papal divorce decrees were based upon
the so-called Petrine privilege which was said to be implicit
in Jesus' word to Peter "I will give you the keys to the
kingdom of heaven and whatever you bind on earth shall be
bound in heaven, and whatever you loose on earth shall be
loosed in heaven".[36] This was interpreted as giving authority
to Peter and subsequent Popes to loose the bonds of matrimony in special circumstances. In addition, reliance was on
the Pauline privilege which was based upon the passage in 1
Corinthians 7:10–15 and which was said to give the Pope
authority in respect of mixed marriages.

Papal divorce decrees ceased to have any legal effect in
England in 1553. Nonetheless, marital relationships still
broke down and the wealthy continued to press for some
means of ensuring that their estates did not pass to estranged
wives. In time a cumbersome and expensive means of parliamentary divorce emerged; the first being granted in 1668. As
John Wade points out, "a parliamentary divorce cost between six hundred pounds and a thousand pounds in times
when a soldier earned about fourteen pounds per year and a
tradesman about forty-five pounds per year. Truly respectable divorce was the privilege of the healthy".[37] This situation led to considerable criticism exemplified, perhaps, by a
splendidly sarcastic judgement attributed to Mr Justice
Maule in 1884,

Prisoner, you have been convicted of the grave crime of
bigamy. The evidence is clear that your wife left you and
your children to live in adultery with another man, and

that you then intermarried with another woman, your wife being still alive. You say that this prosecution is an instrument of extortion on the part of the adulterer. Be it so; yet you had no right to take the law into your own hands. I will tell you what you ought to have done; and, if you say you did not know, I must tell you that the law conclusively presumes that you did. You ought to have instructed your attorney to bring an action against the seducer of your wife for criminal conversation. That would have cost you about a hundred pounds. When you had recovered (though not necessarily actually obtained) substantial damages against him, you should have instructed your proctor to sue in the Ecclesiastical Courts for a divorce *a mensa et toro*. That would have cost you two hundred or three hundred pounds more. When you had obtained a divorce *a mensa et toro* you should have appeared by counsel before the House of Lords in order to obtain a private Act of Parliament for a divorce *a vinculo matrimonii*, which would have rendered you free and legally competent to marry the person whom you have taken on yourself to marry with no such sanction. The Bill might possibly have been opposite in all its stages in both Houses of Parliament and, altogether you would have had to have spent about a thousand or twelve hundred pounds. You will probably tell me that you never had a thousand farthings of your own in the world; but, prisoner, that makes no difference. Sitting here as an English Judge, it is my duty to tell you that this is not a country in which there is one law for the rich, and another for the poor. You will be imprisoned for one day, which period has already been exceeded as you have been in custody since the commencement of the Assizes.

In 1857 the English Parliament enacted the Divorce and Matrimonial Causes Act which effectively transferred the divorce jurisdiction from the ecclesiastical courts and Parliament to secular courts. That Act plainly embraced a double standard. A husband could divorce his wife on the grounds of adultery but a wife could only divorce her husband on the ground of aggravated adultery such as adultery coupled with cruelty.

Thereafter the law was amended from time to time on a piecemeal basis until the Matrimonial Causes Act 1937 introduced extensive new grounds for divorce, judicial separation and annulment of marriage. Whilst the range of misconduct which could be considered as grounds for divorce was progressively widened, there was no provision made for "no fault" divorce until 1973.

A great many Christians still lament the demise of laws which, in the main, required some kind of matrimonial fault to be proven before a decree of dissolution could be granted. However the resulting legal proceedings almost invariably did more harm than good.

In the first place the overwhelming majority of petitions were undefended. This meant that in any case where one party was prepared to lie and the other was prepared to allow the allegations to remain unchallenged a couple could quickly obtain a decree whatever the true position may have been. For the private investigators who made a living in providing real or imaginery evidence in adultery cases this was a goldmine. Sometimes they would earn their fees by battering down doors with a sledge-hammer so that a couple of strongarmed men and a photographer could burst into a bedroom to take photographs. In other cases they would engage in the deliberate deception of a court by arranging for a photograph to be taken of the husband sitting up in bed with a model hired for the purpose.

In the second place the procedure followed made any reconciliation almost impossible. It also produced the most incredible anguish and heartache not only for the parties but frequently for their children or other members of their family. The proceeding commenced with a petition in which one party not only nominated the ground relied upon but set out in graphic detail the allegations to support it. In practice that meant a recitation of all of the real or imagined misdeeds committed by the other party over the past fifteen years of

marriage. The document was filed in court and a copy was
served upon the other party, who usually filed an "answer".
The "answer" usually dismissed the allegations in the petition as a tissue of lies and set out a litany of complaints about
the party who had filed it. The first party then responded by
filing a "reply" in a similar vein. By the time each party had
virtually exhausted the supply of mud to be thrown an
atmosphere of extreme hostility had usually been created.
Furthermore, as the case approached the date for hearing it,
it was customary to enlist the aid of friends and relatives to
give substance to the allegations raised. Perhaps, most tragic
of all was the tendency for one parent to call a child to give
evidence against the other. I can only say that those who look
back on this appalling system with nostalgia must never have
seen a heartbroken child of thirteen or fourteen leaving the
witness box.

In the third place the system was concerned with establishing particular kinds of fault rather than with the question
of who was primarily responsible for the breakdown of the
marriage. The proceedings frequently established the husband drank and the wife nagged but whether he drank
because she nagged or she nagged because he drank was
anybody's guess. In fairness it should be said that it is
doubtful whether any sort of legal proceeding could be
expected to resolve that question, at least without placing a
prohibitive cost burden upon the community. However, it is
clear that the law did not achieve many of the things claimed
for it.

The present law in England is governed by the Matrimonial Causes Act 1973 which provides a sole ground for
divorce, namely that the marriage has irretrievably broken
down. In accordance with the law's predilection for recognising only matters which fit into precisely defined
pigeonholes, the Act provides that the Court may not find
that the marriage has broken down irretrievably unless:

(a) one party has committed adultery and the other finds it
    intolerable to live with him or her;

(b) one party's behaviour has been such that the other cannot reasonably be expected to live with him or her;

(c) one party has deserted the other for at least two years;

(d) the parties have been separated for at least two years and consent to the divorce; or

(e) the parties have been separated for five years.

Perhaps the end result of this gradual evolution towards divorce based, not upon fault, but upon breakdown of the relationship, will be a system similar to that now operating in Australia as a result of the Family Law Act 1975. Since 1 January 1976, if the parties have been living separately and apart for twelve months then the court will conclusively presume the marriage to have broken down. There has been much criticism by the church about this single ground but in its defence is the fact that the overwhelming majority of reconciliations occur within the first twelve months of separation. The first person for whom I acted under the new Act had not seen his wife for more than sixteen years. Neither he nor his wife had ever expressed any interest in reconciliation but neither had sought to obtain a decree against the other because they had too much integrity to suggest that the marital breakdown was all the other person's fault. The barren legal shell had remained but it was fanciful to regard it as a marital relationship in any real sense.

CHAPTER TWENTY-TWO

Custody of Children

The law governing the custody of children and the manner in which the court will exercise its discretion to order access to them has also changed during the last century. In England, the present position concerning the custody of children is governed by the Guardianship Act, 1973.

The general principle now followed is that the children's welfare is paramount. That principle was also enshrined in earlier legislation but in the last two or three decades considerable changes have occurred in judicial attitudes to the custodial care of children. Initially the judges finding matrimonial fault found it almost impossible to prevent that finding from spilling over into questions of custody of children. Consequently, although no lawyer nor judge would have had the effrontery to refer to the custody of children as a reward or consolation to the innocent party, there was no doubt that "matrimonial fault", prejudiced a party's chances of obtaining custody. This occurred in two ways. In the first place judges took the view that while the welfare of the children was the paramount consideration it was not the only one. Accordingly, when the evidence suggested that either party would be a suitable parent judges felt entitled to take into account such concepts or whether one "deserved" to have custody. In the second place, some judges placed great emphasis on personal morality in determining a person's ability to be a custodial parent.

With the evolution of a more permissive moral climate and a different perception of the needs of children came a series of judicial decisions which progressively eroded the role of fault in relation to custody and access.

The Act has now abolished the so-called "preferred role" of the mother, a concept described by Glass J. A. in the case of *Epperson* v. *Dampney* in the following terms:

> ". . . the bond between a child and a good mother . . . expresses itself in an unrelenting and self-sacrificing fondness which is greatly to the child's advantage."[38]

This attachment was said to be "biologically determined by deep genetic forces". Whilst few would cavil at the assertion of a close bond between mother and child, any adoptive parent could refute the judge's suggestion of a biological basis for it.

An increasingly used development in this area of divorce law is the idea of joint custody, whereby the formal legal custody is given to both parents, but by necessity the day to day "care and control" only to one. It is a form of order used only when there is a good prospect of continuing cooperation between the parents, as it presupposes a willingness to communicate and to share in the making of the important decisions about the child's future. The purpose behind such an order is to seek to ensure the involvement of both parents in the child's upbringing, to the benefit of the children and both parents.

However, not only is such an order sometimes impractical, but also there are occasions when parents who are agreed on the principle of joint custody disagree as to whom should be given care and control. In these circumstances the principles applied by the court in deciding the issue will be the same as in an "ordinary" custody dispute. The present position may be summarised as follows:

(a) The welfare of the children is the paramount consideration and virtually excludes other considerations such as what particular parents may need or deserve.

(b) Accordingly, evidence of a misconduct will not be admitted unless it is of a kind which reflects upon a party's fitness as a parent.

(c) The mother is no longer regarded as having any kind of "preferred role" even in respect of relatively young children. At least that is the position in theory. In practice, young children will usually remain with the mother although the judge may be compelled to express himself with some care in order to avoid criticism.

(d) The "welfare of the child" will not necessarily be best served by the parent who can provide the most financial security or the best physical surroundings.

   The courts are more concerned with which parent can provide the emotional nurture or mothering which the children need.

(e) Whilst a divorce makes it inevitable that the children be deprived of the opportunity of living with both parents together it does not make it necessary for children to be separated from their siblings. Consequently, the court takes the view that brothers and sisters should not be split up unless there are compelling reasons.

(f) The courts will not usually take into account the religious beliefs of the parties or their desires to have their children brought up in particular religious environments. In some cases, however, the particular religious environment may result in a child being subjected to social isolation or risk of physical neglect. Consequently whilst the courts have steadfastly refused to become involved in disputes about whether one religion or denomination is preferable to another, they have frequently placed great importance on the practical implications of adherence to the more extreme sects. For example, a parent who is a member of the Exclusive Order of the Plymouth Brethren may have difficulty in retaining custody because of the risk that the child might be directed to break off all contact with the non-believing parent.

(g) In many cases the decision of the court will involve the preservation of the status quo.

This simply means that where a child has been in the care of one parent for a substantial time and the evidence discloses that he is well cared for and leading an emotionally stable life then the court will award custody to that parent unless there are compelling reasons for changing custody. This has been somewhat cynically referred to as an example of the old maxim that possession is nine-tenths of the law. It is important to remember, however, that any change of custody can be emotionally distressing to a child and, for that reason alone, it is undesirable to change custody unnecessarily. Furthermore, no judge can know with any degree of certainty whether any custody change will ensure that a child's emotional needs are adequately fulfilled. Accordingly, when the judge is faced with a need to make a decision about custody in circumstances where both parties look to be good custodial parents he will be tempted to leave the child with the parent who has already cared for him for a substantial period of time. After all, the judge knows he is doing well in that parent's care. He may feel that the child would do equally well in the care of the other parent but giving that parent custody involves an inevitable period of disruption and there is always the risk that he might be wrong. Under those circumstances a judge is likely to ask himself, "Why take a risk when I don't have to?"

Overall, it is still true to say that more mothers obtain custody than fathers. To some degree that may reflect an underlying bias in favour of mothers at least in the minds of some judges. On the other hand, it may reflect nothing more than the social conditions in which the parties find themselves. There are, for example, far more mothers than fathers who subsist on social security benefits of some kind or who do part-time work only. The court is frequently asked to decide whether the custody of a young child should be awarded to his mother who will be available to look after him twenty-four hours a day or to his father who will be at work for about ten of the fourteen hours in which the child will be awake each day. Although it is not the hapless father's fault, the contest is largely one between the natural mother and the baby-sitter or day-care centre who will care for the child should the father be granted custody. In those circumstances it is scarcely surprising if the mother succeeds.

The wishes of the children will also be taken into account by the court and will be given increasing weight as they get older. From the ages of thirteen or fourteen onwards they will normally be conclusive.

The principle that conduct will be considered relevant only if it reflects upon a person's fitness as a parent has caused much heartburn. It means that a parent who has selfishly, and even capriciously, broken up the marriage and treated his or her responsibilities with contempt may still gain custody. Equally a loving and concerned parent of impeccable character may lose it. It is small wonder that people leave the court with a burning sense of injustice. Yet children are not mere chattels to be awarded to the most "deserving". They are the innocent casualties of marital breakdown. Their emotional nurture and support is always important. When their parents have just separated it is crucial. In these circumstances it is only right that the child's interest be treated as paramount even if that means award-ing custody to a parent who, in one sense, does not deserve it.

Because custody proceedings usually take months to ripen into a full-blown hearing, courts are frequently faced with applications for interim custody, that is, for an order that one party or the other have custody of the children until the time of the hearing. The pressure of work often means that a judge is forced to make a decision, at least on a temporary basis, which is little more than a snap judgement based upon what he is told by the lawyers appearing for the parties. A judge may literally have thirty cases in his list for the day and at three o'clock in the afternoon be confronted by two parents each seeking immediate custody of a child. Clearly someone has to take the child home at the end of the day, yet adequately to canvass the question of who would be the best custodial parent might ultimately require two or three days of evidence. In the circumstances, all that the judge can do is to glean the main facts from the lawyers appearing for each party and make a snap judgement which will at least resolve the dispute until there is more time to consider it. He may ask for a tentative report from a counsellor, if practical, or may adjourn the matter to permit such a report to be obtained. In that event he may direct the parties to canvass the matter further on some subsequent date when the court has a spare forty-five minutes or an hour in which to hear evidence as to the arrangements proposed by each side for the care of the child until the custody hearing can be concluded. Even on a hearing of that nature, however, the court will not have time to embark upon a detailed examination of the merits of the respective parties. Consequently a judge will usually seek to limit the scope of the enquiry to such matters as the proposed accommodation, schools and other matters not substantially in dispute.

In hearings of this kind the guiding principle is that the *status quo* should not be changed unless there are compelling reasons for doing so. In practice, it usually means that if one party leaves the matrimonial home and the other remains with the children the court will leave them there. On the other hand, if the children go with the departing spouse and remain with him or her for three or four weeks the court will not usually order their return. This reliance upon the *status quo* has been criticised for the reasons I have already mentioned but it cannot be denied that in the emotionally volatile period immediately following the separation of their parents, children need to remain in a situation which is as stable as possible. For this reason the courts try to limit the number of possible changes of custody by leaving the child where he is until his custodial needs can be determined at a proper hearing. If it then becomes clear that a change of custody is in his interests then that will be ordered. However, the court does seek to avoid having a child taken from one parent or another on an interim basis and then returned after a final hearing. To adopt any other policy is to run the risk of children changing hands with such frequency that they feel like relay batons.

CHAPTER TWENTY-THREE

Access

As previously mentioned the courts take the view that it is in a child's interest to maintain a continuing relationship with both parents save in the most exceptional circumstances. For this reason a court will almost always grant the non-custodial parent access to his or her children. The precise form of the order will depend upon such factors as the ages of the children, the availability of overnight accommodation and the distance which the non-custodial parent lives from them.

In many cases the only order made by the court is that the husband or wife have reasonable access to the children. Such an order leaves it to the parties to make their own arrangements as to the duration and frequency of access visits. If the parties are mature and sensible people who appreciate their children's needs and are able to communicate with one another about them then this arrangement is probably the best since it allows a degree of flexibility not permitted in a more closely defined order. It may also convey to the children the subtle message that their parents may have separated but they still have sufficient respect for one another to be able to sit down together and make joint decisions concerning their welfare.

If an order of that nature is not successful and the parties find they are unable to agree on access periods then the only alternative is to approach the court to have access defined by a judge. Each side will be at liberty to set out its case in the form of affidavits and they may be cross-examined on oath before the decision is made. In the end result the judge will make an order stipulating precisely when access is to occur and imposing any conditions which he considers desirable. A typical order would be one permitting the non-custodial parent to have access from, say 6 pm each Friday until 6 pm Sunday and during half of the school holidays.

The court's policy of granting access to non-custodial parents, save in exceptional circumstances has, from time to time, attracted considerable criticism. It has been suggested, for example, that non-custodial husbands who refuse to pay maintenance should be denied access. It has also been suggested that parents who have endeavoured to kidnap their children or who have failed to look after their children during the periods of access should be denied further contact with them. Applications have frequently been made by one parent to have the other parent's access terminated upon the grounds that the non-custodial parent is an alcoholic, a drug addict or an immoral person. When such applications fail, as they do in the overwhelming majority of cases, people frequently leave the court with a great sense of injustice and frustration.

As understandable as those feelings may be, however, they reflect a basic misunderstanding of the reasons for which access orders are made. Access has been said to be not a right of the parent but a right of the child. That is not merely a trite piece of verbiage designed to justify a denial of justice. It reflects the underlying truth that each child has a deep-seated emotional need to be able to identify with both parents and to maintain a relationship with them. When that opportunity is denied the child usually suffers some kind of emotional deprivation. The problem is compounded because small children are totally incapable of appreciating the reasons for such a step. Accordingly, a small boy may have a father who is irresponsible, unreasonable or even psychiatrically disturbed. He may make no attempt to support him and may be likely to have a bad influence on the boy. He may be, in short, the sort of person who does not "deserve" to see his son. Yet if the mother succeeds in denying him access to her son the boy will understand nothing of that. All he will understand is that his father whom he loves and, perhaps, idealises does not come to see him. Why doesn't he? Obviously because the poor little fellow is not worthy of the great man's time. The mother may have been trying to protect him by obtaining such an order but he may end up feeling hurt and rejected.

Furthermore, even if the mother succeeds in persuading him that his father is a "bad man" that will not be the end of the problem. Children need to look up to their fathers. It is an important element in the process of self-evaluation and ultimately in the development of their own feeling of identity and self-confidence. If a well-meaning mother constantly disparages the child's father he comes to feel that a certain shamefulness associated with his father impinges in some indefinable way on his own life. His own emotional development may be inhibited to a degree as a result. Any acceptance of his father's "badness" is also likely to be of a temporary nature. It may last for several years but there will usually come a time when he is no longer willing to accept his mother's assurance and will endeavour to make contact with his father so that he can resolve the matter for himself. If, at this point, he discovers that his father is not such a bad person after all and comes to feel that, in preventing access, his mother was acting more out of spite than out of any legitimate attempt to protect him, he may feel a strong sense of betrayal. That may cause a serious breach in the relationship between mother and son. The resulting estrangement will not necessarily be spontaneously healed by a subsequent disillusionment with his newly found father.

A judge before whom I was arguing a case some years ago put the dilemma succinctly when he asked my opponent, "What is your client going to tell her son when he asks why his father never comes to see him? Is she going to lie to him and say that his father doesn't care about him and doesn't want to see him? In that case she will only succeed in making him feel that he is not worthy of his father's love. Or is she going to tell him the truth, namely, that she fought tooth and nail to stop his father from seeing him? In which case he will ultimately end up hating her for having deprived him of one of the two most important relationships in his young life".

Once it is understood that children perceive deprivation of access in such a damaging manner, it can readily be appreciated that judges resort to such a step only when they have been persuaded that it is necessary. There are many alternatives available to the court which reduce the need for such a step. For example an alcoholic who is prone to go out drinking until the early hours of the morning may be incapable of looking after his children for a whole weekend, but may be perfectly capable of caring for them between 9 am and 6 pm on Sunday.

In extreme cases where a judge harbours the belief that a non-custodial parent cannot cope at all he may order that access be permitted under supervision or at a particular home made available for the purpose.

Difficulties frequently arise where the children do not wish to see the non-custodial parent. It seems to be generally accepted, and I believe rightly so, that they should be encouraged to try to establish some relationship with that parent and to try and come to terms with their feelings about him. In this kind of situation judges will frequently try to resolve it by referring both the parties and the children to a Divorce Court welfare officer who will try to ascertain the basis of the children's reluctance and endeavour to overcome it. Frequently it is nothing more complicated than allegiance to the custodial parent and an adoption of his hostility. In other cases it may have stemmed from a feeling of betrayal when one party left the matrimonial home thereby "deserting" them. In other cases there may be a litany of complaints ranging over many years. In others, the problem may have been caused by unpleasant incidents during earlier periods of access. In all of these situations the counsellor will endeavour to bring parent and children together. He will try to assist each person to communicate with the "other side", to overcome misunderstandings and to try again. The counsellor may also point out to the custodial parent the degree to which his or her attitude is being reflected in the attitudes displayed by the children and the manner in which attitudes of that kind are likely to prove harmful to them in the long run.

If counselling is not effective the dilemma will ultimately be resolved by a judge. His decision will depend very much upon the particular circumstances. In some cases he may decide that it is not in the children's interest to remain in an environment of unremitting bitterness on the part of the custodial parent. In that event, he may try to resolve the matter by changing custody in the hope that the other parent will be more reasonable about access and that the child may yet have a relationship with both parents. In other circumstances, he may seek to resolve the matter by making firm orders for limited access and threaten various sanctions if they are frustrated by any conduct on the part of the custodial parent. Finally, if all else fails, and the children have maintained an implacable refusal to see the non-custodial parent, the judge may find himself faced with only two options. He must either refuse access or require the children to be dragged kicking and screaming out to the non-custodial parent's car thrust into it and tied down. In those circumstances, he may feel obliged to concede defeat and refuse access. Access is for the benefit of the child. If the evidence discloses that a particular child would be better off without it then it will be refused.

CHAPTER TWENTY-FOUR

Property and Maintenance Orders

In addition to any rights under the Married Women's Property Act, 1882, a person seeking a decree of divorce, nullity or judicial separation may also seek orders for the transfer of property and/or maintenance under the provisions of the Matrimonial Causes Act, 1973. The Act provides the Court with wide powers in relation to the detention, custody, possession and sale of property. It also enables orders to be made for the benefit of children as well as former spouses.

In considering an application for an order adjusting the relative entitlements of the parties to property, the Court is enjoined to take into account the following factors:

(a) The income, earning capacity, property and other financial resources which each of the parties to the marriage has or is likely to have in the foreseeable future, including in the case of earning capacity any increase in that capacity which it would in the opinion of the court be reasonable to expect a party to the marriage to take steps to acquire.

(b) The financial needs, obligations and responsibilities which each of the parties to the marriage has or is likely to have in the foreseeable future.

(c) The standard of living enjoyed by the family before the breakdown of the marriage.

(d) The age of each party to the marriage and the duration of the marriage.

(e) Any physical or mental disability of either of the parties to the marriage.

(f) The contributions which each of the parties has made or is likely in the foreseeable future to make to the welfare of the family, including any contribution by looking after the home or caring for the family.

(g) The conduct of each of the parties, if that conduct is such that it would in the opinion of the court be inequitable to disregard it.

(h) In the case of proceedings for divorce or nullity of marriage, the value to each of the parties to the marriage of any benefit (for example, a pension) which, by reason of the dissolution or annulment of the marriage, that party will lose the chance of acquiring.

It may be seen that the court is specifically directed to take into account non-financial contributions involved in caring for a home and family. The view is frequently taken that the contribution which the wife makes as a homemaker should be regarded as equivalent to her husband's contribution as the family breadwinner. In many cases the applicant receives somewhere between forty per cent and sixty per cent of the marital assets. It should be stressed, however, that the court is obliged to take into account all of the factors referred to above and that the distribution of assets in any particular marriage will depend upon the circumstances.

A twenty-year old girl who seeks a property settlement after a six-month marriage to a sixty-year old millionaire will be unlikely to succeed in wresting half of his fortune from him. On the other hand a woman with a number of young children living in a house registered in joint names but paid for almost entirely by her parents may succeed in obtaining an order that the whole property be transferred to her without any compensatory payment to the husband.

The courts possess very wide powers and can prevent the sale or transfer of properties until the other party's claim can be determined. If it finds that property has been transferred to someone else when an application was pending or contemplated then it can actually set aside the transfer and place the legal title back into the name of the original owner so that the application may not be thwarted.

The court will almost invariably make orders requiring that the non-custodial parent contribute to the maintenance of the children but the precise amounts will depend upon factors enumerated in the section and in particular upon the ability of that person to pay.

Spouse maintenance (there is in theory no reason why a husband cannot be maintained by his wife) is a little more complicated. The courts will not generally require a party to pay maintenance to a wife who goes to work and supports herself unless there are compelling reasons for doing so. The most common reason for such an order is that the wife has young children to care for but that is by no means the only reason that the court may accept as satisfactory. A judge has wide powers and where the need is demonstrated, may order payment of a lump sum to cover some particular need.

The court may make orders for urgent maintenance on short notice or, if the situation is really desperate on an *ex-parte* application.

CHAPTER TWENTY-FIVE

Injunctions

The court also has the power to grant injunctions, that is, orders restraining the other party from doing something. Such orders are usually granted to preserve the marital property or to protect one of the parties or the children from some threat. The court's power to make injunctions offers a quick and effective means by which a wife can obtain protection from violence and harassment on the part of an estranged husband. In such circumstances the police may not usually intervene because they take the view that domestic disputes should be sorted out by the parties' solicitors and the Divorce Court rather than in courts exercising criminal jurisdiction. One may protest until one is blue in the face that the law does not condone assaults merely because the victim is married to the assailant but, in many cases, the police will merely shrug their shoulders and refuse to become involved. It is possible for the person concerned to conduct a private prosecution but the proceedings may take several months and are unlikely to produce any more serious sanction than a fine. Proceedings of that nature obviously offer very little protection against the possibility of further assaults.

In England and Wales there are special statutory provisions designed to protect women and children from domestic violence. However a wife may also apply for an injunction restraining her husband from assaulting her, molesting her or approaching her place of residence during the court proceedings. If there are grounds for expecting that the wife may be in imminent danger then an order of that kind can be obtained almost immediately, at least on an interim basis. If the husband ignores that order and assaults or harasses the wife she may have him brought before the court, by force if necessary, to show cause why he should not be dealt with for contempt. If it is the first time he has breached such an order he will usually be permitted to "purge his contempt" by apologising and promising not to offend again. If he does so, he may escape punishment. It is possible for the court to release him only upon the condition that he enters into a recognisance to be of good behaviour for a stipulated period of time. If he continues to disregard the order then the court may inflict quite serious penalties upon him, including if necessary, terms of imprisonment. However, it is rarely necessary for the court to resort to that measure. Usually the mere fact of being dragged before the court and hearing his lawyer talking about the need to bring his toothbrush next time offers sufficient deterrence.

Injunctions are also a very important remedy if all of the property is in the husband's name and the wife fears that he may sell it and simply disappear. In those circumstances the wife can effectively freeze the property by obtaining appropriate injunctions.

CHAPTER TWENTY-SIX

Lawyers

Lawyers, like politicians, have been described as the "finest body of men that money can buy". It is said that they will fight zealously to protect your fortune from your enemies so that they may take it for themselves. Shakespeare penned the immortal line, "First . . . let's kill all the lawyers"[39] and generations have shouted "Amen!". Yet most of the criticisms of lawyers as a class have been exaggerated to say the least. Of course there are particular lawyers who are dishonest, greedy, lecherous, incompetent or simply uncaring. Lawyers are simply men and women and they are prone to the same frailties as the rest of the community. Nonetheless, it is true to say that the overwhelming majority of lawyers genuinely try to achieve the best result for their clients. In fact, lawyers trade upon their reputation and by and large reputations are built up by obtaining results.

Furthermore, most lawyers make far less money than the daily paper would suggest. Most solicitors find that their overheads approach eighty per cent of their gross fees and that their bad debts cause more stress than their mothers-in-law. Legal aid is available in divorce cases to assist in meeting the legal bills, but the financial criteria for obtaining it are increasingly stringent, and many people have to meet some or all of the costs themselves. Indeed, even for those with the benefit of legal aid, the system has a way of clawing back money advanced under the scheme from property won or preserved during the course of the proceedings. However, if you obtain legal aid the rates charged by your lawyers are fixed and determined by the government. If you do not qualify for legal aid it is sensible to shop around or at least insist upon having the hourly rate of fees specified in advance. That is not to say that it is wise to engage the cheapest lawyer available. Many legal firms have an unfortunate policy of allocating family law matters to the most junior member of the firm. Of course, everyone has to start somewhere and new solicitors are often conscious that they are at the threshold of their careers and consequently take great pains to ensure that their duties are discharged diligently. Unhappily, diligence and enthusiasm are not enough. If the matter is at all complicated it requires sound judgement and experience and in the long run you will do better to pay a little more for an experienced practitioner.

On the other hand, there are firms which have built up impressive reputations on the basis of their commercial work and have become accustomed to charging very high fees for virtually all that they do. Unfortunately those firms frequently share the policy of the more humble ones in allocating family law matters to the more inexperienced solicitors. This means that clients frequently pay for a degree of competence and experience which the solicitors who actually handle their cases do not possess.

Finally there are always one or two fashionable solicitors who are in great demand because of a flamboyant manner and, sometimes, wide connections. They may charge several times the fees charged by their less pretentious colleagues but rarely achieve better results.

As a general rule of thumb it may well be worthwhile to pay twenty or thirty per cent more for an experienced lawyer but one who wants three or four times as much as his less experienced colleagues is unlikely to be worth it. There are exceptions to every rule and if you have a complicated estate worth millions it may be worth paying even a very high fee for a leading Queen's Counsel.

Despite the cost it really is wise to have a lawyer represent you unless you have been able to reach an amicable agreement with your former spouse about everything. Even if you had the necessary knowledge of the law and were confident that you could effectively cross-examine the other party's witnesses it would still not be prudent to act for yourself. You are likely to become far too emotionally involved to exercise sound judgement. In fact, the worst clients to act for seem to be other lawyers. They make outbursts and do all kinds of imprudent things that they would never permit a client to do. A number for whom I have acted over the years have later approached me, ruefully shaking their heads and apologising for being such difficult clients. At least most of them have had the good sense not to act for themselves.

The best way to find a good solicitor is by personal recommendations preferably from other family law clients. Having made a tentative selection sit down with your solicitor, go through the situation with him in general terms and ask him to explain what is likely to occur. A competent solicitor should be able to explain the procedure and to give you some reasonably clear idea of how long the matter is likely to take to get to court, the results you are likely to achieve and the ultimate cost in fees. Of course he will be basing his estimates on only one side of the case and would be very rash to make precise promises but he should be able to provide some idea of the cost on the basis of what you tell him. Such a discussion will give you badly needed information and will also give you an opportunity to evaluate the expertise and commonsense of your solicitor.

Keep in mind the following suggestions:

(a) Don't ignore the advice of your lawyers. You are paying good money for them to act for you.

   If you are dubious about the advice your solicitor has given you then by all means seek a second opinion from another solicitor or ask your solicitor to take a barrister's advice. Whatever you do don't take advice from friends who assert that they have been through an identical situation. If you or someone with sufficient knowledge were to probe deeply enough you would almost certainly find that the situations were far from identical. It is one of the banes of a lawyer's existence to find his advice ignored because the client finds that the guy who puts petrol in his car at the service station or the woman behind the counter at Woolworths expressed a contrary view. More than once I have argued cases involving the distribution of marital property because although the opposing counsel and I agreed as to the inevitable result neither of us could persuade our clients to accept our advice. The cases had to be fully presented and the clients then found they had wasted thousands of dollars in order to obtain results that should have been obtained by agreement.

(b) Before agreeing to any final financial settlement, discuss the matter with your solicitor.

That is not to say that your decisions must be dictated by your legal rights. You are free to act in a generous fashion or to compromise the situation because of family considerations should you wish. It is simply prudence, however, to take advice first.

(c) If you are concerned that your husband or wife may engage in some devious or underhand manoeuvre tell your solicitor about it. There may be some means of preventing it.

(d) If you are concerned about any aspect of your solicitor's performance raise the matter with him.

There may be an explanation but it is foolish to simply sit back and hope that things will get better.

(e) On the other hand, bear in mind that court proceedings take a considerable amount of time even if everyone concerned moves as quickly as possible.

The courts are inevitably choked with a long backlog of cases and all litigants want their cases heard quickly.

Furthermore, you will normally get only one chance to present your case and your solicitor needs to take adequate time to marshal whatever evidence is necessary to substantiate your claim. Another continuing problem for most barristers is being called upon to argue appeals against decisions in cases which were poorly presented. Such appeals are often hopeless attempts to close the stable door after the horse has bolted.

(f) Remember that your lawyer sells his time. Any time you ring him up or go to see him he will make a note of the amount of time spent talking to you and will ultimately charge you for it.

That is not unreasonable. His time is all that he has to sell. If you want to keep your legal expenses down then don't waste his time. Make a list of things that you wish to discuss with him and run through them in a logical and concise fashion. Remember that while he may be sympathetic he is neither an old friend nor a counsellor. There are other people who will be happy to talk the matter over with you and provide emotional support without charge.

(g) At an early stage in the proceedings try making a personal approach to your husband or wife about the issues between you. State candidly what you want, tell him that you've consulted solicitors and that the legal fees on each side may run to thousands of pounds.

Remember that if you can come to some sort of amicable agreement at an early stage of the proceedings then you will avoid the acrimony often engendered by contested proceedings and save a large amount of legal fees. Be careful, however, to make it a ground rule of the discussion that no firm deal will be concluded until the matter has been discussed with your solicitor.

(h) Barristers have been described as a special branch of the theatrical profession and there is an air of the theatre about every court case.

Don't assume the lawyer on the other side hates you. He is simply fulfilling a role in accordance with his instructions. Equally try to avoid seeing your husband or wife as the "enemy". You are not fighting a battle but merely resolving a dispute in court. Arguments put to the court by lawyers do not necessarily reflect the innermost feelings of their clients. Witnesses frequently say many things out of sheer defensiveness.

(i) Finally, when the process is over, don't brood about it and don't participate in endless recriminations with the other party.

Legal proceedings are emotionally draining exercises at the best of times. When they involve sorting out the rights and obligations of people after a divorce they are also an unpleasant reminder of the old relationships. They seem to hang over one's head for months or years and constantly intrude upon attempts to make a new life. When they are finally completed be grateful that they are out of the way and that even if you did not achieve all that you had hoped for you are nonetheless free to start again.

A Word to the Church

The response of the church to the problem of marital break-down and divorce has been almost bewilderingly diverse. On the one hand it has produced marriage guidance and counselling organisations that have offered troubled people great compassion and sound common sense. On the other hand it has at times produced scathing renunciations that have caused enormous distress to people who were already amongst the ranks of the "walking wounded".

It is true, of course, that there will always be the risk of a perceived ambivalence due to a desire to "hate the sin but love the sinner". Yet that is a fine distinction and one which has not always been made clear. Condemnation of particular people may not be intended but the fire and brimstone sermon denouncing the moral laxity of our times and, in particular, the evils of divorce will bring cringes of guilt to the heart of every divorced person in the congregation. That does not mean that the subject should never be mentioned, but references to the prevalence of divorce and the cavalier manner in which some people treat their marriage vows should be balanced by sensitivity towards separated or divorced people in the congregation.

One frequently hears a minister speak a word of rebuke, having in mind the sort of person who simply deserts his spouse and perhaps his children in order to run off with someone else. Unhappily, sitting in the congregation there may be a frightened woman who fled in terror from a drunken and violent husband or a man who was deserted by his wife in precisely the same manner as the victim in the example which the speaker has in mind. Such people are likely to assume that the speaker's comments are directed at them or that they apply to them with equal force even if that was not intended. Consequently, we have an ironic situation in which the victims are very often the ones who are wounded by barbs intended for the "offenders". Those who really do have a cavalier attitude towards their marriage vows usually don't hear the stinging rebukes offered in church or if they do, shrug them off. Many sermons also carry the implication that there is always at least one villain in a broken marriage. You get the impression that marriages are made in heaven and fail only if one party goes to the Devil. This is overly simplistic and unfair.

Lest I fall into the same error by making sweeping generalisations, let me acknowledge that the church does contain a small percentage of people who seem capable of acting in a thoroughly immoral manner and somehow rationalising their behaviour to their own satisfaction. There may be circumstances in which some rebuke is perfectly justified. Jesus certainly did not shrink from condemning the hypocrisy of the Pharisees who claimed to be pillars of moral rectitude but whose hearts were full of selfishness and deceit.[40] More commonly, however, he evoked repentance by simply demonstrating his love and compassion for people. Look at the story of the woman taken in adultery or of Zaccheus the tax collector who gave half of his wealth to the poor simply because Jesus called him by name and was prepared to eat with him.[41] Jesus sought out those who were regarded, with some justification, as the dregs of society. Although he never compromised the standards of behaviour which he expected from those who followed him, he rarely condemned people. Indeed he said that he did not come to condemn the world but that through him the world might be saved. He showed these people both compassion and understanding and that produced a change of heart. Whilst it is true that he condemned hypocrisy, I have never been able to find even one instance in the New Testament in which Jesus bludgeoned someone into the kingdom of heaven by threats or bitter denunciations of their sinfulness. Perhaps it is time that the church reconsidered its position and tried things his way.

It must be conceded that the church is right to be concerned about the divorce rate. Nearly forty thousand divorces a year in Australia and nearly 154,000 divorces in England and Wales indicates an incredible amount of human misery caused by the fragmentation of families. The Bible also makes it plain that God hates divorce, that is, he hates to see families broken up. Consequently, it is perfectly right for the church to be trying to do something to halt the tide of marital breakdown. The problem is not one of intention but of direction. Much of the problem seems to stem from misunderstanding and oversimplification. For example, many Australian Christians assert that the divorce rate has doubled or tripled over the past ten years as a result of the "devaluation" of marriage due to the introduction of the Family Law Act. "Everyone knows" that this is symptomatic of a moral decline and that the problem gets worse every year. "Everyone" also knows that the overwhelming majority of families in which the children live with one parent are casualties of divorce. In reality none of those propositions is true. In fact, in 1975 the year before the Australian Family Law Act (equivalent to the English Matrimonial Causes Act of 1973) came into operation, there were some 24,307 divorces in Australia. In 1985 there were 39,830. In other words, in the ten year period immediately following the introduction of the Family Law Act the divorce rate increased by about sixty-four per cent. That is admittedly sufficient to cause concern but it is by no means the dramatic increase constantly asserted in our churches. In fact the rate increased steadily in the years prior to 1975 and has declined steadily since 1982. The Institute of Family Studies which monitors these trends reports that whilst demographic projections based upon the 1982 figures suggested that forty per cent of all marriages would end in divorce that figure had dropped to thirty-five per cent by 1986. Of course those figures are still disturbing but they indicate that things are not continuing to go to the dogs year by year.

Furthermore, there have been many social trends within the last ten years which go a long way toward explaining the increase since 1975.

In the first place there has simply been an increase in the size of the population.

In the second place there has been an enormous increase in the degree of unemployment in Australia and in various economic difficulties which have imposed great strains upon families. In large cities like Sydney where it is possible to compare socio-economic groups in various suburbs one can see a marked correlation between increases in unemployment and increases in the divorce rate.

These kinds of pressures have been reflected in other social ills such as an increase in consumption of alcohol and addictive drugs and a marked increase in the suicide rate.

As observed earlier patterns have been radically altered by the development of feminism and an increasing willingness by women to assert their rights. Whilst this has produced positive changes it has also meant that, in some marriages at least, there has been a degree of conflict and dissatisfaction which would not otherwise have occurred.

Many males have felt threatened by women who have been able to surpass them in terms of their career advancement and other achievements. These problems have not received the attention which they should. The conservatives have been content simply to deprecate the changes whilst the progressives have frequently been preoccupied with the need for progress and have swept aside these problems with the assertion that people "should not feel that way". That may be so but marital conflict emerges because of the way people do feel rather than the way they should and these kinds of conflicts cannot be simply swept under the table.

Many migrant families, who arrived in Australia from countries in which the husband is traditionally accepted as

having almost unlimited authority, have also experienced
enormous emotional upheaval as a result of a cultural clash.

It is also incorrect to assume that easy divorce laws are
responsible for the overwhelming majority of single parent
families. Helen Glezer's study for the Family Research Unit
of the University of New South Wales[42] established that the
marital status of the single parents was as follows:

	Male	Female
Divorced	16.6%	21.2%
Separated	44.7%	39.5%
Widowed	34.9%	26.0%
Never Married	2.9%	12.5%
Other	1.0%	1.0%

When allowance is made for the fact that there were nine
female "single parents" for every male "single parent", itself
an interesting statistic, it is evident that, on an across the
board basis, approximately one single parent in five is
divorced. In other words if one were to assume that none of
the divorced parents would have separated from their
spouses unless they were able to obtain a divorce and divorce
had been totally abolished overnight then eighty per cent of
the families surveyed would still have had only one parent.

In fact, it seems overwhelmingly likely that the vast
majority of people would have separated from their spouses
even if they were unable to obtain a legal divorce. Much of
the increase in divorce figures since 1975 may be attributable
to nothing more significant than that the people who would
previously have terminated their marriages by separating
without proceeding to a formal dissolution by a court are
now taking that further step. As I mentioned earlier the first
person for whom I appeared in an application for a dissolution under the Family Law Act had not seen his wife for
sixteen years. He would consequently have appeared as a
statistic in the post Family Law Act figures when in fact the
marriage had been at an end many years before.

When all these factors are balanced it is clear that the
increase in the incidence of divorce is largely a symptom of

serious underlying problems. The church would be far more effective if it sought to address those problems rather than simply making sweeping and condemnatory statements. Of course there are irresponsible and selfish people who betray their marriage vows without a qualm. Some of them may be found in our churches. Such people should be censured, though I would suggest privately rather than from the pulpit. But it is time the church recognised that such people are in the minority. Most of the divorced and separated people in our churches are among the ranks of the hurt and ashamed. They do not need intemperate diatribes to bring home to them a consciousness of guilt; they are racked by it. To come to Christ with their hurt and their guilt should be a liberating experience. Jesus came to heal the broken-hearted. We have been entrusted with his great commission to proclaim the good news that all may be forgiven and reconciled to their Father. Yet like the Pharisees we so often bind heavy burdens on their shoulders which we make little effort to help them bear.

I fully recognise that theological opinions differ on this subject and people are entitled to their own views. Nonetheless it seems to me that there is an urgent need for the church to endeavour to become the kind of caring and accepting community in which people with broken marriages can have their wounds bound and can receive assistance and encouragement in forging a new life. This is a challenge which the church has largely failed to take up or even recognise. I pray God that each of us will see it as our own challenge and seek to make that kind of caring community a reality.

Notes

1. "Divorce, the Bible and the Law", B. Ward Powers and John Wade, AFES Graduates Fellowship Sydney 1978, page 12
2. Genesis 24:67
3. John 2:1–11
4. Malachi 2:14
5. Concise Oxford Dictionary
6. Mishnah Gittin 9:10
7. Matthew 5:31–32
8. "Divorce, the Bible and the Law" supra, page 16
9. Matthew 5:17
10. John 8:7
11. Matthew 23:37; Luke 13:34
12. Matthew 5:32
13. "Divorce, the Bible and the Law", supra, page 17
14. Matthew 19:29
15. Romans 8:17
16. John 3:27
17. "How the Balance of Power is Changing in Marriage", Bettina Arndt, the *Bulletin*, 6 April, 1985, page 64
18. The *Canberra Times* Wednesday Magazine, 20 May, 1987
19. Supra page 60
20. Supra pages 62–3
21. 2 Samuel 12:17
22. John 21:15–17
23. Matthew 23:37
24. Matthew 7:3
25. 1 John 1:9 (AV)
26. Proverbs 22:6
27. Ephesians 6:4
28. Job 12:15
29. Matthew 19:14
30. 2 Corinthians 6:14 (NEB)
31. Job 3:25
32. 2 Corinthians 6:14 (AV)
33. *Donoghue* v *Stevenson* (1932) AC 562
34. 1974 Vol. 2, pages 86–8
35. *Divorce*, Rayden, 11th edition, London, Butterworths, page 3
36. Matthew 16:19
37. "Divorce, the Bible and the Law", supra, page 16
38. *Epperson* v *Dampney* 1. FLN No. 29
39. *King Henry VI*, Pt 2, III, ii, line 232
40. John 8:3–11
41. Luke 19:2–8
42. "Families in Australia—a profile", Family Research Unit, University of NSW, 1978